INTIMACIES AND CULTURAL CHANGE

To Hyunju, for sharing special moments.

Daniel Nehring

To René and Ana, who are always close.

Rosario Esteinou

This book is dedicated to my family for giving me the support and inspiration to accomplish this work and to the people of Mexico whose intimate lives have had to coexist with every day violence in recent years.

Emmanuel Alvarado

Intimacies and Cultural Change
Perspectives on Contemporary Mexico

Edited by

DANIEL NEHRING
Pusan National University, South Korea

ROSARIO ESTEINOU
*Research and Higher Studies Centre in
Social Anthropology, Mexico City*

EMMANUEL ALVARADO
Palm Beach State College, USA

Routledge
Taylor & Francis Group

LONDON AND NEW YORK

First published 2014 by Ashgate Publishing

Published 2016 by Routledge
2 Park Square, Milton Park, Abingdon, Oxfordshire OX14 4RN
711 Third Avenue, New York, NY 10017, USA

First issued in paperback 2016

Routledge is an imprint of the Taylor & Francis Group, an informa business

British Library Cataloguing in Publication Data
A catalogue record for this book is available from the British Library

The Library of Congress has cataloged the printed edition as follows:
Nehring, Daniel.
  Intimacies and cultural change : perspectives on contemporary Mexico / by Daniel Nehring, Rosario Esteinou and Emmanuel Alvarado.
     pages cm
  Includes bibliographical references and index.
  ISBN 978-1-4094-6183-8 (hardback)
1. Interpersonal relations--Mexico. 2. Intimacy (Psychology) 3. Love--Mexico. 4. Social change--Mexico. I. Title.
  HM1106.N424 2014
  302.0972--dc23

                                                            2013041454

ISBN 13: 978-1-138-27493-8 (pbk)
ISBN 13: 978-1-4094-6183-8 (hbk)

Contents

List of Figures and Tables

Figures

Tables

Notes on Contributors

Emmanuel Alvarado received his PhD in Comparative Studies with a concentration in Hispanic Studies from Florida Atlantic University. Currently, Dr Alvarado works as Professor of Spanish at Palm Beach State College. He has published numerous articles and presented various conference papers in the fields of Sociolinguistics and Latin American Cultural Studies. Some of his publications include 'Mexico's Poor: Contextualizing Poverty and Inequality in the Post-NAFTA Years', published in the *Delaware Review of Latin American Studies*. Subsequent articles include 'Attitudes Toward Immigrants and Multiculturalism in Contemporary America: The Role of Foreign Language Fluency', published in *Sociation Today* as well as 'Intimacy, migration, and cultural change: Latinos and American Fertility', published in *Revista de Estudios Sociales* In addition to his own research, he has also served as senior editor of the Florida Atlantic Comparative Studies scholarly journal (*FACS*), an interdisciplinary peer-reviewed humanities journal, and oversaw the publication of its three most recent volumes.

Rosana Blanco-Cano (PhD Tulane University) is an assistant professor of Spanish in the Department of Modern Languages and Literatures and co-director of the Women's and Gender Studies Program at Trinity University, San Antonio. She has published several articles in the areas of (trans)national Mexican cultural studies, gender and performance studies, Latin American cinema and Spanish cinema. She is co-author of the book *100 Years of Spanish Cinema* (Blackwell 2008), and author of the book *Cuerpos disidentes del México imaginado: Cultura, género, etnia y nación más allá del proyecto posrevolucionario* (Iberoamericana/Vervuert 2010).

Héctor Carrillo received his doctorate degree in Public Health (DrPH) from the University of California, Berkeley (1995). He currently works as Associate Professor of Sociology and Gender Studies at Northwestern University and is also a member of the Governing Board of the Latina and Latino Studies Program. Before joining the Northwestern faculty in 2009, his previous affiliations included the Department of Sexuality Studies at San Francisco State University and the Department of Medicine, Center for AIDS Prevention Studies, at the University of California, San Francisco. He is the author of *The Night Is Young: Sexuality in Mexico in the Time of AIDS* (University of Chicago Press 2002). He is currently investigating the intersections of sexuality, migration, and heath among Mexican gay and bisexual men who have relocated to California, as well as the meanings associated with adult male circumcision as an HIV prevention strategy among Mexican immigrant men. In collaboration with the San Francisco AIDS Foundation and San Francisco

State University, he is also studying the influence of spatial mobility on late testing and access to medical and HIV prevention services among Latino/a migrants. He was co-chair of the Social, Behavioral, and Economic Science track of the XVII International AIDS Conference (Mexico City, August 2008). He is a member of the editorial boards of Sexuality Research and Social Policy, Sexualities, and Sexualidad, Salud y Sociedad: Revista Latinoamericana. He also has a history of involvement in HIV/AIDS community-based organizations.

Rosario Esteinou is a professor at the Centro de Investigaciones y Estudios Superiores en Antropología Social (CIESAS) in Mexico City. She received her PhD in Sociology from the University of Turin in 1989. She has taught and conducted research in family studies for more than two decades. Since 2008, she has been a member of the Mexican Academy of Sciences. Her work has included studies on middle and low class families, kinship, family history, family strengths, assisted reproductive technologies, parenting and couple relationships. Currently, she is involved in research on parental education and adolescent social competence. She has published two authored books: *Familias de Sectores Medios: Perfiles Organizativos y Socioculturales* and *La Familia Nuclear en México: Lecturas de su Modernidad. Siglos XVI al XX*, and edited four other books.

Dubravka Mindek PhD in Anthropology, Escuela Nacional de Antropología e Historia, México D.F.). After graduating in ethnology and Spanish language and literature from the University of Zagreb, Croatia, she pursued post-graduate studies in anthropology in Mexico. Her research interests include family, kinship, development and gender in rural areas. Since 2008 she has been in charge of the research division at the *Centro de Investigaciones y Estudios Superiores en Antropología Social* (CIESAS), Mexico.

Daniel Nehring is currently Visiting Professor at the Department of Global Studies at Pusan National University in South Korea. His research concerns dynamics of intimate life in the context of globalization and rapid social change. In particular, he is interested in contemporary transformations of intimacy in East Asia and Latin America. At present, he is working on a book on the globalization of psychotherapeutic discourses of personal life.

Olga Rojas holds a BA in Sociology from the Universidad Autónoma Metropolitana, as well as an MA in Demography and a PhD in Population Studies from El Colegio de México, where she currently works as a research professor. Her areas of interest in research are families, gender, and reproduction. She has published numerous works in these issues, including journal articles, book chapters, and the very recent book *Paternidad y vida familiar en la ciudad de México* [*Fatherhood and Family Life in Mexico City*] (El Colegio de México 2009).

Bladimir Ruiz (PhD) is Associate Professor of Spanish and Chair in the Department of Modern Languages and Literatures at Trinity University, San Antonio. His research interests are focused on issues of gender and sexuality in contemporary Latin American literature and culture, and nation-building and ideology in nineteenth century Venezuelan narrative.

Katie Willis works as professor of human geography and director of the Centre for Developing Areas Research (CEDAR) at Royal Holloway, University of London. Her main research interests lie in the fields of gender, migration and health, particularly in the contexts of neoliberalism and state restructuring. She has significant research experience in a number of countries, including Mexico, Peru, Singapore and China. She is the author of *Theories and Practices of Development* (Routledge 2005) and *Geographies of Developing Areas: The Global South in a Changing World* (with Glyn Williams and Paula Meth, Routledge 2009). She has also edited five books, including *Gender and Migration* (with Brenda Yeoh, Edward Elgar 2000). In 2009, she was awarded the Gill Memorial Prize by the Royal Geographical Society (with the Institute of British Geographers) for her contribution to development geography.

A Brief Introduction

Daniel Nehring, Rosario Esteinou and Emmanuel Alvarado

Transformations of Intimate Life in Contemporary Mexico

Over the past four decades, Mexican society has experienced important changes that have had a profound impact on Mexicans' intimate lives. Long-held certainties about love, sexuality, marriage and family life have come to be questioned, and deeply rooted norms, values, and beliefs about intimate relationships have come to be challenged. Earlier in the twentieth century, the Mexican Revolution had already brought about significant changes in the social organization of gender relations, both in the public and in the private sphere. However, state and society in the post-revolutionary period remained in many ways grounded in patriarchal cultural narratives and Catholic morality[1] (Monsiváis 2006, Esteinou 2008). In recent years, the consensus that existed around these patriarchal narratives has waned. At the same time, recent research has pointed to the growing importance of egalitarian, companionate forms of understanding, experiencing and practising intimate relationships (Hirsch 2003, Rojas Martínez 2008).

Historical research has uncovered highly diverse practices of intimate life throughout Mexican history (Stern 1995, Olcott et al. 2006). However, the legitimacy of these practices was closely circumscribed by dominant norms grounded in Catholic morality, and forms of intimate life that contradicted these norms often remained invisible, unspeakable and barely tolerated (Irwin et al. 2003, Rubenstein 2006, Cano 2006). This pattern characterizes much of the period following the Mexican Revolution in 1910. Until the 1970s, mass media, the state and the Catholic Church successfully promoted cultural narratives that posited a particular model of family life as the central pillar of social stability. While the post-revolutionary politics of intimate life were highly complex (Olcott

---

1   We use the term Catholic morality to refer to norms, values and beliefs about gender relations that are rooted in Catholic doctrine. These norms, values and beliefs have exerted a pervasive influence across Mexican history. Nonetheless, they should not be understood as a uniform and unchangeable cultural system, as they have varied notably over time and across different locations and sectors of Mexican society. In this context, see, for example, Stern's (1995) work on morality and practices of gender relations in late colonial Mexico and Voekel's (2002) analysis of transformations of Catholic faith and everyday religious practices in the late eighteenth and early nineteenth century. On contemporary conservatism and Catholic sexual morality, see González Ruiz (1998) and Rodríguez (2005).

et al. 2006, Gutiérrez Castañeda 2002), it is possible to summarize basic elements of this model. To begin with, the post-revolutionary family model was characterized by a gendered division of labour between a father-husband-bread winner and a devoted mother and housewife. The role of the former lay in supporting his family through extra-domestic labour, while the latter's primary duties were to take care of her children and create a harmonious domestic environment (Esteinou 2008). Women's increasing ability to participate in paid labour from the mid-twentieth century onwards did not fundamentally change this (Monsiváis 2006). Heterosexual courtship and marriage were presented as the only sites in which romantic love and sexual desire could be legitimately expressed. However, while romantic love was idealized in post-revolutionary culture (de la Mora 2006), strict norms regulated the roles which women and men had to fulfil in everyday life and limited expressions of emotional closeness (Esteinou 2005).

Since the 1970s, Mexican society has undergone important changes. The economic crisis of the late 1970s and early 1980s led to neoliberal reforms that undermined the patriarchal division of labour and pushed women into the labour market in an effort to supplement family income and, in many cases, to ensure basic family needs (Fernández-Kelly 1983, González de la Rocha and Escobar Latapí 1991). The family planning policies of the Mexican government and long-term demographic trends entailed a reduction of the average number of children born to women by the age of 44 from 6.3 in 1970 to 3.3 in 2005 (INEGI 2000, INEGI 2005). This development has considerably reduced the amount of time women dedicate to childcare across the lifecycle and facilitated their incorporation into the labour market and public life. Moreover, mortality rates have steadily declined and life expectancy has gradually increased since the 1970s, allowing Mexicans to experience more complex intimate relationships along their life course (Esteinou 2008). At the same time, the proliferation of mass media and the Internet, as well as the greater ease of long-distance travel and the growing frequency of transnational migration, have resulted in greater exposure to diverse cultural narratives among contemporary Mexicans (Nehring 2009, Hirsch 2003). In response to these developments, the nature of couple relationships, marriage and family life has come to change, as women and men increasingly prioritise emotional attachment and personal satisfaction when they make choices about their intimate lives (Esteinou 2008).

Questions and Agendas

In this book, we ask how the outlined changes have shaped the ways in which Mexicans today experience love, marriage, intimate attachment and family life. Recent years have witnessed the emergence of a rich body of scholarship on contemporary transformations of gender relations in Mexico. However, a socio-economic focus is predominant in this literature, and there is still relatively little research on the cultural dynamics of intimate life (Nehring 2005). Subject matters such as the consequences of shifts in the Mexican labour market for the domestic division of labour and power have been extensively debated[2] over the past three decades (e.g. García and de Oliveira 1994, 1995, 2005). At the same time, there are very few studies on changes in public discourses about intimate life in Mexico (Salles and Tuirán 1998, Salles and Valenzuela 1998). Likewise, only a few major studies have explored in depth cultural understandings and experiences of intimate relationships in a rapidly changing Mexican society (Gutmann 1996, Gutmann 2007, Hirsch 2003, Carrillo 2002, Amuchástegui 2001). Furthermore, relevant academic debates on this subject have been dispersed across different disciplines, often without informing each other's research agendas and conceptual apparatus.

This book is based on the assumption that a cultural perspective is necessary to fully understand the patterns and dynamics of intimate life in Mexican society. On the one hand, this means that greater attention needs to be devoted to the public discourses, debates, controversies and struggles that shape the meanings of intimacy pervasive in society at large. What discourses of love, sex, marriage, couple relationships, family, and so forth are prevalent in Mexico today? How are these discourses re-worked, modified, contested and challenged by alternative, subordinate narratives? On the other hand, there is a distinct need for a better understanding of the ways in which Mexicans draw on these discourses to account for their everyday experiences and practices of everyday life. A few seminal ethnographies (e.g. Carrillo 2002, Hirsch 2003, Gutmann 1996) have explored these issues. However, these studies are concerned with quite specific geographical regions and social groups,[3] and a need to explore the everyday dynamics of intimate life across the country in a much more comprehensive manner remains.

In this book, we respond to these concerns with a set of interdisciplinary studies that explore both public discourses and everyday experiences and practices of intimate life. These studies are built around two questions:

1. How have contemporary processes of globalization, modernization and social change transformed public discourses and cultural models of intimate life in Mexican society?

---

2   These debates began as a response to the collapse of the Mexican economy in 1982 and neoliberal reforms of Mexican society in the 1980s and 1990s. They have explored issues such as household survival strategies in the context of economic crisis (e.g. González de la Rocha and Escobar Latapí 1991), the consequences of women's massive incorporation into the labour force for domestic gender relations (e.g. Fernández-Kelly 1983), and adjustments in gendered divisions of labour and power in the domestic sphere (e.g. García and de Oliveira 1994).

3   These studies have tended to focus on the urban working class (e.g. Gutmann 1996), as well as certain sectors of rural society (e.g. Hirsch 2003). Other sectors of Mexican society, such as the urban middle classes, have largely been ignored in extant research.

2. How do contemporary Mexicans draw on generalized public discourses of intimate life to account for their respective everyday experiences and practices?

Addressing these questions, it is our aim to offer a panoramic view of the cultural dynamics of intimacy in contemporary Mexico. The following nine chapters offer an in-depth analysis of both public discourses (chapters 1 to 4) and everyday understandings (chapters 5 to 9) of intimate life. They explore intimate life among different sectors of society in both urban (chapters 5 and 6) and rural (Chapter 7) spaces. Moreover, they combine empirical research in Mexico with studies on intimate life among Mexican Americans (Chapter 8) and Mexican immigrants (Chapter 9) in the USA. By incorporating research on Mexicans and Mexican Americans into this book, we seek to highlight the increasingly transnational scope of Mexicans' intimate lives and highlight conceptual and empirical connections in research conducted in Mexico and the USA. Bringing together contributions from sociology, anthropology, demography, geography, literature and film studies, we moreover aim to bridge prevalent disciplinary barriers and combine achievements and perspectives of different fields of study.

The authors in this volume draw on and add to three strands of academic debate. First and most immediately, the following chapters build on the outlined literature about intimate life in Mexico. Second, they add to debates on cultures of love and intimacy in the Global South (Padilla et al. 2007, Hirsch and Wardlow 2006, Jankowiak 2008), by highlighting the ways in which Mexicans are reworking their understandings and experiences of intimate life in the context of globalization and modernization.

Finally, the chapters in this book resonate with Ken Plummer's (2003) account of the contentious nature of intimate citizenship in the contemporary world. Plummer's argument stems from the assumption that hegemonic grand narratives of intimate life are slowly fading away:

> Of course, no society has ever had just one narrative about how life is to be lived [...]. Societies have always been ambiguous, variable, conflictual, changing. But societies have typically sought to provide one overarching cultural paradigm that seems to plausibly hold together the world and its history – often by means of a God or gods. [...] But just as they always have been, religious traditions are riddled with schisms, conflicts, disbelievers, and critics. These days, however, such conflicts are much more visible and public – and for many people this makes religious tradition less and less plausible as the source of the "one grand story" of the world. Yet, the very fragility of these traditions can ironically lead them to adopt stronger and stronger positions, to claim more and more authority, generating a powerful sense of tribal fundamentalisms over life. Religious tradition is one – indeed, probably the major – source of conflict and tension around how to live life today. Most of the new intimacies, and the choices they make available, are vehemently opposed by religions of all kinds. Despite this,

people seem increasingly aware that this "one way" is visibly crumbling in the postmodern world. Our formerly strong conviction of unity, permanence, continuity – of one moral order under God – has started to collapse, and what we now find instead are fragmentations, pluralizations, multiplicities. (Plummer 2003: 18)

At the same time, social, cultural and technological changes have given rise to a broad range of 'intimate troubles' and contentious choices, from new forms of family life that seek legitimacy to the scope and moral limits of new reproductive technologies (Plummer 2003: 4ff.). Plummer uses the concept of 'intimate citizenship' to refer to arenas of intimate life that are thus becoming publicly visible as sites of uncertainty, doubt and contention as to their meaning and social legitimacy. Intimate citizenship concerns the decisions which individuals make about their bodies, emotions and social relationships while it also refers to the choices – moral, legal, and so forth – which societies make in considering the legitimacy of different practices of intimate life (Plummer 2003: 12ff.).

Academic debates about intimate citizenship emerged in the United Kingdom in the course of the past decade, and they have so far largely limited themselves to considering transformations of intimacy in European societies (e.g. Roseneil 2010, Ryan-Flood 2009, Oleksy 2009, Gunaratnam 2013). In spite of its Eurocentric origins, intimate citizenship is an obviously useful conceptual tool for the study of cultural transformations of intimacy in Mexico. The concerns Ken Plummer identifies in the quotations above resonate in obvious ways with contemporary struggles about the moral, social and legal legitimacy of dimensions of Mexicans' intimate lives. Recent high-profile controversies between various political parties, civil society groups, state actors and the Catholic Church as to the legalization of gay civil unions (de la Dehesa 2010) and access to abortions (Human Rights Watch 2006, Kulczycki 2007) are of obvious importance in this context. Moreover, research during the past two decades has highlighted pervasive and often acrimonious 'culture wars' between religious-conservative and secular social movements about the politics of sexuality in Mexico (González Ruiz 1998, Rodríguez 2005, de la Dehesa 2010, González Ruiz 2002).

This book explores intimate troubles, public and private choices, and struggles about intimate life in diverse sectors of Mexican society. It offers a panoramic perspective on this subject matter under the scope of one central argument: since the 1970s, a contradictory pluralization and fragmentation of discourses of love, sexuality, marriage and family life has taken place in Mexico, in which the cultural commonalities, tensions, and contradictions between emergent and historically established narratives of intimate life are played out in different ways in a variety of localized arenas. This pattern of contradictory pluralization is predicated upon significant recent economic, demographic, and political changes. It involves a limited trend towards companionate logics of intimacy grounded in tendentially individualistic understandings of intimate attachment. This trend entails shifts in women's and men's understandings and experiences of power and production divisions, as well as matters of sexuality, in close interaction with equally important patriarchal cultural models. The latter seem to have lost their hegemonic status in many sectors of Mexican society, but nevertheless are forcefully reasserted in public life by parts of the media, political groups, and the Catholic Church.

Outline of the Book

The book addresses these concerns in three steps. Chapters 1 and 2 set the stage for our argument, by developing a macro-level analysis of changes in the cultural contours of intimate life in the context of broader structural transformations of Mexican society. Chapter 1 explores shifts in cultural models and public discourses of intimate life in Mexico over the past 50 years. Chapter 2 then examines the patterns of intimate life in Mexican families across the twentieth century.

Drawing on case studies on literature and film, chapters 3 and 4 then analyse public discourses of sexuality, couple relationships, and intimate life in contemporary Mexican society. The book's latter chapters present a series of case studies that explore the ways in which Mexicans draw on these discourses in their everyday life to account for their experiences and practices of couple relationships, marriage, love, and sexuality. These case studies are organized around major analytic axes that differentiate contemporary Mexicans' experiences of intimacy: differences in socio-economic status, socio-cultural differences between rural and urban spaces, generational differences in cultural meanings of couple relationships and sexuality, and, finally, the impact of transnational migration on experiences of intimate life.

In Chapter 1, Katie Willis provides an introduction to processes of globalization and modernization in Mexico in recent decades and how these have framed public discourses and collectively-shared cultural models of intimate life. The chapter focuses on shifts since the late 1960s, stressing the diversity of Mexico's population and the need to recognize how and why experiences of social change have varied socially and spatially. In particular, the chapter draws out differences between rural and urban populations, the importance of class distinctions and variations in economic and political processes which play out at the level of individual states. The chapter is structured around six main themes: economic transformation; migration; state policies; health and education services; social movements and non-governmental organizations; and media and technology. These have been selected as the main drivers of social change within Mexico (and the wider world). As well as outlining and explaining the key trends associated within each theme, the chapter also provides indications of how they are associated with shifts in cultural models or public discourses of intimacy.

In Chapter 2, Rosario Esteinou provides an overview of processes of globalization and modernization in Mexico in the twentieth century and discusses how these have shaped public discourses and cultural models of intimacies in the context of family life. Intimate life extends beyond family relationships in many ways, and the study of intimacies must not be conflated with the study of families. However, across much of Mexico's history, public discourses and dominant cultural models have defined family as a central and exclusive space for intimate relationships. Therefore, in order to understand intimacies in contemporary Mexican society, it is important to understand how these discourses, as well as the lived realities of family life, have changed and developed. Rosario Esteinou provides a clear background for readers unfamiliar with contemporary Mexican history and society, as well as a link between theoretical debates on intimate citizenship and empirical research on intimate life in Mexico. Drawing on contemporary academic debates at the international level, Esteinou analyses how intimacy in Mexican families developed across three periods: 1900 to 1950, 1950 to 1970 and 1970 to 2000. Her argument examines cultural, economic, legal and socio-demographic processes that have shaped intimate life in families across different sectors of Mexican society. On the one hand, her aim is to identify some features of twentieth century Mexican society that point towards different types of intimacy, taking as a criterion for classification the balance between the bonds of family obligation and freedom of choice in establishing those bonds. On the other hand, she considers whether the twentieth century witnessed a trend towards increasing disclosure and democratization in the construction of intimate relationships.

In Chapter 3, Rosana Blanco analyses the film *Así del precipicio* (Teresa Suárez 2006) to examine discourses of intimate citizenship in cinematic representations of lesbian identity in Mexico today. Cinema, Blanco argues, plays a central part in the construction of symbolic meanings of couple relationships and sexuality in Mexican society. *Así del precipicio*, in this context, can be seen as an emblematic representation of the *nuevo cine mexicano* and filmmaking in the early twenty-first century. Blanco argues that contemporary Mexican cinema's vision of intimacy is grounded in neoliberal discourse and right-wing political agendas. *Así del precipicio* is concerned with a supposed moral decline of Mexican society. It seeks to document this decline through the stories of a group of young, privileged women who identify themselves as lesbian, thus challenging their society's customary normative regulation of sexuality. Exploring the ways in which the film constructs these stories, Blanco reflects on the limits and contradictions in its representation of lesbian intimate citizenship. Acknowledging sexual difference, *Así del precipicio* seeks to assert the modernity and globality of contemporary Mexican society. At the same time, however, its narrative forcefully reasserts patriarchal cultural representations of lesbian sexualities.

The analysis of discursive representations of intimate life in Mexico continues in Chapter 4 with Bladimir Ruiz's discussion of youth sexualities in Naief Yehya's 1994 novel *Camino a casa*. Its young narrator is subjected to social pressures, and culturally accepted sexual scripts become a source of conflict and inner turmoil with which he needs to cope. Central themes in Ruiz's analysis of this narrative are the development of youth sexual identity, the formation of hegemonic masculinity, as well as the role of music and consumerism in shaping youth subjectivities. His argument in this context focuses on the cultural construction of youth identities and intimate citizenship, exploring the cultural processes by which the hegemonic ideologies of gender and masculinity are appropriated and resisted.

In Chapter 5, Olga Rojas explores understandings and experiences of marital life and sexuality among urban middle and working class men. Existing research on the subject indicates that, for Mexican men, sexual activity both within and outside marriage constitutes a central representation and assertion of masculinity. In response to this argument, Rojas's chapter considers cultural trends towards egalitarian marital relationships based on love and intimate attachment. Her chapter points to a possible reformulation of masculine identity, based on intimate, loving relationships with their spouses, rather than their role as bread-winners and the exercise of compulsive sexuality. Rojas concludes that a traditional model of sexuality seems to prevail among working-class men, while a tendency towards companionate intimate relationships is identifiably emerging among more affluent socio-economic groups.

Chapter 6 begins a series of case studies on Mexicans' everyday experiences of intimate life. In Chapter 6, Daniel Nehring explores the narratives of couple relationships, love and intimate attachment among young female professionals from Mexico City. His study is based on 21 life story interviews conducted in Mexico City with women between 25 and 34 years of age employed in a variety of white-collar, professional occupations. The intimate lives of these women were generally built around the notion of autonomously defined life plans. Within these life plans, they expressed both deep and lasting intimate attachment to a partner and to the pursuit of individually fulfilling careers. Marriage and the fulfilment of familial and parental expectations continued to be desirable for most, but were framed as a matter of individual choice and satisfaction, rather than the outcome of social pressure and expected sanctions. In this sense, his findings point to the emergence of a 'negotiated familism', within which central elements of patriarchal familism continue to serve as meaning-giving traditions while losing a significant part of their coercive power.

In Chapter 7, Dubravka Mindek considers the emergence of new companionate cultural models of intimate life in the rural town of Tehuitzingo, Puebla, and the impact of these on the town's courtship practices, conjugal life, and the dissolution of couple relationships. Her argument is based on ethnographic fieldwork in Tehuitzingo, including participant observation, formal and informal interviews, and the analysis of relevant documents, such as court records on marital problems and dissolution. Mindek analyses the town's most salient avenues of close contact with wider society, such as migration, work, formal education, and mass media. Her findings point to notable gender differences in the appropriation of new cultural models, women of all generations being far more likely than men to profess a desire for love and companionship. The chapter contrasts these attitudes and desires with actual practices of intimate life in Tehuitzingo. Mindek's findings suggest that new cultural models of intimacy do not automatically override established traditional cultural patterns. In particular, Mindek points to a complex pattern of coexistence, complementation, and mutual adaptation resulting from a network of interactions, interests, and motivations.

Chapters 8 and 9 then turn to the transnational worlds of Mexican Americans and Mexican immigrants in the USA. In Chapter 8, Emmanuel Alvarado looks at cultural contexts behind the fertility choices of educated Mexican American women. His study is based on 36 in-depth interviews conducted in various towns throughout South Texas. He identifies some emergent themes that explicitly address the motivations and cultural influences that shape their reproductive choices. The themes are grouped into three major categories: patriarchal/ egalitarian relationships, familism, and professional success and ambition. The findings presented by Alvarado suggest that family size choices among educated Mexican American women result from the dynamic interaction between the history and cultural traditions of Mexican Americans, on the one hand, and the pressures of socio-economic and cultural assimilation, on the other. As a result, cultural understandings surrounding the fertility choices of college-educated Mexican American women reflect the hybridity and complexity found within their liminal space of American social life as well as challenge assimilationist assumptions about the future of Hispanic fertility in the USA.

Héctor Carrillo in Chapter 9 focuses on the mutually constitutive relationship between sexual globalization and transnational migration. His argument draws on a qualitative study with gay and bisexual Mexican immigrant men in California, involving both ethnographic observation and in-depth interviews with 150 participants. Carrillo analyses how his participants' experiences of migration contribute to the globalization of sexuality. He argues that their motivations for transnational migration are shaped by the ways in which they imagine gay cultures in urban spaces in the USA. In cross-cultural intimate relationships in the USA, Mexican gay immigrant men provide their US-born partners access to sexual ideologies and practices learned during their earlier lives in Mexico, asserting their worldviews in a society in which they often find themselves in marginal social positions and tentatively formulating alternative gay sexual identities. At the same time, returning to Mexico, these men articulate cultural understandings and practices of sexuality discovered in the USA, thus legitimizing their decision to move abroad and contributing to the globalization of sexuality in Mexico.

Bibliography

Amuchástegui, A. 2001. *Virginidad e iniciación sexual, experiencias y significados.* México D.F.: EDAMEX.

Cano, G. 2006. Unconcealable Realities of Desire: Amelio Robles's (Transgender) Masculinity in the Mexican Revolution, in *Sex in Revolution: Gender, Politics, and Power in Modern Mexico*, edited by Olcott, J., Vaughan, M.K. and Cano, G. Durham: Duke University Press.

Carrillo, H. 2002. *The Night is Young: Sexuality in Mexico in the Time of AIDS*. Chicago: University of Chicago Press.

de la Dehesa, R. 2010. Global Communities and Hybrid Cultures: Early Gay and Lesbian Electoral Activism in Brazil and Mexico, in *The Politics of Sexuality in Latin America*, edited by Corrales, J. and Pecheny, M. Pittsburgh: Pittsburgh University Press, 175–96.

de la Mora, S. 2006. *Cinemachismo: Masculinities and Sexuality in Mexican Film*. Austin: University of Texas Press.

Esteinou, R. 2005. The Emergence of the Nuclear Family in Mexico. *International Journal of Sociology of the Family*, 31(1), 1–17.

Esteinou, R. 2008. *La familia nuclear en México: lecturas de su modernidad. Siglos XVI al XX*. México D.F.: CIESAS/Miguel Angel Porrúa.

Fernández-Kelly, M.P. 1983. *For We Are Sold, I and My People: Women and Industry in Mexico's Frontier*. Albany: State University of New York Press.

García, B. and de Oliveira, O. 1994. *Trabajo femenino y vida familiar en México*. México D.F.: El Colegio de México.

García, B. and de Oliveira, O. 1995. Gender Relations in Urban Middle-Class and Working-Class Households in Mexico, in *Engendering Wealth and Well-Being: Empowerment for Global Change*, edited by Blumberg, R.L. et al. Boulder: Westview Press, 195–210.

García, B. and de Oliveira, O. 2005. *Dinámica Intrafamiliar en el México Metropolitano*. México D.F.: El Colegio de México.

González de la Rocha, M. and Escobar Latapí, A. (eds) 1991. *Social Responses to Mexico's Economic Crisis of the 1980s*. San Diego: Center for US-Mexican Studies.

González Ruiz, E. 1998. Conservadurismo y sexualidad en México, in *Sexualidades en México, Algunas aproximaciones desde la perspectiva de las ciencias sociales*, edited by Szasz, I. and Lerner, S. México D.F.: El Colegio de México, 281–305.

González Ruiz, E. 2002. *La sexualidad prohibida: intolerancia, sexismo y represión*. México D.F.: Plaza y Janés.

Gunaratnam, Y. 2013. Roadworks: British Bangladeshi mothers, temporality and intimate citizenship in East London. *European Journal of Women's Studies*, 20(3), 249–63.

Gutiérrez Castañeda, G. (ed.) 2002. *Feminismo en México: Revisión histórico-crítica del siglo que termina*. México: PUEG/UNAM.

Gutmann, M. 1996. *The Meanings of Macho: Being a Man in Mexico City*. Berkeley: University of California Press.

Gutmann, M. 2007. *Fixing Men: Sex, Birth Control, and AIDS in Mexico*. Berkeley: University of California Press.

Hirsch, J. 2003. *A Courtship After Marriage: Sexuality and Love in Mexican Transnational Families*. Berkeley: University of California Press.

Hirsch, J. and Wardlow, H. (eds) 2006. *Modern Loves: The Anthropology of Romantic Courtship and Companionate Marriage*. Ann Arbor: University of Michigan Press.

INEGI. 2000. *XII Censo General de Población y Vivienda 2000: Resultados Definitivos*. [Online]. Available at: http://www.inegi.org.mx/sistemas/comu nicados/default.aspx?c=16951&s=est [accessed: 16 July 2013].

INEGI. 2005. *Conteo de Población y Vivienda 2005*. [Online]. Available at: http://www.inegi.org.mx/est/contenidos/proyectos/ccpv/cpv2005/default. aspx [accessed: 16 July 2013].

Irwin, R.M., McCaughan, E. and Nasser, M.R. 2003. Introduction: Sexuality and Social Control in Mexico, 1901, in *The Famous 41: Sexuality and Social Control in Mexico, 1901*, edited by Irwin, R.M., Nasser, M.R. and McCaughan, E. New York: Palgrave Macmillan, 1–20.

Jankowiak, W.R. (ed.) 2008. *Intimacies Love and Sex Across Cultures*. New York: Columbia University Press.

Kulczycki, A. 2007. The Abortion Debate in Mexico: Realities and Stalled Policy Reform. *Bulletin of Latin American Research*, 26(1), 50–68.

Monsiváis, C. 2006. When Gender Can't Be Seen amid the Symbols: Women and the Mexican Revolution, in *Sex in Revolution: Gender, Politics, and Power in Modern Mexico*, edited by Olcott, J., Vaughan, M.K. and Cano, G. Durham: Duke University Press, 1–20.

Nehring, D. 2005. Lo mismo, pero diferente: Reflexiones sobre el estudio del aspecto cultural de las relaciones de género. *Papeles de Población*, 45, 221–46.

Nehring, D. 2009. Cultural models of intimate life in contemporary urban Mexico: A review of self-help texts. *Delaware Review of Latin American Studies*, 10(2).

Olcott, J., Vaughan, M.K. and Cano, G. (eds) 2006. *Sex in Revolution: Gender, Politics, and Power in Modern Mexico*. Durham: Duke University Press.

Oleksy, E.H. (ed.) 2009. *Intimate Citizenships: Gender, Sexualities, Politics*. London: Routledge.

Padilla, M.B., Hirsch, J., Muñoz-Laboy, M., et al. (eds) 2007. *Love and Globalization: Transformations of Intimacy in the Contemporary World*. Nashville: Vanderbilt University Press.

Plummer, K. 2003. *Intimate Citizenship: Private Decisions and Public Dialogues*. Seattle: University of Washington Press.

Rodríguez, G. 2005. Las trincheras del conservadurismo en la educación sexual, in *Los rostros del conservadurismo mexicano*, edited by de la Torre, R., García Ugarte, M.E. and Ramírez Saíz, J. M. México D.F.: CIESAS, 289–308.

Rojas Martínez, O.L. 2008. *Paternidad y vida familiar en la Ciudad de México: Un estudio del desempeño masculino en los procesos reproductivos y en la vida doméstica*. México D.F.: El Colegio de México.

Roseneil, S. 2010. Intimate Citizenship: A Pragmatic, Yet Radical, Proposal for a Politics of Personal Life. *European Journal of Women's Studies*, 17(77–82).

Rubenstein, A. 2006. The War on Las Pelonas: Modern Women and Their Enemies, Mexico City, 1924, in *Sex in Revolution: Gender, Politics, and Power in*

Modern Mexico, edited by Olcott, J., Vaughan, M.K. and Cano, G. Durham: Duke University Press, 57–80.

Ryan-Flood, R. 2009. *Lesbian Motherhood: Gender, Families and Sexual Citizenship*. London: Palgrave Macmillan.

Salles, V. and Tuirán, R. 1998. Cambios demográficos y socioculturales: familias contemporáneas en México, in *Familia y relaciones de género en transformación*, edited by Schmukler, B. México D.F.: EDAMEX, 83–126.

Salles, V. and Valenzuela, J.M. (eds) 1998. *Vida familiar y cultura contemporánea*, México D.F.: Consejo Nacional para la Cultura y las Artes (CONACULTA).

Stern, S.J. 1995. *The Secret History of Gender. Women, Men & Power in Late Colonial Mexico*. Chapel Hill: The University of North Carolina Press.

Voekel, P. 2002. *Alone Before God: The Religious Origins of Modernity in Mexico*. Durham: Duke University Press.

Chapter 1

Intimate Citizenship and Social Change in Contemporary Mexico

Katie Willis

This chapter provides an introduction to processes of globalization and modernization in Mexico in recent decades and how these have framed public discourses and collectively-shared cultural models of intimate life. The chapter focuses on shifts since the late 1960s, stressing the diversity of Mexico's population and the need to recognize how and why experiences of social change have varied socially and spatially.

Since the 1950s, national data for Mexico reveal significant changes in marital status (see Table 1.1), with a decline in marriage and an increase in individuals remaining single or living together without legal marriage (consensual union in the language of the census). At first glance this suggests a transformation in a particular form of intimate life, revolving around couple relationships, sexuality and in some cases parenting. However, this chapter will argue that these assumptions about widespread change in attitudes and practices need to be considered more carefully.

Ken Plummer (2003: 30) states that:

> The world over, people continue to confront inequalities that shape their most intimate lives: pronounced inequalities, major imbalances of power between genders, social marginalization based on ethnicity and race, age stratification, and the exclusion of all manner of people who are disabled or otherwise perceived as "different". Experiences of the intimate – loving, child rearing, sexualities, the body, our feelings – need to be mapped onto these dimensions.

Despite significant progress in some sectors, Mexico remains a highly unequal country and, as Plummer suggests, axes of inequality need to be considered when investigating the nature of discourses and practices of intimacy. This chapter draws out differences between rural and urban populations, the importance of class distinctions and variations between different states within the federal system.

The chapter is structured around six main themes: economic transformation; migration; state policies; health and education services; social movements and non-governmental organizations; and media and technology. These have been selected as main drivers of social change within Mexico (and the wider world). Some of these are familiar in examinations of intimate life, but as Plummer (2003: 15) argues in relation to intimate citizenship more generally: 'Along with

Table 1.1   Trends in marital status, 1950–2010

	% in each category[a]		
	1950[b]	**1990[c]**	**2010[d]**
TOTAL			
Single	27.9	40.6	35.2
Married	47.5	45.8	40.5
Consensual union	11.8	7.3	14.4
Separated	No data	1.2	3.8
Divorced	0.4	0.7	1.4
Widowed	7.3	3.5	4.4
No data	4.8	0.7	0.3
MEN			
Single	29.7	43.4	37.8
Married	50.6	46.1	41.7
Consensual union	12.2	7.2	14.8
Separated	No data	0.6	2.4
Divorced	0.3	0.4	1.1
Widowed	3.6	1.5	2.0
No data	3.4	0.7	0.4
WOMEN			
Single	26.2	37.9	32.7
Married	45.3	45.4	39.4
Consensual union	11.6	7.5	14.1
Separated	No data	1.8	5.0
Divorced	0.6	1.0	1.8
Widowed	10.6	5.7	6.6
No data	5.7	0.7	0.2

Note: [a] Percentages do not always add up to 100 per cent due to rounding up and down; [b] Calculated from data in INEGI *Censos de Población y Vivienda*, 1950–1970; [c] Calculated from data in INEGI *Censos de Población y Vivienda*, 1990; [d] Calculated from data in INEGI *Censos de Población y Vivienda*, 2010.
Source: www.inegi.org.mx.

the classical (usually male) public sphere of political participation, several newish spheres also require analysis. These include the new social movements, the mass media and cyberspace' (Plummer 2003: 15).

Given the range of material which will be covered in this chapter, I can only provide a brief overview of trends under the different headings. In their introduction to *Love and Globalization*, Mark Padilla et al. (2007: xii) stress that engaging with globalization processes does not mean that forms of intimacy correlate with political-economic forms in a simple way: 'we cannot predict the social expressions of love and intimacy solely on the basis of the material structures within which they operate'. However, in writing this chapter, I have followed Matthew Gutmann's argument in relation to intra-household relationships: 'The diverse ways in which power is manifested and wielded at the household level do not, however, prevent us from recognizing recurrent elements in the wider sociological context' (1996: 8).

As well as outlining and explaining the key trends associated within each of the six themes, the chapter also provides indications of how recent political, economic, social and technological changes are associated with shifts in cultural models or public discourses of intimacy. Many of these ideas are then picked up in much more detail in later chapters.

Economic Change

In the broader context of shifting concepts and practices of intimacy, the role of economic processes has been highlighted (see for example Hirsch and Wardlow 2006, Hirsch et al. 2009). Within Mexico, the national economy has experienced significant restructuring since the 1980s, with a concomitant shift in the nature of work and the profile of workers; most notably the increase in women in the economically active population.

After the Second World War, Mexico's industrial policies focused on import substitution industrialization and significant state ownership was associated with rapid economic growth particularly in urban areas. For example, GDP grew on average 7.2 per cent per annum in the period 1960–1970 (World Bank 1980: 113). This generated substantial flows of rural to urban migration and levels of urbanization in the country rose significantly from 41.7 per cent in 1950 (INEGI 2013) to 51 per cent in 1960 and 67 per cent in 1980 (World Bank 1980: 149). In 1965 the Border Industrialization Program was established in parts of northern Mexico, to attract foreign investment into assembly factories (*maquiladoras*) producing electronic goods, clothing and other products for the US market. While the original plan was to create jobs for men who may have previously travelled to the USA through the *bracero* programme, which ran 1942–1964, in reality it was women who were often the preferred labour force (Fernandez-Kelly 1984, Salzinger 2003, Wright 2006). However, in the 1980s male participation in the labour force increased greatly and by 2000 about 40 per cent of the *maquila* workforce in Cuidad Juarez were men (Lugo 2008). In the late twentieth century there was also significant state investment in the tourist industry, most notably in Cancún (Torres and Momsen 1995), along with private sector investment in tourist resorts on both the Caribbean and Pacific coasts, which again provided new job opportunities for female labour (Chant 1991, Castellanos 2007).

As part of the strategy of working alongside (some would say co-opting) workers' movements, the unions (in the form of the *Confederación de Trabajadores de México*, CTM) were a key part of the governance approach of the *Partido Revolucionario Institucional* (PRI), particularly until the 1980s. Union membership was overwhelmingly male, reflecting the heavy industry profile of the formal economy. Wage demands were framed around the concept of a 'family wage' to cover all household expenses. Workers in the informal sector, within which women were largely employed, were largely excluded from union activities and the wage and work benefits which accrued to union members.

In the 1970s, Mexican economic growth began to slow down and the government's ability to repay its foreign loans, taken out during the boom period, was threatened. Finally in 1982, the government defaulted on its debt repayments. As part of IMF financial support, structural adjustment programmes were introduced, reducing the role of the state and opening up the Mexican economy to much greater foreign competition and investment. Investment was spatially concentrated, particularly in the *maquiladoras* of Northern Mexico and in key tourist locations. Meanwhile foreign competition was undermining domestic industry and the rising cost of imports, due to currency devaluation, contributed to increasing economic stress for many households. Additionally, the rolling back of the Mexican state, not just as an employer, but also through provision of subsidies to poorer households, exacerbated the rising poverty levels.

Within this context of rising demand for female labour in certain parts of the country and increasing household need for income, women's involvement in the paid labour force increased significantly (Chant 1991, 1992). Between 1970 and 1990 the proportion of the population aged 12 and over who were economically active increased from 42.6 per cent to 43.04 per cent. However, this increase was due to the rising percentage of women entering the paid labour force as the proportion of men who were economically active declined (see Table 1.2). The relationship between the growth in women's paid labour and the nature of intimacy is not a simple one, not least because of the heterogeneity of women, intimate relations, and employment sectors. Assumptions are sometimes made that entry into the paid labour force provides women with new opportunities to challenge patriarchal norms in the household, whether that be in relation to a husband, partner, father or other male kin. However, as Sharon McClenaghan (1997) argues in relation to the Dominican Republic, this is a simplistic and romantic vision of the empowering nature of paid work. In some contexts, however, there is evidence of shifts in domestic life associated with women's paid work. Altha Cravey (1998) for example, compares what she terms the 'new factory regime' of both men and women in paid employment in Nogales with the 'old factory regime' of the lone male breadwinner and full-time housewife in Ciudad Madero.

Table 1.2   Rates of economic activity in the population aged 12 and over by gender, 1970–2010

	% Economically active (aged 12 and over)		
	Total	Men	Women
1970	42.6	69.7	17.5
1990	43.0	68.0	19.6
2000	49.3	70.3	29.9
2010	49.2	72.1	32.2

Note: Calculated from data in *INEGI Censos de Población y Vivienda*, 1970, 1990, 2000, 2010.
Source: www.inegi.org.mx.

Leslie Gates (2002) outlines a more detailed study of bargaining strategies within households where wives and/or daughters work in factories in Ciudad Juarez. While entry into the paid labour force may represent a shift in widely-practised, but not universal, gender divisions of labour, the operation of patriarchal norms within bargaining practices suggests that intimate relations may not have been transformed as much as some might claim. In Gates' study, women who 'withdrew services' as a bargaining strategy with their male partners or fathers were much less likely to be successful than those who 'provided services'. For example refusing to have sex, or do particular domestic chores were less successful for women negotiating with their partners than promising they would have sex or complete chores. While the economic language of bargaining and negotiation may seem somewhat divorced from intimate relations which are often idealized with regard to emotions such as love, it does reflect the give and take of social interactions and the mundane dimensions of intimacy. Of course, in some heterosexual couple relationships, women's entry into the labour force can lead to increased tensions and domestic violence as men feel undermined or threatened by women's move into the sphere of paid work (López and Salles 2006: 461).

Rising women's participation in the paid labour force often provides opportunities to both meet people and to find out about other perspectives, for example about relationships. This is similar to the role of educational spaces discussed below. However, not all forms of employment facilitate encounters with potential partners or socializing with other workers. Domestic service is, for example, notable in its potential isolation, particularly for domestic workers who live in their employers' homes (Goldsmith 1989). Additionally, while household members may be happy with women entering paid employment outside the home, discourses around inappropriate behaviour, dress and relationships may be mobilized to critique particular groups of women. Melissa Wright (2005) in her work on the campaigns around the 'femicide' in Ciudad Juarez, discusses the framings about 'good women' that are mobilized by different groups. For those calling the authorities to account for the failures in finding the perpetrators, notions of 'good daughters' stressing modesty and hard work are used. This is to counter claims that murdered women 'deserved it' because they were promiscuous. Wright uses the term 'paradox' to encapsulate the tensions between feminist organizations and individuals who are campaigning for women's rights to choose the lives they want, while having to use models of women's behaviour that fit conservative, patriarchal norms.

Migration

Migration, both internationally and internally, can provide new possibilities to engage in practices of intimacy which would be disapproved of in the community of origin. Escaping from the surveillance of family and neighbours by moving from a village to an urban area can provide the freedom individuals may seek to break with prevailing norms, for example, about homosexual practices (Cantú Jr 2009), pre-marital sex, or female household headship. While social approbation of all of these activities is declining in Mexico overall, there are still contexts within which there could be social disapproval or outright antagonism, especially around homosexuality.

Migration may also expose migrants to new practices of intimacy, whether this in be in relation to couple relationships or parenting. These practices may, in turn, be adopted by migrants, hybridized with existing practices and taken 'back home' in the form of what Peggy Levitt (1998) terms 'social remittances'.

As discussed above, Mexico's boom period for rural-urban migration within the country was in the post-war period. While rural-urban migration is still occurring, what is more common is the engulfing of rural settlements in urban areas as they expand. This has been particularly important since the shift in Article 27 of the Mexican Constitution regarding the potential for communally-held *ejido* land to be passed to individual ownership and sold (Jones and Ward 1998). Urban-urban migration is increasing, particularly to key locations within the country that are seen as economically buoyant (PNUD 2007).

International migration from Mexico to the United States has long been a characteristic of the country's demography. The *bracero* programme formalized a form of seasonal low-skilled migration but since the end of that programme in 1964 migration northwards has continued often in the form of undocumented migration. According to the US Census Bureau as of 2011 there were approximately 11.7 million Mexican-born residents in the USA (US Census Bureau 2011).

Of course, migration is not spatially or socially evenly spread. According to the UNDP the Mexican municipalities with the highest rates of outmigration are those in the middle-income categories. The residents of poorer municipalities do not have the economic or social capital to migrate, while those of richer municipalities have less reason to move (PNUD 2007).

Migration does not inherently create spaces of freedom to experiment with or be exposed to new forms of intimacy. In some cases practices travel with migrants and are embedded in their social interactions despite spatial dislocation. This may be because of intra-household relations, surveillance from fellow migrants or diaspora members, or continued transnational links to family and friends in the community of origin (Ariza and D'Aubeterre 2009). Pierette Hondagneu-Sotelo and Ernestine Avila (1997) discuss the construction of 'transnational motherhood' through interviews with Mexican and Central American domestic workers in the United States. For many of these women, while they were physically distant from their children the emotional and material connections remained, but in a different form. Rather than performing a mothering role through intimacy within the home, mothering continued at a distance through sending money and providing advice and emotional support where possible. Technological developments, particularly the internet and cellphones, have made it much easier for contact to be maintained across international borders (Ariza and D'Aubeterre 2009).

Migration may also enable individuals to meet new partners. This could also contribute to the move away from living with or very near to extended families after marriage (Esteinou 2006). Shifts away from living with or near parents or in-laws are also facilitated by income received from remittances. For example, Julia Pauli (2008) examines how financial autonomy due to men's remittances from the USA allows women to live away from their mothers-in-law in new-built houses in rural areas. This is often a welcome relief as it allows them to escape what they often perceive as a tense environment with frequent conflict.

State Policy

States play very significant roles in shaping discourses and practices of intimacy. Within Mexico, some attention has been placed on these themes, particularly in recent years with very high-profile debates around abortion and gay rights. Given the federal system in Mexico, examinations of the state and intimacy need to recognize the different scales at which state policies operate. International institutions, most notably the United Nations, have also played a key role at the supra-national level in shaping national policy.

The separation of church and state in nineteenth century Mexico led to civil, rather than religious, marriage being the only legally recognized form of union. Similarly divorce has been legal in all Mexican states, with some variations, since the Mexican Revolution. This contrasts greatly with many other Latin American countries, such as Brazil and Argentina, where divorce remained illegal until the latter part of the twentieth century. Despite the legality of divorce, divorce rates remain low (see Table 1.1). Esteinou (2006: 98–9) argues that this reflects social norms regarding cohesion and the role of the family, rather than processes of individualization. She also identifies however, that there are class and age differences, with divorce more common among younger cohorts and middle classes. In Gutmann's study of masculinity in Santo Domingo and Mexico City, he also examines the low rates of divorce (1996: 141). While he identifies Catholic faith as one reason for negative attitudes toward divorce, many of the other factors link more to the operation of the legal system. The relatively high financial cost of divorce, combined with issues around access to children and custody battles, especially for fathers, and the complexities of land and housing rights in the case of divorce, were all given as reasons by Santo Domingo residents for the low divorce rate. This does not necessarily mean that married couples continue to live together; Gutmann provides a number of examples of couples who have separated, live with other partners, but do not get divorced.

State policies regarding homosexuality are more heterogeneous, reflecting the social and spatial diversity of the country. While homosexual practices are legal in all states and the age of consent is the same as for heterosexuals, many other aspects of intimate life are constrained by legalization; most notably marriage and parenting. In November 2006 the Distrito Federal Assembly legalized same-sex civil unions, with the law coming into effect in 2007. Same-sex marriage became legal in the Distrito Federal in 2010. Gay couples are also allowed to adopt children in the DF. The legal changes in Mexico City followed a prolonged campaign by LGBT campaign groups, which was met by significant opposition from a range of conservative institutions, within which the Catholic Church was a major element (Encarnación 2011). Before the same-sex marriage law came into effect it was challenged in the Supreme Court by other states, but the challenge was rejected. While same-sex civil unions and marriages conducted in Mexico City have to be recognized elsewhere in the country, it is only in Coahuila, Colima and Quintana Roo that same-sex civil union or marriage ceremonies have been explicitly approved through legislation (as of August 2013). However, there are increasing challenges to state policies regarding gay marriage, following a Supreme Court ruling in December 2012 which stated that forbidding same-sex marriage went against federal law of 2001 and 2003 outlawing discrimination on the basis of sexual orientation (Justice in Mexico Project 2013).

As Omar Encarnación (2011: 115–16) is careful to point out, despite the rise in legal gay rights in Mexico and other Latin American countries, attitudes to homosexuality vary greatly. He quotes the 2008 Americas Barometer survey which found that 30–40 per cent of Mexicans surveyed had a 'high tolerance' of homosexuality; for example they had no problems with openly gay people being able to run for public office. High levels of hostility and lack of tolerance were more likely to be found among people with a religious faith, particularly those from the non-Catholic Christian churches, and those with lower levels of formal education. He also cites the levels of violence against members of the LGBT community, including murders. Thus, while state policies at both federal and individual state level may reflect a growing inclusion of diverse forms of partnership and family, this does not automatically translate onto more inclusive practices on the street.

A final key element of intimate life into which the state has increasingly interjected is in relation to domestic violence. The focus has been on male violence against women, but domestic violence usually encompasses all forms of physical and psychological violence within the domestic sphere regardless of the individuals involved. The changing forms of intimacy discussed in this volume often involve shifts in power relations within couple relationships. As López and Salles (2006: 390) demonstrate, intimate relations are not just about emotional support and solidarity, but also conflict and antagonism. Violence is a particularly extreme way in which power can be exercised and has frequently been constructed as an inherent part of masculine behaviour and normalized within domestic life. While this has never been as ubiquitous as the one-dimensional constructions of the Mexican *macho* and the self-abnegating Mexican woman suggested (Gutmann, 1996), attitudes to violence against women and within the home have experienced significant changes. Feminist organizations and NGOs have been important in raising these issues (see below) and elements of the media have also been part of presenting alternative ways of living. State responses, to both domestic and international pressures have also contributed to changing attitudes and practices, although there are clearly significant limitations.

Mexico is a signatory to the 1980 UN Convention on the Elimination of All Forms of Discrimination Against Women (CEDAW) and ratified the Convention in 1981. In 1997 federal law was changed so that physical and psychological violence within the family was explicitly recognized as a crime which could be punished by a jail sentence. Additionally, the law recognized that rape could occur within marriage. These legal changes demonstrated the willingness of governments to intervene directly in the so-called domestic or private sphere (Torres Falcón 1999). In 2006, the *Ley de Acceso a las Mujeres a una Vida Libre de Violencia* (Law for Women's Access to a Life Free of Violence) came into force. This law specially mentioned indigenous women as an identified vulnerable group (Ortiz-Barneda et al. 2011). Despite legal protection and significant campaigns, domestic violence remains a significant problem in many parts of Mexico. For example, Wright (2005: 282) cites Esther Chávez, then director of the Casa Amiga centre in Ciudad Juarez who claimed that 70 per cent of women in Chihuahua state had been victims of domestic violence. In Mexico City, rape and intimate partner violence was the third most important cause of morbidity and mortality for women at the end of the twentieth century (Ascensio 1999 cited in Garcia-Moreno and Watts 2011: 2).

Health and Education Policy

New forms of intimacy, particularly those considered more individualistic, are influenced not purely by direct interventions in intimate life through state policies on marriage, divorce and homosexuality, but also through education and health policies at both the federal and individual state level. Rosario Esteinou (2006: 83) outlines the importance of expanded school education in the twentieth century (see Table 1.3), as contributing to new models of intimacy and new opportunities

Table 1.3   School attendance by age and gender group, 1950–2010

	% of age group attending school/college/university			
	1950[a]	1970[b]	1990[b]	2010[b]
6–12				
Male	38.2	66.1	89.2	96.1
Female	35.4	65.4	88.8	96.4
13–15				
Male	41.0*	57.7	71.7	85.3
Female	33.0*	47.5	67.2	86.4
16–19				
Male	14.5**	27.5	38.1	50.7
Female	9.4**	19.0	36.6	51.7
20–24				
Male	3.6	12.7	17.9	22.8
Female	2.1	6.6	13.8	21.3

Note: * Aged 13–14; ** Aged 15–19.
Source: [a] Calculated from data in *INEGI Censos de Población y Vivienda*, 1950; [b] From table 'Población que asiste a la escuela 5 y más años según sexo, 1970 a 2010', www.inegi. org.mx.

for couple relationships outside the previous formalized rituals of courtship and gendered spatial divisions. The school can be seen as a new agent of socialization in comparison with parents and the family more broadly (2006: 85). Additionally, more diverse forms of schooling are available, including pre-school institutions and non-Catholic schools.

Secondary school attendance increased significantly in the latter part of the twentieth century as provision improved and qualifications became more important for entry into particular employment sectors. Additionally, in 1993 the Mexican constitution was changed so that secondary education was compulsory, but as Bradley U. Levinson (2001) observes, this change was often symbolic due to the lack of resources at state or household level. While this situation has improved since the early 2000s, with over 85 per cent of 13–15 year olds attending school in 2010 (see Table 1.3), this still means that nationally about 15 per cent of young people in this age group are not attending school. The figures also do not take into account completion or attainment (Parker and Pederzini 2000). There are also significant regional differences. In the Distrito Federal 92.5 per cent of women and 91 per cent of men in the 13–15 age group were enrolled in school in 2010, while the figures for Chiapas were 76.8 per cent and 81.2 per cent respectively (INEGI 2010).

Attendance in post-compulsory education, including universities, has also increased; nationally over 50 per cent of 16–19 year olds were in education in 2010, while the figure for 20–24 year olds was about 20 per cent (see Table 1.3). Regional differences are particularly striking in the non-compulsory education sector. In 2010 about 65 per cent of 16–19 year olds in the Distrito Federal were in education, but in Michoacán figure was about 40 per cent (INEGI 2010). These differences both reflect and contribute to different transitions to adulthood which Gabriela Mejia Pailles (2012) has identified based on an analysis of the Mexican National Youth Survey ENAJUV) 2000. Looking at the sample of 20–29 year olds, she identified rural-urban differences in leaving education, with young people in urban areas much more likely to combine entry into the labour force with continued education, while in rural areas this was much less common. Limited access to non-compulsory educational opportunities in rural areas, financial difficulties and social norms (around both paid work and family formation) all contribute to explain this pattern.

The gender gap in education has fallen significantly in Mexico since the 1970s (Parker and Pederzini 2000 and Table 1.3), however, again there continue to be differences between rural and urban areas. In rural areas young women are more likely to leave school earlier than young men, while in urban areas women's educational enrolment rates are often equal, or even greater than those of men. For example, in the Distrito Federal in 2010 65.6 per cent of women aged 16–19 were in education, whereas for young men the figure was 64.9 per cent (INEGI 2010). In relation to patterns of intimacy, Mejia Pailles (2012: 266) concludes that higher educational attainment among women is associated with later family formation.

Parker and Pederzini (2000: 113) have identified the importance of income in explaining gender differences in school attendance. The conditional cash transfer scheme, Oportunidades (previously Progresa-Oportunidades) seeks to encourage children's school attendance in rural areas, and lower-income urban districts. Cash payments, usually to mothers, are made on condition that children attend health centres and school. There is a sliding payment system with more money given for girls' attendance at secondary school. While there has been significant debate about the way in which women as mothers have been incorporated into this scheme (see, for example, Molyneux 2006), the results in terms of children's health and school attendance have been very positive (Escobar Latapí and González de la Rocha 2008).

The role of educational spaces in changing/ reinforcing patterns of intimacy is very important. They can provide opportunities for young people to meet away from family surveillance and to be exposed to different ideas, both formally through the curriculum, but also informally through conversations with fellow students. Formal sex education in schools has been on the curriculum since the 1970s, but, as in many countries, sex education in Mexico has tended to focus on biological processes, rather than wider social debates around relationships and emotions

(Gutmann 2007: 123–5). Additionally, as with the debates around gay rights (see above), the role of the Catholic Church in framing sex education debates has often been important.

Within the sphere of health care, improved access to family planning services has also meant that sexual intimacy between heterosexual couples is less likely to be framed by the risk of pregnancy. Nationally, the total fertility rate (TFR) has decreased dramatically since the 1970s (see Table 1.4), although this hides the variation from the Distrito Federal (lowest TFR of 1.8) to Chiapas and Guerrero, with the highest TFR of 2.5 in 2009 (INEGI 2013). The desire for smaller families is also driven by women's labour force participation and the opportunity costs (in terms of income, but also ideas of identity and self-worth) of pregnancy and childcare. In 1976, 30.2 per cent of women of fertile age were using contraception, but by 2009 the figure was 72.5 per cent (INEGI 2013). As with most social indicators in Mexico, there are significant regional differences; in 2009, 79.6 per cent of fertile age women in the Distrito Federal used contraception, compared with 54.9 per cent in Chiapas (INEGI 2013). While free family planning services are provided in state medical facilities, access to and the nature and quality of services available in such facilities, varies greatly. There are also debates about the focus of family planning services on women which fails to recognize the negative implications of excluding men. Excluding men both reinforces a construction of men as irresponsible and unreliable (Gutmann 2007), but is can also leave women unable to negotiate the use of contraception with male partners who are unwilling to entertain the idea.

The widespread use of contraception among a population which still widely identifies as Catholic (89.3 per cent in 2010, INEGI 2013) is a clear indication of how individuals and couples flexibly interpret religious doctrine within their sphere of intimacy. However, in other sexual and reproductive health debates, the role of the Church has been much more forceful. Debates around the provision of abortion services, for example, demonstrate this very clearly. There are no federal regulations about abortion, but in most Mexican states, abortion is illegal, or is only legally permitted in very specific circumstances, such as when pregnancy is the result of rape. An estimated 500,000 abortions are carried out annually in Mexico (Kulczyci 2007). However access to abortions (either legally or illegally) differs greatly both spatially and socially. Additionally, while emergency contraception was legalised throughout the country in 2004, knowledge of this service and access to it is also very variable (Sánchez Fuentes, Paine and Elliott-Buettner 2008).

In April 2007, abortion up to 12 weeks of gestation was decriminalized in the Distrito Federal (Sánchez Fuentes, Paine and Elliott-Buettner 2008). Public hospitals in the capital can now provide a termination in early pregnancy for free for women who request one. Sánchez Fuentes et al. (2008) outline how the legal change came about. Key aspects included the role of civil society organizations (see below for a wider discussion of the role of such organizations in changing discourses of intimacy in Mexico) such as the *Grupo de Información en Reproducción Elegida* (GIRE/Reproductive Choice Information Group) and

Table 1.4   Total fertility rate 1976–2013

	Mean number of children per woman aged 15–49
1976[a]	5.7
1990[b]	3.4
2000[b]	2.6
2013[c]	2.2

Note: [a] SPP-IISUNAM Encuesta Mexicana de Fecundidad, 1976 (Mexico DF, 1979); [b] CONAPO Estimaciones de la población 1990–2010 (www.conapo.gob.mx); [c] CONAPO Proyecciones de la población 2010–20150 (www.conapo.gob.mx).
Source: INEGI (2013).

Católicas por el Derecho a Decidir (Catholics for the Right to Choose). Within political parties, the abortion debate could be used as a tool within wider strategies. As Sánchez Fuentes et al. conclude: 'Though abortion is usually viewed as a politically risky subject for legislators, in this case, the left-wing party [the PRD] identified it as a pillar of a democratic, secular and progressive society, and used it to define their values in contrast to the right wing' (2008: 356).

Social Movements and NGOs

Outside state institutions, civil society organizations in the form of social movements and non-governmental organizations (NGOs) have played an important role in framing discourses around intimacy within Mexico, particularly since the 1960s. As indicated above in the discussion of abortion and gay marriage, civil society organizations come in many forms, including those which seek to maintain what are viewed as 'traditional' morals and behaviours. The massacre at Tlatelolco in 1968 was a key moment in the development of social movements within Mexico, but other events, such as the 1985 Mexico City earthquake (Gutmann 2002) and the murders of women in Ciudad Juarez (see above) have triggered significant mobilizations. The challenge to PRI hegemony represented by the election of Vicente Fox of the *Partido Acción Nacional* (PAN) to the presidency in 2000 provided an opportunity for the opening up of more democratic and inclusive forms of government, but there has been limited progress in this regard.

Adriana Ortiz-Ortega and Mercedes Barquet (2010: 113) argue that, 'it was not until the beginning of the 1970s that women began organizing on their own to discuss the specificities of their social standing as women in Mexican society'. Women had long been involved in campaigns to access community services, particularly in the expanding informal settlements which emerged as Mexico's towns and cities expanded, and women played a significant role in the student movement of the late 1960s, but this mobilization was around meeting their roles as wives and mothers ('practical gender interests' in Molyneux's 1985 terms), rather than more strategic action for wider social change in relation to women's rights. The 1970s feminist organizations were largely constituted by educated women from higher socio-economic groups and were based in urban areas, particularly Mexico City. The focus of much of their campaigning was on sexuality and reproductive rights, particularly abortion and access to contraception.

These campaigns remained important in the 1980s, but the devastating effects of the economic crisis and restructuring (see above) resulted in employment and living conditions receiving greater attention. The importance of the grassroots mobilization of women in rural areas and low-income urban areas around communal services expanded massively and increased the visibility of women in the public sphere (Ortiz-Ortega and Barquet 2010). In some cases women's involvement in such actions were associated with a growing recognition of their wider social position as women in Mexican society, with restricted rights and opportunities (Craske 1994). The diversity of women's mobilization has continued to the present day, including high profile groups such as the Zapatistas in southern Mexico, where the involvement of indigenous women is noteworthy (Stephen 1995). Groups that explicitly identify as 'feminist' have been crucial in lobbying political parties and government for legal change (see discussion above regarding abortion).

International collaboration has been a key part of aspects of the Mexican feminist and women's movement. Mexican organizations have played an important role in the Latin American and Caribbean feminist *Encuentros* which have been held regularly since 1981 (Sternbach et al. 1992). The 1987 meeting was held in Taxco and in 2009 it was held in Mexico City. These meetings demonstrate the diversity of Latin American feminism and the importance of recognizing the development of regionally-specific forms of feminism and women's activism. While Mexican women's organizations have increasingly linked into international feminist networks, particularly in the USA (see for example the Ciudad Juárez violence against women actions, Staudt 2008), activities and approaches are framed by the specific Mexican context within which the organizations are operating, rather than being a simple translation of 'Western' feminism.

The gay rights movement has experienced an expansion and trajectory similar to that of the feminist movement since the 1970s. While there are numerous debates around terminology, particularly the term 'gay' in a Mexican context (see, for example, Carrillo 2003), I am using it here as a useful shorthand. In the 1970s organizations such as the Grupo Orgullo Homosexual de Liberación (GOHL) and the Frente Homosexual de Acción Revolucionario (FHAR) were established in major urban centres. GOHL was based in Guadalajara and FHAR in Mexico City (Balderston 1997). The emergence of HIV/AIDS in the 1980s was particularly important in mobilization around gay rights, with the provision of sexual health services and education linked with a growing awareness of the need to campaign for greater rights for LGBT individuals. Currently, organizations such as Letra S continue to campaign in this field and have played significant roles in the legal changes described in earlier sections of this chapter (www.letrase.org.mx).

The first LGBT pride parade took place in 1978 in Mexico City and it now takes place annually attracting thousands. Similar marches and public expressions of collective LGBT identity are now held in many parts of the country. In June 2009 the first 'sexual diversity march' was held in Oaxaca City attracting a few hundred participants who paraded through the city centre on a Saturday afternoon before holding a rally in the central square. While some of the marchers wore masks to hide their identity, most were happy to be seen walking behind banners and rainbow flags. Oaxaca City, with its growing middle class population, large tourist industry and significant university student population, is not indicative of the state as a whole. However, the very public display of diverse forms of sexual identity and demands for equal rights for LGBT individuals was an obvious indication of how attitudes in one of Mexico's most conservative states have changed. Oaxaca is also one of the states where same-sex marriages have taken place following the Supreme Court ruling in December 2012 (see above).

The rise of NGOs, particularly as service providers, has been an observable trend in many parts of the world since the 1980s, due largely to the adoption of neoliberal policies by governments and international financial agencies (Lewis and Kanji 2009). As the state withdraws provision of services, e.g. health and housing, and private sector providers step in, poorer communities are excluded. NGOs may step in to fill this gap. Additionally, NGOs may operate in places or in sectors where the state was never a significant provider. With regard to services linked to understandings and practices of intimacy, Mexican NGOs have been particularly important in the field of sexual health, with some working in partnership with government organizations (Gómez-Juregui 2004). As well as organizations such as Letra S working in field of sexual rights, other NGOs, such as Salud y Genero, have focused on incorporating heterosexual men into reproductive and sexual health education and support. This recognizes the importance of men's roles as partners and fathers in and of itself, as well as the need to engage with men to achieve greater gender equality (Chant and Gutmann 2000).

Media and Technology

The role of media in highlighting aspects of intimate life in Mexico and presenting alternative forms of couple relationship and family relationships is the final main theme I want to address in this chapter. Media can be highly effective in challenging prevailing social and cultural norms, particularly when framed as 'entertainment'. Newspapers and magazines have been important channels through which themes such as women's rights and sexuality have been addressed in Mexico. For example, the feminist magazine, *fem* was included as a supplement to the *Uno Más Uno* newspaper in the early 1990s (Gutmann 1996: 93), and *Letra S* focusing on sexual rights and HIV/AIDS has been a supplement in *La Nacional* and later

La Jornada (www.letrase.org.mx). However, it is television and film which have been particularly influential in relation to debates about intimacy within Mexico in recent decades. New technologies have also expanded opportunities for accessing information and ways in which relationships can be played out.

While concepts such as 'cultural globalisation' sometimes suggest that countries in Latin America, Asia and Africa are engulfed by Hollywood or US television programmes, within Mexico and in many parts of Latin America, the long-standing role of the *telenovela* (soap opera) must be recognised (Lopez 1995). Some soap operas were explicitly developed in conjunction with government departments, something which was more feasible during the period of state-owned television channels prior to the privatisation and deregulation of the 1980s. *Acompáñame* (Accompany Me/Come With Me) was broadcasted by Televisa in the late 1970s and focused on the reproductive choices of three sisters. This was part of a family planning campaign by CONAPO, the state population council (Soto Laveaga 2007). Soap operas have often engaged with 'controversial' issues to attract attention and have provided a way of presenting alternative forms of intimacy to millions of Mexicans across the country. For example, *Lo Que es el Amor* aired 2001–2 on TV Azteca. It focused on the lives of upper-middle-class urban professionals working in finance and dealt with issues such as divorce, homosexuality and infidelity (Pearson 2005).

However, films and television programmes produced outside Latin America also receive a large audience. Within television, the massive expansion in the number of available channels due to deregulation of the television sector means that viewers with satellite connections can access a wide array of programming. Domestic channels also import foreign shows, or produce Mexican versions of international shows such as *Big Brother*.

Unsurprisingly the expansion of mobile telephones and the Internet has provided new spaces and channels for the expression of intimacy and opportunities to explore possible alternative forms of living or being in a couple relationship. In 2010, Mexico had 98.1 fixed and mobile telephone subscribers per 100 people (UNDP 2013: 187), but this varied greatly within the country. In 2011, 77.4 per cent of the population of Baja California Sur used mobile telephones, while the figure for Guerrero was only 31.1 per cent (INEGI 2012). The figures for Internet users are similarly wide-ranging. Nationally in 2010 there were 31.1 Internet users per 100 people (UNDP 2013: 187). However, there are significant differences, reflecting what has been termed a 'digital divide'. In gender terms slightly more men (51 per cent) than women (49 per cent) were Internet users in 2011 (INEGI 2012). Socio-economic divides are much starker (Mariscal et al. 2011), and this is also seen in geographical differences, with figures for the Distrito Federal standing at 53.6 per cent and the lowest internet use in Chiapas with 22.0 per cent. Internet use is also concentrated in the 12–34 age group, with only 4 per cent of the population over 55s using the Internet in 2011 (INEGI 2012).

Emailing and the use of social networking sites such as Facebook and Twitter are among the main reasons Mexicans use the Internet (INEGI 2012). This provides potentially new fora within which to meet potential partners and also to develop new forms of intimacy. It is also potentially part of trends towards a growing sharing and expression of emotions beyond close family and friends, something which 'confessional' forms of television shows have been engaged in for some time.

Conclusion

This chapter has provided a brief overview of key recent economic, social and political shifts in Mexico. While these may be seen as part of a homogenizing and hegemonic process of modernization within early twenty-first century global capitalism, the chapter has highlighted social and spatial variations. Additionally, the chapter has highlighted the agency of Mexican individuals and communities in both shaping and resisting certain interventions or influences. However, what is also clear is that dimensions of inequality continue to frame Mexicans' lives, including the choices that they make about their intimate lives.

Bibliography

Ariza, M. and D'Aubeterre, M.E. 2009. *Contigo en la distancia* ... Dimensiones de la conyugalidad en migrantes mexicanos internos e internacionales, in *Tramas Familiares en el México Contemporáneo: Una Perspectiva Sociodemográfica*, edited by C. Rabell Romero. Mexico D.F.: UNAM/El Colegio de México, 353–91.

Balderston, D. 1997. Excluded middle? Bisexuality in *Doña Herlinda y Sus Hija*, in *Sex and Sexuality in Latin America*, edited by D. Balderston. New York: New York University Press, 190–99.

Cantú Jr., L. 2009. *The Sexuality of Migration: Border Crossings and Mexican Immigrant Men*, edited by N.A. Naples and S. Vidal-Ortiz. New York: New York University Press.

Carrillo, H. 2003. Neither machos nor maricones: Masculinity and emerging male homosexual identities in Mexico, in *Changing Men and Masculinities*, edited by M. Gutmann. Durham: Duke University Press, 351–69.

Castellanos, M.B. 2007. Adolescent migration to Cancún: Reconfiguring Maya households and gender relations in Mexico's Yucatan Peninsula. *Frontiers: A Journal of Women's Studies*, 28(3), 1–27.

Chant, S. 1991. *Women and Survival in Mexican Cities: Perspectives on Gender, Labour Markets and Low Income Households*. Manchester: Manchester University Press.

Chant, S. 1992. Women, work and household survival strategies in Mexico, 1982–1992: Past trends, current tendencies and future research. *Bulletin of Latin American Research*, 13(2), 203–33.

Chant, S. and Gutmann, M. 2000. *Mainstreaming Men into Gender and Development*. Oxford: Oxfam.

Craske, N. 1994. Women and regime politics in Guadalajara's low-income neighbourhoods. *Bulletin of Latin American Research*, 13(1), 61–78.

Cravey, A. 1998. *Women and Work in Mexico's Maquiladoras*. Lanham, MD: Rowman & Littlefield.

Escobar Latapí, A. and González de la Rocha, M. 2008. Girls, mothers and poverty reduction in Mexico: Evaluating Progresa Oportunidades, in *The Gendered Impacts of Liberalization: Towards Embedded Liberalism?*, edited by S. Razavi. New York: Routledge/UNRISD, 435–68.

Esteinou, R. 2006. Una primera reconstrucción de las fortalezas y desafíos de las familias mexicanas en el siglo XXI, in *Fortalezas y Desafíos en las Familias en Dos Contextos: Estados Unidos de América y México*, edited by G. Esteinou. Mexico D.F.: CIESAS, 75–109.

Fernandez-Kelly, M.P. 1984. *For We Are Sold, I and My People: Women and Industry in Mexico's Frontier*. New York: SUNY Press.

Garcia-Moreno, C. and Watts, C. 2011. Violence against women: An urgent public health priority. *Bulletin of the World Health Organization*, 89(1), 2–3.

Gates, L.C. 2002. The strategic uses of gender in household negotiations: Women workers on Mexico's northern border. *Bulletin of Latin American Research*, 21(4), 507–26.

Goldsmith, M. 1989. Politics and programs of domestic workers' organizations in Mexico, in *Muchachas No More: Household Workers in Latin America and the Caribbean*. Philadelphia: Temple University Press, 221–44.

Gómez-Jáuregui, J. 2004. The feasibility of government partnerships with NGOs in the reproductive health field in Mexico. *Reproductive Health Matters*, 12(24), 42–55.

Gutmann, M. 1996. *The Meanings of Macho: Being a Man in Mexico City*. Berkeley: University of California Press.

Gutmann, M. 2002. *The Romance of Democracy: Compliant Defiance in Contemporary Mexico*. Berkeley: University of California Press.

Gutmann, M. 2007. *Fixing Men: Sex, Birth Control, and AIDS in Mexico*. Berkeley: University of California Press.

Hirsch, J.S. and Wardlow, H. (eds) 2006. *Modern Loves: The Anthropology of Romantic Courtship and Companionate Marriage*. Ann Arbor: University of Michigan Press.

Hirsch, J.S., Wardlow, H. Smith, D.J., et al. 2009. *The Secret: Love, Marriage, and HIV*. Nashville: Vanderbilt University Press.

Hondagneu-Sotelo, P. and Avila, E. 1997. 'I'm here but I'm there': The meanings of Latina transnational motherhood. *Gender & Society*, 11(8), 548–71.

INEGI. 2010. *Censos de Población y Vivienda, 2010* [available at: www.inegi.org.mx].

INEGI. 2012. *Estadísticas sobre Disponibillidad y Uso de Tecnología de Información y Comunicación en los Hogares* [available at: www.inegi.org. mx]. México DF: INEGI.

INEGI. 2013. INEGI statistics online [available at: www.inegi.org.mx, accessed 15 July 2013].

Jones, G.A. and Ward, P.M. 1998. Privatizing the commons: Reforming the ejido and urban development in Mexico. *International Journal of Urban and Regional Research*, 22(1), 76–93.

Justice in Mexico Project. 2013. First gay marriage celebrated in Oaxaca following Supreme Court's December ruling, 8 May 2013 [available at: http:// justiceinmexico.org/2013/05/08/first-gay-marriage-celebrated-in-oaxaca-following-supreme-courts-december-ruling/].

Kulczycki, A. 2007. The abortion debate in Mexico: Realities and stalled policy reform. *Buletin of Latin American Research*, 26(1), 50–68.

Levinson, B.U. 2001. *We Are All Equal: Student Culture and Identity at a Mexican Secondary School, 1988–1998*. Durham: Duke University Press.

Levitt, P. 1998. Social remittances: Migration driven local-level form of cultural diffusion. *International Migration Review*, 32(4), 926–48.

Lewis, D. and Kanji, N. 2009 *Non-Governmental Organizations and Development*. London: Routledge.

Lopez, A.M. 1995. Our welcomed guests: Telenovelas in Latin America, in *To Be Continued ... Soap Operas Around the World*, edited by R.C. Allen. London: Routledge, 256–75.

López, M. de la Paz and Salles, V. 2006. Los vaivenes de la conyugalidad, in *Fortalezas y Desafíos en las Familias en Dos Contextos: Estados Unidos de América y México*, edited by G. Esteinou. Mexico DF: CIESAS, 385–435.

Lugo, A. 2008. *Fragmented Lives, Assembled Parts*. Austin: University of Texas Press.

Mariscal, J., Gil-Garcia, J.R. and Aldama-Nalda, A. 2011. Policies on access to information technologies: The case of e-Mexico. *Information Technologies and International Development*, 7(2), 1–16.

McClenaghan, S. 1997. Women, work and empowerment: Romanticizing the reality, in *Gender Politics in Latin America*, edited by E. Dore. New York: Monthly Review Press, 19–35.

Mejia Pailles, G. 2012. *A Life Course Perspective on Social and Family Formation Transitions to Adulthood of Young Men and Women in Mexico*. PhD thesis, Department of Social Policy, London School of Economics and Political Science [available at: http://etheses.lse.ac.uk/357/].

Molyneux, M. 1985. Mobilization without emancipation? Women's interests, the state and revolution in Nicaragua. *Feminist Studies*, 11(2), 227–54.

Molyneux, M. 2006. Mothers at the service of the new poverty agenda: Progresa/ Oportunidades, Mexico's conditional transfer programme. *Social Policy & Adminstration*, 40(4), 425–49.

Ortiz-Barreda, G., Vives-Cases, C. and Gil-Gonzáez, D. 2011. Worldwide violence against women legislation: An equity approach. *Health Policy*, 100(2–3), 125–33.

Ortiz-Ortega, A. and Barquet, M. 2010. Gendering transition to democracy in Mexico. *Latin American Research Review*, special issue, 108–37.

Padilla, M.B., Hirsch, J.S., Muñoz-Laboy, M., et al. 2007. Introduction: Cross-cultural reflections on an intimate intersection, in *Love and Globalization: Transformations of Intimacy in the Contemporary World*, edited by M.B. Padilla et al. Nashville: Vanderbilt University Press, ix–xxxi.

PNUD. 2007. *Informe Sobre Desarrollo Humano México 2006–2007: Migración y Desarrollo Humano* [available at: www.undp.org.mx]. México D.F.: PNUD.

Parker, S.W. and Pederzini V.C. 2000. Género y educación en México. *Estudios Demográficos y Urbanos*, 15(1), 97–122.

Pauli, J. 2008. A house of one's own: Gender, migration and residence in rural Mexico. *American Ethnologist*, 35(1), 171–87.

Pearson, R.C. 2005. Fact or fiction? Narrative and reality in the Mexican telenovela. *Television and New Media*, 6(4), 400–406.

Plummer, K. 2003. *Intimate Citizenship: Private Decisions and Public Dialogues*. Seattle: University of Washington Press.

Salzinger, L. 2003. *Genders in Production: Making Workers in Mexico's Global Factories*. Berkeley: University of California Press.

Sánchez Fuentes, M.L., Paine, J. and Elliott-Buettner, B. 2008. The decriminalisation of abortion in Mexico City: How did abortion rights become a political priority? *Gender & Development*, 26(2), 345–60.

Soto Laveaga, G. 2007. 'Let's become fewer': Soap operas, contraception and nationalizing the Mexican family in an overpopulated world. *Sexuality Research and Social Policy*, 4(3), 19–33.

Staudt, K. 2008. *Violence and Activism at the Border: Gender, Fear and Everyday Life in Ciudad Juárez*. Austin: University of Texas Press.

Stephen, L. 1995. The Zapatista Army of National Liberation and the National Democratic Convention. *Latin American Perspectives*, No. 88, 22(4), 88–99.

Sternbach, N., Navarro Aranguren, M., Chuchryk, P. and Alvarez, S.E. 1992. Feminisms in Latin America: From Bogotá to San Bernardo. *Signs*, 17(2), 393–434.

Torres, R.M. and Momsen, J.D. 1995. Gringolandia: The construction of a new tourist space in Mexico. *Annals of the Association of American Geographers*, 95(2), 314–35.

Torres Falcón, M. 1999. Gender and law: Mexican legislation on domestic violence. *Journal of Gender, Social Policy and the Law*, 7(2), 343–53.

UNDP. 2013. *Human Development Report 2013: The Rise of the South: Human Progress in a Diverse World* [available at: www.undp.org]. New York: UNDP.

US Census Bureau. 2011. *American Community Survey* [available at: http:// factfinder2.census.gov/faces/nav/jsf/pages/index.xhtml].

World Bank. 1980. *World Development Report 1980*. New York: Oxford University Press.

Wright, M.W. 2005. Paradoxes, protests and the *Mujeres de Negro* of northern Mexico. *Gender, Place and Culture*, 12(3), 277–92.

Wright, M.W. 2006. *Disposable Women and Other Myths of Global Capitalism*. New York: Routledge.

Chapter 2
Intimacy in Twentieth-Century Mexico

Rosario Esteinou

Intimacy is a relatively recent theme in international literature. It is also a difficult area of sociological research since it relates to affection, emotions, feelings and subjective interactions, all of which are difficult to grasp. This chapter aims to analyse intimacy in Mexican society throughout the twentieth century, specifically in family settings. The discussion is organized as follows: I first examine some of the theoretical assumptions which guide the contemporary study of intimacy in Mexico and at the international level. Second, I trace some of the characteristics intimacy has assumed in three periods: from 1900 to 1950, from 1950 to 1970, and from 1970 to 2000.

Intimacy and Personal Life as Emerging Themes in Contemporary Debate

Over the past three decades there has been an increasing interest in analysing more deeply the quality of relationships and how they have changed through time. Although intimacy first began to be discussed as an issue in the late seventies, mainly in connection with sexual life (Gabb 2010), Anthony Giddens' book, *The Transformation of Intimacy* (1992) represented a turning point that promoted a debate in Western societies, especially in the United States and the United Kingdom. He proposed that since the sixties there had been changes in the patterns of intimate relationships, from being basically structured around familial ties of obligation, towards a democratization of interpersonal relationships. He argued that the separation of sex from reproduction has promoted the possibility of a 'pure relationship' in which men and women are equals. The result is that whether relationships are sustained or not these days depends on the rewards that they provide. When these do not materialize, couples split up by mutual consent. Giddens' view of intimacy is an optimistic one, since change has brought a democratization of intimate life. However, there are other accounts in which negative aspects of these changes also appear. Beck and Beck-Gersheim (1995) and Bauman (2003) illustrate how personal life becomes difficult when faced with the task of establishing long term relationships, and consequently a sphere of intimacy. These authors observe that contemporary interpersonal relationships are based on latent, insecure, frail and impermanent bonds of love. Risk, anxiety and uncertainty are central in their viewpoint. These conceptual positions have been questioned for not taking into consideration the power that companionate love has in structuring couple and family relationships, regardless of the role that risk and processes of individualization play (Smart 2007, Smart and Shipman 2012, Millán 2009).

Following these studies, other researchers (Jamieson 2002, Smart 2007) have pointed out the importance of intimacy and *personal* life as distinctive aspects of contemporary interpersonal family relationships. Under this scope, families can be understood as affective spaces of intimacy within which family members build meanings and experiences in a specific historical and socio-cultural context (Smart 2004). In other words, everyday family practices constitute a sense of relatedness, no matter whether we are talking about single parents, step-parents, blended or choice families. This diversity of family forms testifies to the reconfiguration of traditional forms of intimacy and interpersonal relationships. At the same time it reinforces the underlying nature of families as social units in which affection and emotions reside.

Jamieson (2002) has pointed out that although intimacy varies between and within societies, there is at least a very minimal level of intimacy in all societies: 'If intimacy is defined as any form of *close association* in which people acquire familiarity, that is *shared detailed knowledge* about each other, then it is impossible to conceive of a society without intimacy' (Jamieson 2002: 8). Growing up and the process of becoming a member of a society typically involves close association between children and adults, siblings and partners, and this provides people with a privileged knowledge of each other which no one else has. In some circumstances, people in close association feel emotionally close even if they say little to each other, but they must sense that they share a common view of the world and mutually benevolent views of each other. According to Jamieson, close association and privileged knowledge may be aspects of intimacy, but they are not sufficient conditions to ensure intimacy as it is understood today. The terms *knowing* and *understanding* suggest nowadays not just cognitive knowledge and understanding, but a degree of sympathy or emotional understanding which involves deep insight into an inner self (Jamieson 2002: 8). In fact, in contemporary European and North American culture it is assumed that to really know and understand a person, an intense interaction is required, and that the privileged knowledge resulting from this is only permitted to those who are loved and trusted. Therefore, trust is today a more fundamental dimension of intimacy than knowing and understanding. However, it is a deep knowing and understanding, which particularly characterizes what can be described as disclosing intimacy (Jamieson 2002: 9). At the heart of the current debate as summarized above, is the issue (among others) of whether the democratization of interpersonal relationships (Giddens' proposal) or the development of disclosing intimacy (Jamieson's conceptualization) are extensive in contemporary Western societies or not. Both authors conclude that, in fact, there is an increasing change towards disclosing intimacy, but differ – as Gabb (2010) observes – on the extent to which this democratization of intimacy is actually prevalent, particularly in terms of gendered and generational power relations within family interactions. According to Jamieson, there is no clear evidence that disclosing intimacy is increasingly the key organizing principle of people's lives. In Giddens' view, however, there is.

There has been little research on intimacy as such in contemporary Mexican society. Indeed, over the last four decades, most of the research regarding family relationships has focused on three aspects. First, there have been numerous studies on the impact socio-demographic and socioeconomic dynamics have on family units and household organization. These studies analyse how family life is connected to labour market dynamics, economic development models, mortality, fertility and marriage rates, as well as other demographic variables. Even though they have generated important findings, they are lacking in their analysis of the quality of family relationships and the ways in which family bonds are created and sustained. In this sense, they have failed to describe the specific aspects associated with the family as a special social group that differs from the economic realm and has its own logic of configuration and function. They have also failed to explore in depth the sociocultural aspects that structure family life.

Second, studies on gender differences and inequalities have been frequent in recent years. They have drawn attention to the persistence of the gendered inequalities women experience in their everyday lives. While these studies have emphasized unequal gender relations as experienced by specific social groups, they typically lack a detailed account of how these inequalities are situated within broader family relationships and dynamics.

Third, research on contemporary transformations of intimacy in Mexico is defined by studies with highly specific and closely localized subject matters. There is thus a distinct lack of research that would offer a more comprehensive, macro-level perspective on these transformations. There are, for instance, no large-scale longitudinal studies on the development of family relationships. As a result, there is only a fragmented and dispersed understanding of family life in Mexican society today. So far, there have been very few attempts to address these issues (Esteinou 2008).

Therefore, my aim in this chapter is to address these gaps and limitations. Through an analysis of intimacy in twentieth-century Mexico, I seek to grasp the quality of family relationships over a longer period than has been considered in previous research, and to examine the so far under-studied socio-cultural dynamics of family life. My aim here is to explore two aspects of the ideas developed above regarding the Western debate: on the one hand, to identify features of twentieth century Mexican society that point towards different types of intimacy, taking as a criterion for classification the balance between the bonds of family obligation and freedom of choice when making those bonds, and on the other hand, to consider whether over the course of the century there was a trend towards increasing disclosure and democratization when building intimacy; in other words, what kinds of intimate citizenships – to use Plummer's term (2001, 2005) – developed during that century. I accept as a starting point the argument of Jamieson that all societies develop some sort of intimacy grounded on close association and privileged knowledge. Mexican society and family life can be therefore be analysed from this perspective. This will be done mainly by reviewing the socio-cultural narratives and norms that moulded or influenced social life and behaviour.

The Emergence of the Nuclear Family:
Romantic Love and Family Obligations between 1900 and 1950

As Jamieson (2002) observed, all societies develop some sort of intimacy. In the first half of the century, the configuration of Mexican families went through some important changes. Economic, social, demographic and legal factors promoted the formation of specific family relationships associated with the modern nuclear family (Esteinou 2008, 2012). The division of roles between the husband-father-breadwinner and the housewife- mother, and freedom of choice in partner selection began to unfold during this period. A wave of industrialization started at the end of the nineteenth century, and this led to a decrease in handicraft manufacturing and employment for women, and an increase in full time jobs for men. Women retired from work and began to concentrate more on the family. As a result, a specific division of labour developed between men and women. By 1950 this division was clear, since most women of working age were dedicated exclusively to domestic work and to raising numerous offspring (Rendón 1990).

Although the division of labour contributed to the formation of some features of the nuclear family, other demographic trends inhibited the consolidation of some elements associated with modern family relationships. Mortality rates in particular made the formation of complete families difficult; it was very common for a close family member to die, and on average a couple spent around 18 years of marriage together (Tuirán 1996, Gómez de León and Partida 2001). In the forties, mortality rates fell considerably, allowing the formation of complete families that spent long periods of time together and which developed sustained bonds. As a result, during this period families faced constant vulnerabilities and difficulties in relation to intimate daily life.

State policies, especially laws regarding marriage, favoured the formation of modern family relationships, and were underpinned by a particularly normative narrative on this issue. The Civil Codes of 1917 (Poder Ejecutivo 1917) and 1932 (Código Civil 1993) supported greater individualism by promoting freedom in the selection of spouses. Civil marriage became a free contract between individuals and was required before a marriage in the Catholic Church could take place. With this legislation, arranged marriages started to decrease substantially in such a way that by 1930, 48 per cent of people were married under civil law (Quilodrán 1996). Thus, the state promoted a secular pattern of marriage alongside the religious form. The new legislation included more rights and promoted greater equality for women within marriage as well. The promotion and development of a free choice of partner through civil marriage played a central role in shaping particular features of intimacy. Indeed, while arranged marriages implied other kinds of intimacy, of knowing the other, based on daily contact, in traditional norms associated with marriage, emotional attachment was not a structural element of the relationship. In contrast, free choice in the selection of a partner established other grounds for gaining knowledge of the other: the development of romantic love.

However, the civil codes still had significant limitations regarding equality between spouses. Although the Civil Code of 1917 gave women more rights within marriage (for example men and women would have the same authority in the home, both should decide on how their children were educated, women could make their own decisions regarding their assets and how these were administered, and they could appear and defend themselves in court), it reinforced the ties that compelled them to remain almost exclusively at home, by introducing the concept of a division between the public and the private sphere. The former belonged to men, and the latter to women. Accordingly, men were to provide the economic resources for the household and women had the obligation of managing all domestic matters. In particular, women should be in charge of looking after the children and running the home. Furthermore, Article 44 established that only with the husband's permission could the wife render her personal services to another person, have a job or profession, or establish a business (Cano 1995: 22–3). The obligation for women to take care of domestic chores was sustained, almost in the same terms, in the Civil Code of 1928, and prevailed until the seventies when it was eliminated (Cano 1995: 23–4). This legal definition of women's duties implied a strong subjugation to the husband and confinement to the home.

As I mentioned before, these changes were very slow, and were disseminated with different rhythms among different social groups. They promoted the development of some aspects of the nuclear family while at the same time helping to form a narrative about what a family should be. Indeed, the modernization of social and cultural life took a long time to develop, and Mexican society continued to have strong conservative views about gender, the socialization of children and family life. These reinforced ties of obligation over individual interests and freedom. This normative narrative had differing impacts on the population as a whole and on different social groups, as discussed below. It was also reinforced by other discourses arising from other areas of society and social actors, such as the Catholic Church and moralists.

One aspect of the nuclear family promoted by this narrative was the importance of love as an ingredient in forming a family. From the end of the nineteenth century onward, Mexican writers started to develop and disseminate this idea within society, as Dávalos (1995) has pointed out. This aspect has not been sufficiently analysed however. When talking about love in the nuclear family, there is often a reference to romantic love. However, we will see that love had different manifestations. In other words, although couples began to form families based on love (due to the increasing freedom in partner selection), its conceptualization differed from how it is understood today. These conceptualizations represented ideal forms of how intimate relationships were to be established, how couples and parents and children should interact, and what kinds of closeness and knowledge they might have.

The narrative of the nuclear family, formed by love and with a clear division of labour and spheres between husband and wife spread to a greater extent among middle and upper social groups. During this period however these groups were very limited in size; most of the population lived in rural areas. Love was seen as a fundamental ingredient of the relationship, but its definition was strongly moulded by a conservative view arising from the Catholic Church, moralists and prevailing social and cultural norms. Indeed, some documents of the time reveal the view that women, confined to the domestic sphere, should defer completely to their husbands and be obedient. One document established at the end of the nineteenth century, for example, that women should devote themselves to their husbands and children: they should be guided by 'their sweetness, their moral beauties, their virtues, their qualities, their talent and judgement ... because she was born to devote herself completely to create the fortune of others; following that path they [women] find happiness' (Serrano de Wilson E. 1883, *Las perlas del corazón; deber y aspiraciones de la mujer en su vida íntima*, cited in Rocha 1991: 36–7).

Another document pointed out how women should treat and relate to their husbands:

> They [women] have been advised to behave in a way that can provide the most precious of goods: the tranquillity of the home. She has been told that she must be prudent, clean, economical, tender and delicate; that she must study closely the character and customs of her life-long companion, in order to mould herself to his; that she must repress all to avoid her husband becoming upset by seeing her melancholic, sick or violent; and even, that she must preserve her physical charms and skills to flatter not only the sentiment, but also the vanity of her owner. (Los maridos 1888, in *La Convención Radical Obrera*, cited by Rocha 1991: 50–51)

There were other documents in which women were advised of what was expected from them as wives: first of all to love and be faithful to their husbands. Second, a woman was to be discrete, as this would help to avoid conjugal disruption: she should not ask where her husband had been, or where he was going, why he went out or came in; she should not make recriminations, and should be prepared to beg and plead. Third, she should resign herself: 'Does your husband quarrel with you? Suffer and be silent. Is he unfaithful? Cry. Does he abandon and despise you? Cry even more' (Estrella, B. 1885, *El libro de oro de las casadas*, cited in Rocha 1991: 45); and finally, she should be thrifty. These ideas spread during the first half of the century. Even though the revolutionary period (1910–1917) brought many disruptions and other movements produced a shift towards a more secular, liberal and even socialist view of women and family life, the conservative tendency continued to be present, as we shall see.

The narrative of the faithful, devoted wife was complemented by another idea that would sum up the typical female ideal during the first half of the century: the idea of the devoted, self-sacrificing mother. In 1922 *Excelsior*, a renowned national newspaper, launched the idea of having one day dedicated to the celebration, extolment and sublimation of mothers, proposing May 10 as Mother's Day. The newspaper proposed that the Education Ministry should promote this day nationwide (Rocha 1991). These ideas were important, since they came to mould the discourse of the nuclear family, in particular in relation to the idea of women having specialized roles. While it is true that mothers devoted themselves to children in previous times, from now on it was socially and normatively expected that they do so, in addition to carrying out domestic work and being faithful, devoted wives. This narrative about the family and the place of women fell on firm ground, as material living conditions did not allow them much room for action in any case. This was a period when manual labour was required at home, when home appliances had not yet been developed, and sanitary conditions were poor for the whole population. As discussed, however, this narrative of the nuclear family did not spread evenly among different social groups. Some elements in the construction of intimacy developed in different ways among, on the one hand, lower socio-economic groups in the cities, and on the other hand, peasants and Indigenous people in rural areas. In fact, among lower socio-economic groups in the cities the difference between public and private spaces was not clear. Life in general and relationships with *fiancés*, acquaintances, lovers and couples, often took place in public spaces. As Speckman (2006) has shown for Mexico City, most of these groups lived in *vecindades*, a set of very modest houses or apartments which shared a common patio, bathroom and laundry. Families crowded into one or two rooms and adults, young people and children shared the same spaces, making it difficult to establish a sphere of intimacy where two people could exchange emotions, have physical contact or one-to-one interaction without the observation of other people. Even so, different aspects of the narrative of the nuclear family did filter into these groups. For example, Speckman (2006) has pointed out that the expectation of being married and a devoted housewife and mother for women, and of being an economic provider of the household for men, was a norm that moulded and shaped the actions and behaviour of many people in these groups, as did traditional customs, since many of these people came from rural areas. Some colonial customs endured as well. For example, at times, the promise of marriage by men to women was enough to lead to sexual intercourse, whether the couple would marry in the end or not. It was also very common for young women to remain at their parents' home until they married. Afterwards they would follow an indigenous patrilocal pattern of residence (the woman moving in with her parents-in-law), and this often resulted in intense conflicts. The life of peasants and indigenous groups in many ways continued to be moulded by these same ancient customs, where overcrowding and arranged marriages occurred. Even as the idea of freedom in choosing one's partner began to influence the formation of couples, strong ties of obligation to elders and gender differences continued to influence how intimacy was constructed. Indeed, a woman had to submit to her husband's wishes and authority, as did her children.

Freedom in the selection of a partner was a fundamental aspect of how love started to become an ingredient in couple and family formation, and in how a specific kind of intimacy began to develop in family settings. However, as I have pointed out, this kind of romantic love had particular features that were not part of this social and cultural narrative. Two other aspects moulded how love and intimacy were understood and to a great degree lived: a strong expectation that women would keep their honour, and the exercise of violence by men over women. Indeed, during this period women were advised to keep their honour, meaning that they could not have improper physical or sexual contact with their *fiancés*, boyfriends and husbands. Virginity should be kept until reaching marriage (Velasco 1995), and married women should not look for sexual pleasure, since this was considered indecent according to Catholic morality. Instead, they should be willing to fulfil their conjugal duty to their husbands. Indeed, as Dávalos has pointed out, at the end of the XIX century:

> Writers of love stories focused on reinforcing the values that should reign within the intimacy of the family. Worried about educating the population (even though their writings only reached a small part of it), they promoted the idea that marriage without affection was morally reprehensible; partners should keep the flame of love alight always. However, such love should not be based on sexual pleasure, since this treatment of a wife would be similar to that of a prostitute. (Dávalos 1995: 59)

These ideas spread during the first half of the century (and beyond) among different social groups.

Therefore, a certain degree of affection was allowed, but honour and modesty prevented women from disclosing their feelings of physical and erotic love regarding their partners. Deference, obedience and submission to husbands and fathers also created a great distance between partners, and this prevented them from having a closer emotional and physical knowledge of each other. To a large extent, these elements defined entire relationships between couples, and between parents and children, and also, therefore, how intimacy was constructed. It is probable that these same elements contributed to another problem, which was an element of intimacy and strong hierarchical relationships: the exercise of violence by men. This expressed itself differently among different social groups. In relation to indigenous people, peasants and lower socio-economic groups some authors have shown how violence was a common feature within families and how men felt they had the right to 'correct' women's misbehaviour and their failure to fulfil their duties as housewives and mothers, by beating them severely. This problem was present throughout the whole period and even into the seventies (González 2006, Lewis 1951). The fear women had as a result of this probably generated a greater distance between couples and inhibited the creation of relationships based on knowing the feelings and thoughts of the other, direct communication and a disclosure of the self. Duties and obligations were so strong that they forged an intimacy based mostly on the fact that 'each one knew his or her place' (as Jamieson has pointed out) in the relationship and in the institution of the family. In contrast, there is less evidence of how physical violence manifested itself among middle and upper class families. Nonetheless, it has been established that emotional and economic violence at least have played important roles into the present (Esteinou 2013).

Romantic love has been pointed out often as a central ingredient in the formation of the nuclear family, but considering all the elements I have described so far, we cannot think of romantic love as an abstract entity based solely on moral virtue and the religious spirit of love. Romantic love in Mexican society during this period freed many women and men to choose a partner, which represented a fundamentally modern socio-cultural change. But in another sense, it tied men and especially women to the fulfilment of a series of duties and obligations within marriage and the family. It almost entirely subsumed women to the desires of men; it promoted distance between partners, and in many cases it implied violence against women and children. Companionship, as it is understood today, was practically non-existent and a rigid series of duties and obligations framed the social and cultural context in which intimacy could develop.

The Flourishing of the Catholic Nuclear Family: Intimacy from 1950 to 1970

The economic and political conditions of families changed significantly in the forties and particularly after the Second World War, due to rapid economic growth, industrialization, and massive migration from rural to urban areas. The middle classes expanded, and consumption became an important feature of these social groups. Daily life and domestic work in particular changed dramatically as different kinds of home appliances reduced housework and became readily available. Gas and oil displaced coal in kitchens and in heating water; the middle and upper classes would generally use gas stoves while oil stoves were more common among lower socio-economic groups. Refrigerators and blenders modified customs surrounding the preparation of daily meals. Likewise, vacuum cleaners, automatic washing machines and electric irons eased housework. Supermarkets began to appear alongside traditional markets bringing many products together in a single space, along with the convenience of self-service (Matute 2006). If it is true that the American way of life began to spread among upper and middle class social groups and created great expectations among other social groups, it is certain also that it differed a great deal from a socio-cultural point of view, since many of the trends registered so far were also present. As we will see, while many social and cultural standards regarding family life and gender relationships were still very conservative, new features began to emerge.

After the intense social and anti-clerical movements of the twenties and thirties, the differences between the State and the Catholic Church began to settle down and these institutions started to coexist peacefully. Anti-clerical laws were eased, allowing the Church to build up its strength in schools and other associations. Indeed, from 1940 to 1970 there was an important increase in the number of secular organizations dependent on the church, an increase in people taking up religious vocations, a strengthening of parochial private schools, and an increase in religious publications. The *Unión Nacional de Padres de Familia* (National Union of Parents) did not just conform with the religious tolerance exercised by the State, but campaigned to allow religion to be taught in Catholic schools, something which had been forbidden by the Constitution of 1917. The *Acción Católica Mexicana* (Mexican Catholic Action), an organization founded in 1929, reached its greatest power during this period. It was a very strong association and had a significant impact on social and cultural life. After the *Partido Revolucionario Institucional* (Institutional Revolutionary Party) – the largest political party – *Acción Católica* had the highest membership of any association, with representatives all over the country. It published many different types of documents, organized and mobilized Catholics (the majority of Mexicans) around religious practices and developed its own different social and cultural practices (Torres-Septién 2006). It also had an evident influence on family life.

During this period, the Catholic nuclear family flourished, mainly among the upper and middle classes, but it also had a strong influence among other social groups. This type of family differed from the nuclear family characteristic of Western societies. In fact, families were large in size, and their members were strongly religious and family oriented, which meant that parents still had an influence on the selection of partners and on sexual behaviour. The division of roles between men and women was reinforced by the Catholic narrative. Although some women worked, those that did so were usually single. Furthermore, social and cultural narratives and standards only justified this when women had no other economic means of survival. A study of love mailboxes and advice columns (a media genre which appeared and developed during this period and consisted of letters sent to magazines, mostly by women, looking for advice) is an example of how this narrative provided a way of instilling social and cultural norms about relationships between men and women. In regard to working outside the home, the answer to a woman who wanted to continue working when she married but whose boyfriend did not want her to, was: 'Let's analyse the pros: He is right in asking you to devote yourself to your home. The man, if he earns enough, expects you to devote yourself to the noble work of wife and mother ...' (Paquita, no. 1210, Mexico, March 20 1952: 41, cited by Ramírez and Ríos 2007: 112). An answer in another magazine ruled: 'Your studies and constant activity are praiseworthy ... You must remember that our model must be that of the devoted mother who looks after the future of her children and is their spiritual guide. Among human creatures the mother is the most perfect' (Nosotras, no. 80, Mexico, May 1955: 10, cited in Ramírez and Ríos 2007: 113). Being a mother and wife, and being married was the fundamental reason for living. Furthermore, marriage was indissoluble. Divorce was simply out of the question.

Besides the clear division of labour between husband and wife, which was also promoted by the import-substitution economic model of the period, and by legislation on family life, the Catholic nuclear family had other features which differentiated it from the model of the previous period. Lower mortality rates and the consequent increase in life expectancy meant that family members spent more years together without being separated by death. Indeed, while in the previous period 40 per cent of couples survived together until the end of the woman's reproductive life, this proportion increased to 80 per cent between 1960 and 1970. One of the most important consequences was that individuals within the family could order stages of life in a stable way. This allowed them to spend more time together (Tuirán 1996), opening the possibility of developing long term bonds and a certain type of intimacy (Esteinou 2008, 2012). While long term relationships were now more available, the type of intimacy that developed acquired specific features and was conditioned by the social and cultural standards of the time.

Another important feature of the Catholic nuclear family narrative and accompanying social and cultural standards was the emphasis placed on women's virginity before marriage. While this was not new, it now became more visible to the public gaze. Love mailboxes of that time reveal that even at the end of the sixties, losing their virginity created a conflict for women. Their letters showed that even when they acknowledged having lost their virginity, they invented different situations, sometimes absurd, to justify this. Some said that they had fallen, others that their menstrual cycle was irregular. Those who openly acknowledged it lived it as a tragedy. One girl for example wrote: 'I happen to have had a bad moment in my destiny, losing the most precious treasure of a woman ... I would like to leave for another place, find work and remake my life. I would like to enter a convent to purge my sins and pray to God for my conduct' (Confidencias, no. 749, January 1960: 39, cited by Ramírez and Ríos 2007: 115). Around 1965 a great number of letters revealed directly or indirectly that the writers had lost their virginity. For men, this was also a fundamental matter of honour and most of them were not willing to give up their ideals on the matter. One man, for example, who married a girl who previously was with another man and had a child with him, wrote:

> I cannot cease to think that another man was the owner of my now legitimate woman, and that her boy isn't mine. My life is hell and this thought torments me day and night. I had made up my mind to divorce her, but a child is about to be born that is mine and, besides, she is very good to me and all of my family. (Confidencias, no. 749, June 1965: 29, cited in Ramírez and Ríos 2007: 116)

Intimacy was built within the limits of these social and cultural standards and therefore influenced the range of feelings and relationships that were allowed to develop and be shown. I have pointed out that free choice in the selection of a partner was a characteristic of the new nuclear family which developed at the end of the nineteenth century, and that love was a fundamental aspect of this. But love was understood differently from how it is today. In many ways, it took the form of romantic love, where virtue and religion mattered more than physical and emotional attraction. As Ramírez and Ríos (2007) have pointed out, the idea of pure love demanded that the choice of partner be made by excluding completely the issue of sexual or erotic appeal, as established codes and norms condemned this. While intimacy during this period was developed to some extent on these same grounds, there were other aspects which made partner selection and married life a more secular process. On one hand, women continued to be submissive towards their husbands, but on the other, they tried to choose the right or most appropriate partner, which meant a man who had a good job (which could provide for the family's wellbeing) and was considered a 'decent' person. In this sense, physical and sexual attraction could be factors influencing the choice of a spouse but other issues were more important. Women continued to be spiritually virtuous but above all had to specialize in being housewives and mothers, and men in being good providers. That was the basis of love and freedom in partner selection.

The difference with regard to the previous period was that women now started to show their feelings and their concerns about sexual love and emotional closeness more openly. Themes and concerns about virginity before marriage and physical attraction in love relationships were important elements, as shown in love mailboxes, because women were trying to attract back or retain their husbands and boyfriends. Virtuous or romantic love was not enough to fight against men's 'weaknesses', that is, their 'natural' tendency to look for physical pleasure in other women. In order to succeed, it seems that women started to allow more physical and sexual contact, as we can grasp from the fact that at the end of the sixties love mailboxes registered an increasing number of letters which reported that women had lost their virginity before marriage.

Freedom of choice in the selection of a partner should not be understood simply as individuals who chose a partner without any social limits or ties, as Smart and Shipman (2012) have pointed out. During this period, families also intervened, legitimizing the process. Families had to consent to the boyfriend chosen, to the courtship and to the marriage itself. During courtship, for example, not only were women very passive, since they had to wait for boys to approach them and invite them to go out, but they also had to accept the vigilant eye of a sister or brother who would go out with them in order to keep their behaviour within the socially accepted boundaries. Also, owing to the pressure of parents, girls sometimes had to delay marriage in order to find a suitable boyfriend; then, concerned about reaching the socially acceptable age limit for marriage, they did so not out of love, but out of fear that they would not marry at all and be condemned to being spinsters. Therefore, sometimes they married not the man they wanted but one who was acceptable to the family. Boys, too, were under the influence of families when choosing a partner. There was another element that framed or influenced partner selection: the marriage market. Since girls were usually secluded at home and many parents thought that they should not go to universities because their place was in the house, the social environments in which they could meet boys were limited. The opportunities to meet a girl or a boy were social gatherings at the parish, family celebrations and meetings at friends' houses. Social class played an important role as well: boys and girls usually met within the same social group they belonged to. Therefore, homogamy was very high. All these factors are revealed in mail boxes and religious magazines of the time, as Ramírez and Ríos (2007) and Torres-Septién (2006) have shown.

The *Acción Católica* and the Church in general tried tenaciously to reinforce their moral precepts against what they saw as the most dangerous influences and changes: the rapid advance of modern life, especially modern entertainment. In one of the Catholic magazines a boy asked for advice regarding the suitability of his girlfriend. He got this answer:

> When you tell me that she is very good and that she only has these "little inconveniences", I see you are lost. At least you are consulting me and I hope you follow this advice. That woman is not right for you, she is manly. She goes out on excursions dressed like a man, knows how to dance perfectly, swims and rides a motorcycle. She loves the tabloids and novels of dubious morals. No, she is not right for you … It is time that we single men pay attention to good girls that, thank God, are still abundant, and by no means should we celebrate those monsters who sometimes wear a skirt, who always wear make up like a clown, who flirt without reserve, who have their heads full of implausible adventures, who think only about being the heroine of one of those stupid movies where flirtation and immorality pervade. (Boletín Nosotras, September 1951, no. 10: 3, cited in Torres-Septién 2006: 184)

Therefore, despite the fact that Catholic morals pervaded social morality in general, modernization was now also influencing social and cultural life in many ways.

In sum, relationships within the family and between genders experienced some sort of secularization, opening the gate to developing a kind of companionship. In an influential book, Burgess, Locke and Thomes established that companionship was a core element of the American nuclear family. This 'is maintained in mutual affection, emotional interdependence, sympathetic understanding, temperamental compatibility, consensus in family objectives and values, family events, celebrations and ceremonies, and interdependence of family roles' (Burgess, Locke and Thomes 1963: 283). This represents a similar definition to that given by Giddens and Jamieson of intimacy. While companionship during this period in Mexico was in fact far from fitting this definition, some of the elements just described were beginning to emerge. Intimacy was not based on knowing and understanding the self, the disclosure of feelings and sexual pleasure. Intense knowledge and emotional understanding had a very discrete place and marriage was still tied to the ultimate goal of reproduction. Deliberation on rules and objectives was not shared, since women and children were expected to submit to the husband and father. Duties and obligations were still stronger than personal needs, decisions and choices, but some sort of mutual affection, material care, and certainly interdependence of roles did have room to develop. Men and women more often chose to marry for love, and the idea that they complemented and took care of each other and of the children was present. They protected their private sphere from the eyes of others, and the home became a private sanctuary where individuals could live in harmony. And for many people it was real, since they conformed to the Catholic norms and principles. Life and intimacy flowed within these limits, between family gatherings and religious celebrations, and intimate relationships still concealed strong inequalities among family members. As in the past, women were expected to submit to their husbands needs and desires and children required to obey diligently. Violence against women and children was also part of the picture and developed differently – as in the previous period – among different social groups.

Companionship and the Development of Expressiveness: Intimacy between 1970 and 2000

During this period different family forms developed even further and coexisted. Some of these gave rise to different types of intimacy. In this section I analyse some of the new trends emerging during this period. In part these were the result of economic, demographic and socio-cultural changes. From an economic point of view, the most important change was the increasing incorporation of housewives and mothers of small children into the labour market. In 2003, they accounted for 32 per cent of the labour force (García and De Oliveira 1994, INEGI/Instituto Nacional de las Mujeres 2004). This change promoted a flexibilization of the rigid role structure present in the previous period, so the division between husband-father-breadwinner and wife-mother entered into a process of redefinition and negotiation, though not in a radical way.

From a demographic point of view, the most important changes were: a drastic reduction in the fertility rate, from 7.2 per woman in the seventies to 2.4 in 2000 (CONAPO 2002, Mier and Terán and Partida 2001); the number of desired children per woman diminished from five to two (INEGI/Instituto Nacional de las Mujeres 2004, Hernández 2001); the number of years a woman spent raising children was reduced to 15 years (Gómez de León 1998); most Mexicans followed a pattern of freedom in selection of their partner, and civil and religious marriage was the main means under which a family was formed (Quilodrán 1996). Mortality rates remained low, which resulted in an enlargement of the individual and family horizon of experience (for example, a couple today can spend 40 years together). These demographic changes had an important influence on the construction of a variety of relationships and family arrangements. The final decades of the twentieth century witnessed the emergence of nuclear (and even extended) families of small size. Relationships within them also changed. Families and couples had a longer life, and thus enjoyed greater opportunities to develop a higher level of cohesion and intimacy, but also – due to the socio-cultural changes – faced more tensions and conflicts. We also observe a greater level of individualization within the couple and between parents and children, greater levels of equality among them, which facilitated greater closeness and the construction of intimacy that allowed a deeper knowledge of the other, and important changes in practices of upbringing related to the socio-cultural changes experienced during this period.

From a socio-cultural point of view, the most important change witnessed was a greater complexity in social and cultural structure (Millán 2008), to the extent that during this period we can observe a variety of coexisting lifestyles and cultural models about what a couple, a family, children's education, and other issues mean. This led to diversity, but also uncertainty for individuals. The domestic world (the family) started to lose importance as a meaningful space, as a place of certainties and as a stable world. As a result, numerous Mexicans and their families gradually were more exposed, in contrast to what happened in previous periods, to a plurality of cultural codes and patterns that they had to deal with in their daily lives (Esteinou 1999). Family roles became increasingly flexible, and the grounds for marriage and cohabitation started to change as individuals began to assess their marriage and their lives based more on emotional, affectionate and sexual satisfaction (Esteinou 2012). Duties and obligations tied to the rigid Catholic moral norms began to decline or relax, making way for the development of individual choices and decisions.

The changes described so far give us a different and novel view of family life. Many of the families of this period tended to be small in size, they gradually included rational and individuation criteria in their practices and decisions, which before was infrequent. The quality of relationships also registered important changes. Due to increasing socio-cultural differentiation, a new type of intimacy started to develop, which was emotionally and physically more expressive and disclosed. Especially among middle and high social groups, we observe that individuals considered a good relationship to be one in which disclosure of feelings, emotional closeness, open communication and sexual pleasure were the basis of the relationship, more than practical and material forms of love and care. Relationships could thus be more fragile but at the same time potentially more satisfactory. We can grasp some of these features looking at the love mail boxes during this period; through them we appreciate a radical change. Increasing sexual liberation of women resulted from population policies, increasing incorporation of women into the labour markets, the generalized use of contraceptive methods, and more flexibility from the Catholic Church after the Second Vatican Council. In the seventies, there were changes in the images of women projected by female magazines and in the answers the specialists gave to readers about love, sexuality and the position of women with regard to their husbands. They offered an image of a sexually liberated woman, who could choose not to be a mother, to marry or not, regardless of being sexually active; and divorce was presented as an alternative to a bad marriage. In the assessment of behaviour, moral and religious judgments are displaced by ones based on scientific criteria (such as health, psychological and legal precepts) (Corona and De la Peza 2007). The narratives during this period became much more secular therefore.

As all these elements gradually developed and formed a different narrative about couple relationships and family life; companionship – as I have described it above – gained ground. An increasing number of families were developing couple relationships where a more emotionally and socially close companionship was present, as we can grasp from some studies (López, Salles and Tuirán 2001, Vivas 1996, Nehring 2012). This type of intimacy gave greater importance to the sexual relationship. In contrast to the previous period, women strove to have pleasant sexual relationships within marriage or partnerships rather than seeing these, in comparison to previous years, as a conjugal duty (López, Salles and Tuirán 2001, Ramírez 2001, Corona and De la Peza 2007). Nonetheless, in some social groups the practice of husbands having sexual supremacy over their wives (such as deciding when to have sexual intercourse) persisted and other more passive and instrumental sexual practices by women (such as sexually satisfying the husband without looking for pleasure, in order to avoid abandonment) also endured, as Figueroa (1993) and Figueroa and Liendro (1994) documented. Although a double moral standard persisted among many men from lower and middle social groups (De Barbieri 1990), women tended to search for more open sexuality with their partners, in contrast to the women of the fifties and sixties. Even health science and psychology promoted this concept, with narratives about sexuality as a pleasant dimension needed for the development of healthy or adequate couple relationships. This implied a change of attitude on the part of women.

I have pointed out that companionship was part of the Western conceptualization of the nuclear family. This new conception of love had as a core element the individual's search for happiness and self-realization, which could potentially give, in extreme cases, a privileged place to the interests of the individual over the group. In general, however, divorce and separation rates did not reach the levels witnessed in Western countries, even though they increased significantly. The greater importance of individual interests, as well as the development and spread of contraceptive methods, increased women's horizons of freedom of action, relaxing the rigid duties and obligations they previously performed, especially that of having children. Indeed, women tended to distance themselves from the Catholic religious norm of 'having as many children as God sends them', and adopted a more secular position by planning their births and the number of children they would have. Self-realization, and not reproduction, came to the foreground as the main goal of marriage (Esteinou 2012).

However, this type of intimacy was not exempt from inequalities and conflicts. Evidence shows that younger, better educated, and more affluent women whose jobs or careers demanded greater involvement and time commitment were more likely to establish more equal gender relationships. On the contrary, women with lower levels of education and from lower socio-economic groups experienced greater inequality in their gender relationships (García and De Oliveira 1994).

Violence also continued to be an important issue in families and relationships in both rural and urban areas, and among all social groups, as González (2006) and I (Esteinou 2013) have pointed out.

The development of companionship implied changes regarding the relationships between parents and children. During this period, a particular conceptualization of children began to emerge, one which emphasized their value in expressive and emotional terms, rather than in economic terms as had been the case at the beginning of the century. This resulted in a more specialized role of women as mothers. On the other hand, fathers became increasingly involved with their children and tended to show their affection much more through physical and emotional contact (Vivas 1996, Rojas 2006, 2008, Esteinou 2012). Parenting also changed and in different social groups a more democratic parenting style began to emerge (Esteinou 2012, Esteinou and Nehring 2009). All these features imply a different kind of intimacy, characterized by an increase in emotional closeness and more open and direct communication.

Concluding Remarks

The information presented in the three periods allows me to make some comments regarding the two objectives set out at the beginning of this chapter. That is, the importance of duties and obligations and of freedom of choice in moulding intimate relationships or intimate citizenship (Plummer 2001, 2005); and whether there was a trend towards increasing disclosure and democratization when building intimacy. We have seen that different types of intimacy developed in the three periods under study, but the main changing features of intimacy that gradually developed over the three periods analysed are: freedom in partner selection, the development of more equal relationships and the development of intimacy based on disclosure of the self. There was greater continuity in the first two periods, however, due to the prevalence of a strong Catholic morality that moulded relationships and feelings. In this sense, duties and obligations tied individuals to marriage, and to a strict hierarchy within the nuclear family, leaving a very restricted space for the development of other forms of expression. Freedom in partner selection was defined mainly by romantic love, which implied a denial of sexual pleasure and emotional closeness. In the third period, in contrast, we can appreciate more radical changes, related to a strong tendency towards secularization. The democratization of relationships started to develop, expression of emotions was favoured, promoting not only a greater flexibility of roles within family settings but also a more disclosing intimacy in which individuals developed a closer and deeper knowledge of the other. This tendency, however, coexists with other types of intimacy which are still very conservative and similar to those present during previous periods.

Bibliography

Bauman, Z. 2003. *Liquid Love: On the Frailty of Human Bonds*. Cambridge: Polity Press.

Beck, U. and Beck-Gerseheim, E. 1995. *The Normal Chaos of Love*. Cambridge: Polity Press.

Cano, G. 1995. La Soltería y el Desarrollo Intelectual de las Mujeres: ¿Un Matrimonio Bien Avenido? in *Cuidado con el corazón. Los usos amorosos en el México Moderno*, edited by Blanco J., Cano G., Dávalos M., et al. México: Instituto Nacional de Antropología e Historia, 15–26.

Código Civil. 1993. *Código Civil para el Distrito Federal* (62nd edition). Mexico: Porrúa.

CONAPO (Consejo Nacional de Población). 2002. *La Situación Demográfica en México*. Mexico: Consejo Nacional de Población.

Corona, S. and De la Peza Ma. del C. 2007. La Liberación Sexual en Tensión: las Revistas Femeninas de los Años 1970–1980, in *Un Siglo de Educación Sentimental*, edited by S. Corona and Ma. del C. de la Peza. Mexico: Universidad de Guadalajara, Universidad Veracruzana, Universidad Autónoma Metropolitana-Azcapotzalco/Xochimilco, 133–82.

Dávalos, M. 1995. El Amor Eterno y el Efímero Matrimonio, in *Cuidado con el Corazón. Los Usos Amorosos en el México Moderno*, edited by Blanco J., Cano G., Dávalos M., et al. México: Instituto Nacional de Antropología e Historia, 57–64.

De Barbieri, T. 1990. Sobre Géneros, Prácticas y Valores: Notas acerca de Posibles Erosiones del Machismo en México, in *Normas y Prácticas Morales y Cívicas en la Vida Cotidiana*, edited by Ramírez J.M. Mexico: Centro de Investigaciones Interdisciplinarias en Humanidades de la Universidad Nacional Autónoma de México, Porrúa, 83–109.

Esteinou, R. 1999. Familia y Diferenciación Simbólica, *Nueva Antropología*, XVI(55), 9–26.

Esteinou, R. 2008. *La familia nuclear en México: Lecturas de su Modernidad. Siglos XVI al XX*. Mexico City: Centro de Investigaciones y Estudios Superiores en Antropología Social, Miguel Angel Porrúa.

Esteinou, R. 2012. Relaciones Familiares e Intimidad en la Sociedad Mexicana del Siglo XX, in *La Nueva Generación de Familias. Tecnologías de Reproducción Asistida y Temas Contemporáneos*, edited by R. Esteinou. Mexico City: Centro de Investigaciones y Estudios Superiores en Antropología Social, 257–84.

Esteinou, R. and Nehring, D. 2009. Educación Familiar y Estilos Parentales en México: una Exploración de la Encuesta Nacional de la Dinámica Familiar, in *Construyendo Relaciones y Fortalezas Familiares: un Panorama Internacional*, edited by R. Esteinou. Mexico: Centro de Investigaciones y Estudios Superiores en Antropología Social, Miguel Angel Porrúa, 87–128.

Esteinou, R. 2013. Family Violence in Mexico, in *Family Violence from a Global Perspective: Strengths-Based Practice and Research*, edited by J. DeFrain and S. Assay. California: Sage Publications

Figueroa, J.G. 1993. El Enfoque de Género y la Representación de la Sexualidad, in *Cuadernos de Capacitación en Investigación sobre Planificación Familia*, edited by Secretaría de Salud. Mexico: Dirección General de Planificación, Secretaría de Salud.

Figueroa, J.G. and Liendro E. 1996. Algunos Apuntes sobre la Presencia del Varón en la Toma de Decisiones Reproductivas, in *Hogares, Familias: Desigualdad, Conflicto, Redes Solidarias y Parentales*, edited by Ma. de la P. López. Mexico: Sociedad Mexicana de Demografía.

Gabb, J. 2010. *Researching Intimacy in Families*. Basingstoke: Palgrave Macmillan.

García, B. and De Oliveira O. 1994. *Trabajo y Vida Familiar en México*. Mexico: El Colegio de México.

Giddens, A. 1992. *The Transformation of Intimacy*. Stanford: Stanford University Press.

Gómez de León, J. 1998. Fenómenos Sociales y Familiares Emergentes, in *La Familia Mexicana en el Tercer Milenio*, edited by Sistema Nacional para el Desarrollo Integral de la Familia (DIF). Mexico: Sistema Nacional para el Desarrollo Integral de la Familia, 10–27.

Gómez de León, J. 2001. Los Cambios en la Nupcialidad y la Formación de Familias: Algunos Factores Explicativos, in *La Población en México*, edited by J. Gómez de León and C. Rabell. Mexico: Consejo Nacional de Población, Fondo de Cultura Económica, 207–41.

González Montes, S. 2006. Las mujeres y la violencia doméstica en un pueblo del Valle de Toluca, in *Historia de la Vida Cotidiana en México*, edited by A. de los Reyes. Mexico: Fondo de Cultura Económica, El Colegio de México, V(1), 341–63.

Hernández, D. 2001. Anticoncepción en México, in *La Población en México*, edited by J. Gómez de León and C. Rabell. Mexico: Consejo Nacional de Población, Fondo de Cultura Económica, 271–306.

INEGI (Instituto Nacional de Estadística, Geografía e Informática), Instituto Nacional de las Mujeres. 2004. *Mujeres y Hombres en México*. Mexico: INEGI, Instituto Nacional de las Mujeres.

Jamieson, L. 2002. *Intimacy*. Cambridge, UK: Polity Press.

López, Ma. de la P., Salles V. and Tuirán R. 2001. Familias y Hogares: Pervivencias y Transformaciones en un Horizonte de Largo Plazo, in *La Población en México*, edited by J. Gómez de León and C. Rabell. Mexico: Consejo Nacional de Población, Fondo de Cultura Económica, 635–93.

Matute, A. 2006. De la Tecnología al Orden Doméstico en el México de la Posguerra, in *Historia de la Vida Cotidiana en México*, edited by A. de los Reyes. Mexico City: Fondo de Cultura Económica, El Colegio de México, 2, 157–76.

Mier y Terán, M. and Partida V. 2001. Niveles, Tendencias y Diferenciales de la Fecundidad en México, 1930–1997, in *La Población en México*, edited by

J. Gómez de León and C. Rabell. Mexico: Consejo Nacional de Población, Fondo de Cultura Económica, 168–205.

Millán, R. 2008. *Complejidad Social y Nuevo Orden en México*. Mexico: Instituto de Investigaciones Sociales de la Universidad Nacional Autónoma de México, Miguel Angel Porrúa.

Millán, R. 2009. Incertidumbre y Miedo: Visiones sobre la Modernidad, in *Paradojas del miedo. Encuentros con la Ambigüedad, la Incertidumbre y el Absurdo*, edited by F. Pamplona. Mexico City: Universidad Autónoma de la Ciudad de México, 85–136.

Nehring, D. 2012. Love in Changing Times: Experiences of Intimate Relationships Among Young Female Professionals in Mexico City. *Asian Journal of Latin American Studies*, 25(1), 75–96.

Plummer, K. 2001. The Square of Intimate Citizenship: Some Preliminary Proposals. *Citizenship Studies*, 5(3), 237–53.

Plummer, K. 2005. Intimate Citizenship in an Unjust World, in *The Blackwell Companion of Social Inequalities*, edited by Romero M and Margolis E. Great Britain: Blackwell Publishing Ltd.

Quilodrán, J. 1996. El Matrimonio y sus Transformaciones, in *Hogares, Familias: Desigualdad, Conflicto, Redes Solidarias y Parentales*, edited by Ma. de la P. López. Mexico: Sociedad Mexicana de Demografía, 59–69.

Ramírez, Ma. E. 2001. Construcción Social de Valores acerca de la Sexualidad. El Caso de las Señoras de la Tierra de Xochimilco. *Estudios Sociológicos*, XIX(55), 161–84.

Ramírez, E. and Ríos, G. 2007. Revelaciones Amorosas: 1950–1969, in *Un Siglo de Educación Sentimental*, edited by S. Corona and Ma. Del C. de la Peza. Mexico: Universidad de Guadalajara, Universidad Veracruzana, Universidad Autónoma Metropolitana-Azcapotzalco, Universidad Autónoma Metropolitana-Xochimilco, 95–132.

Rendon, T. 1990. Trabajo Feminino Remunerado en el Siglo XX. Cambios, Tendencias y Perspectivas, in *Trabajo Femenino y Crisis en México: Tendencias y Transformaciones Actuales*, edited by E. Ramírez and H. Dávila. Mexico: Universidad Autónoma Metropolitana-Xochimilco, 19–51.

Rocha, M.E. 1991. *El Album de la Mujer. Antología Ilustrada de las Mexicanas*. Mexico: Instituto Nacional de Antropología e Historia.

Rojas, O. 2006. Reflexiones en torno de las Valoraciones Masculinas sobre los Hijos y la Paternidad, in *Ser Padres, Esposos e Hijos: Prácticas y Valoraciones de Varones Mexicanos*, edited by J.G. Figueroa, L. Jiménez and O. Tena. Mexico: El Colegio de México, 95–120.

Rojas, O. 2008. *Paternidad y Vida Familiar en la Ciudad de México*. México: El Colegio de México.

Smart, C. 2004. Retheorizing Families. *Sociology*, 38(5), 1043–48.

Smart, C. 2007. *Personal Life*. Cambridge: Polity Press.

Smart, C. and Shipman, B. 2012. Visiones Monocromáticas: Familias, Matrimonio y la Tesis de la Individualización, in *La Nueva Generación Social de Familias*.

Tecnologías de Reproducción Asistida y Temas Contemporáneos, edited by R. Esteinou. Mexico City: Centro de Investigaciones y Estudios Superiores en Antropología Social, 217–40.

Torres-Septién, V. 2006. Una Familia de Tantas. La Celebración de las Fiestas Familiares Católicas en México (1940–1960), in *Historia de la Vida Cotidiana en México*, edited by De los Reyes, A. México City: Fondo de Cultura Económica, El Colegio de México, 1, 171–206.

Tuirán, R. 1996. Las Trayectorias de Vida Familiar en México: una Perspectiva Histórica, in *Hogares, Familias: Desigualdad, Conflicto, Redes Solidarias y Parentales*, edited by Ma. de la P. López. Mexico: Sociedad Mexicana de Demografía, 7–14.

Velasco, C. 1995. Esa Ilusión Encanto de la Vida: Amores en el Diario de la Abuela, in *Cuidado con el corazón. Los usos amorosos en el México Moderno*, edited by Blanco J., Cano G., Dávalos M., et al. México: Instituto Nacional de Antropología e Historia, 27–42.

Vivas, M. 1996. Vida Doméstica y Masculinidad, in *Hogares, Familias: Desigualdad, Conflicto, Redes Solidarias y Parentales*, edited by Ma. de la P. López. Mexico: Sociedad Mexicana de Demografía, 111–22.

Chapter 3

Intimacy, Lesbian Desire and Representation in Contemporary Mexican Film: *Así del precipicio*[1]

Rosana Blanco-Cano

From the Golden Age of Mexican cinema until the New Mexican Cinema, film has worked as a privileged field that proposes symbolic discourses and practices which confirm or problematize the notion of modernity in Mexico. If Golden Age films transmitted the values of the post-revolutionary system, in the new millennium, the film industry seems to be reflecting the image of the modern, democratic and global Mexico consolidated after the country's political transition in 2000.[2] Movies like *Así del precipicio* (Teresa Suárez 2006), *Niñas mal* (Fernando Sariñana 2007), and *Casi divas* (2008) are directly framed within an environment characterized by rapid changes that connect the notion of modernity, globalization and democracy to flexible gender and sexuality practices. In *Así del precipicio*, the young female protagonists represent the urban upper class and question traditional models of gender through a variety of strategies and approaches to intimacy. The film attempts to highlight and even normalize the experience of characters that claim a lesbian identity. Hence, *Así del precipicio* redefines the membership of the traditional Mexican family, historically defined as heterosexual.

By using a theoretical framework that incorporates cultural studies, gender studies and theoretical concepts like intimate citizenship, this chapter examines discourses and practices that permeate the cinematic representation of lesbian identity in contemporary Mexico. My main interest here is on how *Así del precipicio* depicts the intimate experience of lesbian characters in the light of contradictory cultural practices and discourses that characterize contemporary global Mexico, particularly within the urban upper class context of the film. I am interested in analysing the ways in which *Así del precipicio* open spaces for lesbian identities while, at the same time, presenting a conservative and superficial tone that may undermine the complexity of such representations.

---

1   Teresa Suárez 2006.

2   In the year 2000, the Institutional Revolutionary Party (PRI is the acronym used in Spanish) officially lost political control over the executive and legislative branches of government after clinging to power for over 70 years. For many, this event marks Mexico's transition to modern democratic rule.

The chapter is divided into three sections. The first one explores the symbolic dynamics inherent in film industry production and the boundaries imposed on the female body by the power of visual representation. The second one draws on theoretical formulations of lesbian intimate citizenship and complex models of cultural interpretation to reveal the interdependence of diverse discourses and symbolic practices of individual identity. The last part examines how the movie *Así del precipicio* simplifies complex lesbian intimate citizenships.

Symbolic Dynamics: Film, Tradition, Modernity and Contradiction

Film was undoubtedly one of the most effective symbolic systems in the production of behaviours during the consolidation of the post-revolutionary system between 1930 and 1950.[3] Funded by government initiatives, the film industry constituted, according to Carlos Monsiváis, a 'school in the dark', in which sentimental education was taught. In turn, that education was tied to strict gender practices that would be the foundation of the great Mexican family (Monsiváis 1992: 117). In the traditional cinematic melodrama, the maternal and restrained role of women was performed and privileged. Ana López suggests that the maternal melodrama of Golden Age of Mexican Cinema fulfilled functions which went beyond entertainment and artistic expression; cinematic representations were incorporated into society like documents that reflected the social anxieties of post-revolutionary Mexico. First, they fed on the typical melodramatic tone of three basic meta-narratives of post-revolutionary Mexican culture – religion, nationalism and modernity (López 1993: 256). That is to say, they operated as discourses to shape ideal models of gender and cultural identity. Second, says López, maternal melodramas worked as domains that organized the chaos that resulted from the tension between modernity and tradition, countryside and city, and the clash of poverty and wealth. In a wider sense, as suggested by Julia Tuñón, in the great post-revolutionary family portrayed in those melodramas, 'authoritarianism was encouraged to avoid dissolution, real or imaginary' (1998: 131). Loyalty and cohesion were essential requirements in order to belong to nuclear and extended families and – in a wider sense – to the national family. The controlled maternal body was the stabilizing principle of that loyalty and cohesion since this figure served as a privileged medium for the evocation of passionate feelings about the social order: a body that facilitated the transmission of values and the survival of society at large. The different elements of the gender order seen on screen worked towards the creation and implementation of a symbolic system that embodied the values of the revolutionary project aimed at maintaining, in a nostalgic way, a traditional, authentic, and natural Mexican family. In this context,

---

3   For a valuable reflection on the decades of national and cultural consolidation, see Monsiváis, C. (1978) Notas sobre cultura popular. *Latin American Perspectives*, 5, 98–118.

the emancipation of women would have been seen as a threat to the structure of the patriarchal family, and consequently, to society at large.

Since the consolidation of national culture, cinema has worked to produce and control female bodies and their sexuality. In addition, cinema also has reflected cultural changes and Rozado (1992) suggests that it has played a leading role in the modernization and secularization of Mexican society. Nonetheless, the so-called 'New Mexican Cinema' still represents strict models of women's intimate citizenship, both in terms of female sexuality and in terms of women's participation in political and cultural arenas. Although, since the late 80s, moviemakers such as María Novaro, Marisa Sistach, Busi Cortés, and María Elena Velasco with her popular character 'La India María', have yielded deep reconfigurations of gender and female subjectivity on screen, a nostalgic attitude has certainly prevailed. This nostalgia ran counter to the eagerly awaited democratization of the country at the beginning of the new millennium.[4] As Patricia Torres (2008) suggests in her study of reception and interpretation of contemporary Mexican cinema, the two representative movies of the transitional period towards democracy – *Amores Perros* (Alejandro González Iñárritu, 2000) and *Y tu mamá también* (Alfonso Cuarón 2001) – signify a return to a female body without recourse to political and cultural citizenship. Their discursive power thus remains confined to cultural practices that keep homosocial structures as the foundation of the social order.[5] In this sense, as Torres states, both *Y tu mamá también* and *Amores Perros* give spectators the opportunity to formulate a partially modern identity that still defends traditional models of gender and sexuality as part of their Mexican identity. In Torres' study, young spectators recognized themselves in the main characters of both films, putting emphasis on how Mexican youngsters, both female and male, are indeed 'easy going party animals'. However, there was, at the same time, a double standard in that the film's characters also condemned references to alternative models of masculinity and femininity. At best these two films offer a timid portrayal of such alternative intimacies.

Thus, it is important to analyse to what extent the film industry of the twentieth-first century – in correspondence to globalization and conservative agendas that still prevail in Mexican society – contradicts itself by re-establishing the tension between tradition and modernity that has existed in the movie industry since the Golden Age of Mexican Cinema. As Luis H. Méndez suggests, the implementation of neoliberal economic projects during the presidency of Carlos Salinas de Gortari (1988–1994) affected the political and cultural lexicon by the overexploitation of verbs such as 'open', 'democratize', 'modernize', 'deregulate', and 'rationalize'

---

4   Films that represent the democratization of gender in Mexican cinema are: *Lola* (Novaro 1989), *Danzón* (Novaro 1990), *Las hijas de su madre, Las Buenrostro* (Busi Cortés 2005). See Rashkin, E.J. (2001) *Women Filmmakers in Mexico. The Country of Which We Dream.* Austin: Texas University Press.

5   For an examination of homosocial structures in Mexico see: Irwin, R.M. (2003) *Mexican Masculinities*. Minneapolis: University of Minnesota Press.

(2006: 8). The last decade of the twentieth century established a façade of Mexico as a global and multicultural country, proposing a less patriarchal-authoritative Mexican family in which human rights and the acceptance of differences would be a priority. However, since the beginning of the twentieth-first century, and with the consolidation of Partido Acción Nacional regimes (2000–2012), the 'ultraconservative state disguised as 'global' (Monsiváis 2003), imposed a specific discursive structure on the Mexican film industry in response to the demands of the business sector that contradicted the 'cultural deregulation' that seemed to be in correspondence to global environments. In November of 2001, and with the support of the new conservative PAN government, the business sector exerted considerable political pressure to mandate the Fifth Article of the Federal Law of Radio and Television, 'reinforcing the respect for principles of social morality, human dignity and family ties' (Monsiváis 2003: 19, translated by Serna). A superficial ideological deregulation based on contradictory discourses has thus been produced by the diffusion of new cultural narratives. These narratives consist of a strengthening of conservative family models, as well as of a deregulation of cultural frameworks of national identity that are suggestive of the unshackling of 'cosmopolitan, modern, competitive, rational, unbiased individuals' in Mexican society (idem).

This cultural and political narrative has entailed contradictory consequences. In it, individual freedom takes a leading role, and has given rise to the de-penalization of abortion, the legalization of gay marriages, as well as to the legalization of adoption by non-heterosexual individuals or couples. At the same time, and clearly influenced by neoliberal measures that debilitated the government's economic power, it has created a void in which the state does not take any responsibility for generating and sustaining democratic economic and cultural practices.[6] If a global, modern, cosmopolitan and more tolerant Mexico is depicted in films such as *Así del precipicio*, it is important to emphasize that this reality mainly corresponds to Mexico City's middle and upper class contexts that serve as the background of the film. In this sense, as Ignacio Sánchez-Prado proposes, during the new millennium privileged sectors have clearly obtained more discursive power to redefine new ways of organizing intimate citizenship and national identity. The 'lettered city', in this sense, is still imagining the geographies of the modern subject in contemporary Mexico, demonstrating the 'selective' modernization of global and neoliberal environments (Sánchez-Prado 2009: 125).

---

6   As suggested by José Ortiz Monasterio regarding the uneven modernity: 'Between the totopo and the microchip the state has not been able to incorporate into the modern world more than half of the population, made up of very poor Mexicans; from the current population, even exaggerating our optimism, only 10% will actually go into the XXI century' (Ortiz Monasterio 2004: 30, translated by Serna).

Lesbian Intimate Citizenships: Identity Negotiation in Latin America

Intimate citizenships is a critical perspective that enables the understanding of ways in which individuals negotiate their intimate life decisions, considering the convergence of discourses derived from symbolic systems that circulate from the private to the public and vice versa. As defined by Elzbieta Olesky, based on Plummer's (2003) proposals, '(i)ntimate citizenship theory describes how our private decisions and practices have become intertwined with public institutions and state policies, such as public discourse on sexuality, legal codes, medical system, family policy, and the media, to name just a few' (Olesky 2009: 4). Identity is negotiated in an ongoing manner in reference to the temporal and spatial contexts in which the subject is located. Narratives of intimate citizenship, or 'public identity narratives' (Plummer 2003: 104), are present in every kind of text – literary, visual, cultural, academic – and not just among the private circles of relatives or friends. Therefore such narratives can be defined and interpreted beyond the artificial division between the public and private space. Analysing the ways in which narratives of intimacy are defined through symbolic systems and how film represents these narratives expands our understanding of the ways in which individuals articulate their intimate citizenship in contemporary Mexico. In line with the conceptual proposals of Padilla et al. (2007: ix), it is important to examine the symbolic crossroads that mark the intersections between cultural, economic, interpersonal and emotional factors in the construction of sexual identities. The examination of narratives of love is productive in so far as affection constitutes perhaps the most 'sacred' contemporary discourse of intimacy (Padilla et al. 2007: x).

In order to understand the dynamics of women's intimate citizenship, whether they are lesbian or not, it is essential to account for family dynamics given that many practices central to women's exploitation in the context of patriarchal, heterosexist cultural logics have been constituted by defining familial spaces as private. Moreover, the analysis of the discourses and practices that permeate gender and sexuality may entail important insights which regulate and even assert or deny lesbian identity within societies. In Latin America, silence and invisibility mark the representation of lesbian intimate citizenship. Historically and institutionally, lesbians have been denied their discursive power by cultural practices that punish them because of their courage to break with established cultural models of femininity. The definition and regulation of their gender through the heterosexual norm[7] has always resulted in an uneven contrast with the category

---

7   According to Adrienne Rich, there is the cultural assumption that men as well as women are biologically prone to heterosexuality. This assumption excludes, and punishes, those dynamics that attack heterosexual normativity. Heterosexuality, from the compulsory matrix, is defined as natural, positioning homosexuality as the opposite: unnatural and, therefore, dysfunctional. See Rich, A. (1994) *Blood, Bread and Poetry*. New York: Norton Paperback.

'man'. The 'lack of femininity', according to the heterosexual matrix, also derives from the notion that lesbians break with the sacred task imposed on women, child-bearing. Invisibility, then, as suggested by Torres and Pertusa, has been an intrinsic part of the intimate-social experience of lesbian subjectivities in Latin and Latin American contexts:

> The lesbian experience is characterized by a high degree of invisibility, not only socially and culturally, but also on the personal; invisibility being part of their lesbian identity. [...] This invisibility is real; it is not merely rhetorical. It is the product of dynamics related to the coming out of the closet. Invisibility is the silence imposed on the lesbian who instinctively rejects identities imposed on her by everyone and everything in her life. This silence is intended to destroy a lesbian's sense of self and leads to the formation of 'the space of the closet' – a space that will be impossible to overcome and eliminate because it is part of the construction of the lesbian identity. (Torres and Pertusa 2003: 37)

In this sense, invisibility, which can also be read as a lack of space or an impossibility to gain access to discursive power to write about the lesbian body and intimacy, is defined by innumerable dynamics that imply, on the one hand, a partial, 'hidden', vague, and, in some cases, metaphoric representation (Torres and Pertusa 2003: 1). As suggested by Carmen Tisnado, it is worthwhile to examine representations of the lesbian body in a cultural tradition that systematically has denied the existence of such a body, since the representation of lesbian intimacy is still proposed as 'unpronounceable' in Latin America (2006: 267) Apart from focusing on 'unpronounceability' as a starting point for examining the representation of lesbian intimate citizenship in contemporary Mexican film, it is pertinent to identify symbolic discourses and practices that define such 'unpronounceability' in order to understand the relationship that exists between formation, regulation and practice of this identity. Although lesbian identity and other queer identities are kept enclosed, silent and invisible, they also employ a unique form of resistance: 'Lesbians do not come from outside culture, outside history, or outside class, race and gender to raise the flag for a self-evident version of freedom, justice, and equality. Rather, lesbian resistance consists instead of our determinant stories with an eye to reorganizing its distribution cultural and material resources' (Duggan 2003: 84).

It has been suggested that emotional, i.e. non sexual-genital, relations (Rich 1980) define lesbian identity. However, I would suggest that to recover lesbian sexual identity it is necessary to consider desire and sexual experiences as necessary components of lesbians' intimate and social life. The asexuality of the lesbian body must be transcended to show women's decision-making ability concerning their bodies and sexuality (Martínez 1996: 35). Furthermore, the asexuality imposed on the lesbian body has operated as another means of control and invisibility which must be subverted in favour of opening discursive spaces which help transcend the figure of the tragic lesbian, excluded from the socio-cultural space of Latin America. The analysis of sexual experiences and their representation therefore has significant implications for the complexity of definitions and practices of lesbian intimate citizenship.

The insertion of intimate lesbian citizenship in New Mexican Cinema is of vital interest as it legitimizes the supposed cultural opening of twentieth-first century society that highlights expressions of individual freedom, tolerance towards 'differences' and Mexico's image as a country that has participated in processes of democratization, a key requisite to become a full member of the global community. In this context, the legalization of gay marriages and adoptions in December 2009 undoubtedly points to significant progress for LGBT communities in Mexico. At the same time, it suggests a need to reconsider the intersection between experiences of love and discourses of modernity. According to Padilla et al., notions of family based on love and free choice have been employed to demonstrate, embody, and solidify practices central to Western modernity:

> Because of the global dissemination of this ideal of the love-based family – which became marked as a product of the cosmopolitan West – when regions of the developing world encountered these new (to them) ideas at the same time they are undergoing transformations in their demographic and economic circumstances, people experienced the shifting marital project as a moment of becoming more Western. (Padilla et al. 2007: xvii)

Thus, it is pertinent to reflect on how the sudden inclusion of lesbian characters in Mexican cinema responds to the need to confirm, even if only rhetorically, the so eagerly awaited Mexican westernized modernity which has been interrupted, and only partially attained, in Mexico since the beginning of the twentieth century.

Así del precipicio: Statements of Intimate Lesbian Citizenship?

Written and directed by Teresa Suárez, *Así del precipicio* had its premiere in 2006. The plot of the film includes characters from the upper-middle class in contemporary Mexico City, a place where modernity, globalization and conservatism clearly converge. Narrating the lives of three young women, the film, probably unintentionally, represents the contradictory discourses that mark the middle and upper urban Mexican classes. While it seems to admit ways of life beyond the heterosexual normativity, the film ends up condemning those women who challenge the norms of traditional behaviour assigned to women in Mexican society. As Suárez herself states, this was a project that 'nourishes from reality' as it tells the director's autobiographical experiences, particularly those involving addictions (drugs, sex, destructive relationships) and recovery.[8]

---

8   As Dalila Carreño suggests, several films in the new millennium use 'reality' (characters, events, social dynamics) to create 'invigorating' production formulae. Other

In so far as being gay is one of the movie's main topics, the director stressed that, since sexual diversity is part of contemporary reality, it is essential to include it in a way that breaks with the Mexican society's hypocrisy. Like film producer Eugenio López, Suárez argued that homosexuality 'is something quite respectable' (Povero 2006: 1), and that it must not be denied in Mexico where, according to both producer and director, there is the notion that '[homosexuality] only happens in the United States or in other places' (Olvera 2006: 1). These remarks, said around the time of the movie release, posit the film as a pioneer in the production of discursive spaces for lesbian characters. At the same time, the director and producer's observations point to the contradictions that exist in contemporary Mexico. Although it is supposed to be a modern environment in which there is a 'deregulatory' spirit, the female body remains under surveillance and is associated with the mother-wife role as the true Mexican embodiment of womanhood. In this sense, and clearly depicted in the film *Así del precipicio*, disruptions to the traditional model of Mexicaness are to be accepted in response to the spirit of individual freedom and as a mark of modernity. However, the apparently accepted lesbian identities will have to conform with traditional performances such as femininity, social class values, among other factors that make these characters 'non-threatening' for the heterosexual matrix.

To further understand the contradictory traits of *Así del precipicio*, it is worthwhile to examine the conditions of production of this film. Created in an environment of prevalent co-productions – since funding was mainly provided by the private industry (Cinépolis and Jumex) and supported by Fidecine – this movie displays the complex relationship that currently exists between the film crew, governmental organizations such as Radio, Television and Cinematography (RTC), marketing strategies and film criticism, and distribution and release. With regards to the relationship between this organization and the movie, a number of points deserve attention. First, the movie was classified by RTC as intended for people aged 18 or over – because of explicit drug abuse, physical violence and gay issues. Second, according to the director, the movie suffered attempts at film censorship due to female nudity and lesbian scenes (Hernández 2006: 1). Another factor, as the director stated, was the anticipated effects of releasing a movie with a lesbian character in the same month as the passing of the Ley de Sociedades de Convivencia [Civil Partnership Act] that served for the recognition of same sex unions in some areas in Mexico.[9] Third, Suárez declared that she was threatened several times by influential celebrities who took parts of the film personally and

---

films which follow this formula are: *Ver llover* (Elisa Miller 2006), *El Mago* (Jaime Aparicio 2004), and *Efectos secundarios* (Issa López 2006).

9   On November 9, 2006, The Legislative Assembly of Mexico City signed the Ley de Sociedad de Convivencia [Civil Partnership Act]. This law proposes legal recognition of those households made up of people without consanguinity or affinity. This Law is acknowledged as the basis of recent changes regarding the approval of marriage between non-heterosexual couples and children's adoption in these alternative families.

appealed to the Interior Ministry to stop the film shooting. Former RTC's Javier Cortés' statement stands out: he said that the remarks on film censorship were part of the film's marketing strategy.[10]

Taking into account the aforementioned points, the presentation of these topics on the cinematic screen must be analysed with a cultural perspective that shows the dynamics represented by the lesbian character's intimate citizenship. That is, a character who accepts her sexual and emotional attraction to women as well as the creation of spaces of power that dislocate the heterosexual compulsion – a dominant and organizational narrative in the Mexican cultural structure. Furthermore, the analysis of discourses and aesthetic representation is pertinent in so far as it unravels some of the contradictions presented in the movie. These contradictions end up perpetuating some of the discourses and practices that exclude identities that are not considered as ideal by the some of the matrices that produce and manage cultural meanings in contemporary Mexico – family, church, heterosexuality, television, class, the business sector among others.

Statement 1: '[Heterosexual] Love is a Closet'

Hannah (Ingrid Martz) is a young Mexican woman of Jewish origin who, after a marriage crisis that ends in divorce, finally comes out of the closet claiming her lesbian identity. Her story evolves in relation and contrast to those of two other young women, whose stability is also in crisis. Lucia (Ana de la Reguera), Hannah's college friend, works as an advertising art director assistant and is, as pointed out by the character at her last moment of vindication: 'addicted to destructive [heterosexual] relationships and drugs'. The third main character, Carmen (Gabriela Platas) is a frustrated artist and drug addict who is also in love with her best friend – a man who has recently come out of the closet. After Hannah's imminent marital crisis, she takes refuge in Lucía and Carmen's apartment. This living arrangement allows Hannah to move away, even if only temporarily, as it will be discussed later, from her home references. Hannah's coming out of the closet evolves in parallel with the other two young women falling over the 'cliff' [*precipicio*]. It is peculiar that while Hannah's desire and intimacy contours are defined by several visual and thematic tropes that normalize her lesbian identity within the story, the other two characters end up being punished at the end of the movie – Carmen dies

---

10   As it can be read on Verónica Olvera (*Reforma*, November 26, 2006) and Omar Cabrera's (*Reforma*, April 20, 2005) journalistic notes, members of upper Mexican spheres, who felt alluded to by the last names mentioned on the film (Burillo, Serrano, Romano, or the name Matías [Ehrenberg]) regarding drug use/ homosexuality, attempted to stop the film shooting. According to actors Ana de la Reguera and Rafael Amaya, an advertising campaign of 'apology spots' was generated by the likely offence the film caused to Mexican society's important figures. Hence the alleged outrage is part of the advertising strategy of this film.

and Lucia is forced to vindicate herself after her friend's death. This results in an ambiguously symbolic attitude that condemns women's sexual activity and drug abuse, but accepts the queer character. Even Hannah, in her exploration of the boundaries of her sexual identity, hardly ever suffers homophobia – for instance, from the husband of Sandra (Anna Ciocchetti), the woman with whom she falls in love, or from her own family or husband who disappear from the story. This implies that the lesbian's coming out and self-confirmation depend on herself, since the environment's hostility – an upper-class refined environment – seems to be only a 'charade'. The aggressive and controlling patriarchal masculinity – rather reminiscent of post-revolutionary virility – is depicted when Sandra's husband finds her and Hanna together, and attacks them after their first romantic encounter. Sandra then reassures Hannah, 'Please don't pay attention to him. He considers himself a macho but he doesn't dare do anything'. Hence the regulatory nature of patriarchal discourses is represented in this movie as 'emasculated', in a state of transformation which, in agreement with modern global twenty-first century Mexico, is supposed to reinforce the power of individual freedom, democracy and respect for sexual diversity.

Hannah's self-confirmation as a woman who likes women[11] evolves through the account of her intimate experiences and with regard to her failed marriage, in which her needs and wishes were barely recognized. The narrative of this intimate citizenship in transformation at first includes many scenes defined by closed, intimate, protective and, at the same time, limiting spaces. As she herself says in her therapist's intimate office – and confirmed by a former scene where Hannah confronts her ex-mother-in-law – her marriage was not a fulfilling experience. However, Hannah finds strategies to either contest or negotiate her position as a constrained married woman, simultaneously becoming an agent within spaces of intimate citizenship. This power of agency is used, in the end, to finally come out of the closet, establishing the first sexual and emotional relationship with a woman.

Hannah narrates some of her dynamics of resistance and negotiation to her therapist. The narration of her subversion starts when she states in a delicate voice that she was a dutiful woman trying to establish intimacy with her husband without success: 'I tried by all means to be a good wife; I cooked for him but he was never hungry'. As the narration evolves, however, a second emotion arises as she reflects on her marriage: anger. She recounts the lack of emotional intimacy with her husband and how his urge to get her pregnant made her feel assaulted, suffocated, just like her body was always made available to comply with the heterosexual norm. Hannah, however, defies these coercive dynamics by confirming at the same therapy space, and amid laughter and weeping, that 'obviously Abraham didn't know that I was taking contraceptives'. With this statement, she adopts a more confident attitude, showing a gesture of transformation clearly associated with

---

11   It stands out that the word 'lesbian' is absent in this film. Neither Hannah nor her 'liberal' friends are capable of saying it: they use, instead, the euphemism '*lencha*' to refer to Hannah's probable lesbian identity.

the character's privileged position: she has had access to innumerable resources, among them a therapeutic space where she can assert her intimate citizenship as a lesbian woman. In this sense, her resistance to have children, which, at the same time, is a resistance to heterosexual gender normativity, ends up proving Hannah as a woman who embodies modernity and individuality. Hannah is a clear example of someone who places individual freedom above community values. As suggested by Wardlow and Hirsch (2006: 11), procreation patterns and idealization of individualism will be a key component of contemporary discourses with relation to social subjects' intimacy and modernity.

Hannah's view of her marriage as a restrictive and oppressive space is confirmed in one of the most productive scenes with respect to the discourses that shape experiences of intimate citizenship. After the therapy session – preceded by an apparent truce between Hannah and her husband – she gets ready to watch her wedding video. This happens in Lucía's apartment after the therapy session. Lucía joins her in a meaningful dialogue about upper class women's sex and love experiences in twentieth-first century Mexico City. Their words show the interdependence between public discourses and personal decision-making related to intimate life and their experiences of being women:

> Lucía: What a masochist you are! [After seeing Hannah crying in front of her wedding video]
>
> Hannah: I'm so confused; I don't know what to do.
>
> Lucia: Are you in love?
>
> Hannah: Love is a prison, a closet.
>
> Lucia: No, chiquita [lit. little one, meaning dear], love is sex.
>
> Hannah: I didn't like to have sex with Abraham. He was very coarse.
>
> Lucia: Well, Matías is a magician … [But] I don't want to know anything about men, you know. I want to be OK. Be calm. Drink lots of water. Work out. Be at peace with myself.

The two women's disenchanted view of love is noteworthy since it defines their acceptance or rejection at the end of the movie. This is the case, above all, for Lucía's character: she does not seem dependent on emotional love for her identitary 'stability' as a woman, and ends up being punished for it at the end of the movie.

Statement 2: Spaces, Bodies and Ornaments

One of Hannah's most remarkable aspects as a character is her corporeality. Hannah, a blonde young woman who embodies a traditional model of European beauty, has perfect manners and a gentle voice. She is always dressed in designer clothes of pastel colours and framed in an ornamental position within the different spaces she occupies. In this sense, the character's mobility/ immobility stands out since her body remains mostly rigid or passive throughout the different scenes in which she participates. This is indicative of how space – without forgetting the intersections with gender, sexual orientation, class, among other factors – marks the intimate experience of this character in the process of coming out of the closet. Framed within elegant spaces that also confirm class roles, Hannah maintains throughout the film a corporal composure that implies, at the same time, consumer values, purchasing power, cosmopolitanism, and ornamental function. At the same time, it is relevant to reflect on Hannah's bodily commodification within contemporary cinematic productions that are representing the image of a modern, global, and allegedly democratic Mexico. As a descendant of Jewish immigrants in Mexico, Hannah not only embodies the corporeal aesthetic and idealized requisites set by the neo-colonial imagination, but also embodies modernity, cosmopolitanism, and multiculturality that, combined with Hannah's sexual orientation, confirm the new image of a tolerant global Mexico. As pointed out by Ernesto García Canclini (2007: 178), massive European migrations to Latin America at the end of the nineteenth and the beginning of the twentieth century, as well as those groups' participation on the implementation of modern nations in Latin America, turn out to be privileged developments from which paths to modernity can be traced.

The definition of ornamental and even cultured spheres in which Hannah moves, is shown parallel to the development of the character's intimacy. As Sarah Radcliffe suggests (2007: 22), the temporality and incarnation of modernity are defined by the spaces that build up such a concept. Hannah works in Berger Jeweller's, located in a chic building whose interior is almost totally golden – elevator, banisters, walls – where she sells valuable merchandise (jewellery, precious stones, watches, etc.). The space arrangement of the jewellery store – intimate, full of mirrors and simple but dazzling glass cases – matches Hannah's own representation, whose hair and clothes match the space decoration. Even the scene that shows Sandra's arrival to the jeweller's, where the first encounter between these two characters takes place, makes Hannah look like a 'beautifully trapped' woman in this golden cage. The jewellery store evokes a self-contained space whose display cabinets turn out to be the only form of interaction with the outside world. Even though Sandra's bursting into the store *queers* the space, at the same time, Sandra reinforces Hannah's ornamental character as she is also blonde and dressed in designer clothes. In addition, Sandra is desperate to find a watch that she has been unable to find even in Paris. These two women's modernity and global nature is apparently confirmed through three symbolic dynamics: corporal, spatial and the consumption of luxury goods. In García Canclini's words: 'To be modern, nowadays, is to travel, to communicate, exchange with the world. Goods, messages, and people are considered to be modern if they circulate globally, if they speak various languages, and are attractive in a high number of markets' (2007: 177).

This initial encounter between Hannah and Sandra takes place among mirrors that evoke a constant dynamic of self-reflection. Their attraction to one another, enhanced and revealed by the many mirrors that surround them, according to Wardlow and Hirsch (2006: 15), corresponds to the classic definition of romantic love based on mutual appreciation of individuality. At the same time, the mirrors produce an intimate atmosphere in which Hannah dares to desire a woman when she glimpses Sandra's revealing décolletage. Thus, the relationship between these two women starts in a space designed for the commodification of several aspects. Those aspects intervene significantly in the definition of their intimate citizenship: discourses of love centred on individuals' particularity – a function reinforced with the constant self-reflection allowed by the mirrors; the body's ornamental function and love discourses that relate to the commercial value of jewels within the patriarchal imagination. Jewels serve as a means to reinforce patriarchy and values associated with social class and prestige, assets that these two characters handle.[12] Notwithstanding the fact that Hannah requires no security deposit for a Sandra's watch, the commercial nature of their intimacy is evident in this scene. Even though there is a displacement from the jewellery store to other spaces as they venture on a romantic relationship, throughout the movie both women keep their ornamental and commodified quality, which, at the same time, undermines the complexity of these lesbian characters' emotional and sexual intimacy. Although lesbians, these two characters are packaged in such a way as to be palatable within the visual discourses of heterosexuality: they are defined by their easily consumable, delicate beauty and the ornamental, feminine spaces in which they interact.

Statement 3: Intimate Lesbian Desire or Patriarchal Gaze

Despite the fact that their first encounter in the jewellery store sparks Hannah's curiosity and desire for Sandra, only in her dreams will she be able to further explore such desire. This lesbian erotic dream produces in fact a political, discursive and cultural affirmation: 'Erotic and sexual scenes among women work as political statements and as claims for women's rights to a sexual life. Presenting relations among women in this way is a political act since it subverts the traditional idea that

---

12   For a study on the dynamics of patriarchal control associated with jewellery see: Ching Chan, S. (2006) 'Love and Jewelry: Patriarchal Control, Conjugal Ties, and Changing Identities', in *Modern Loves. The Anthropology of Romantic Courtship and Companionate Marriage*, edited by Jennifer Hirsch and Holly Wardlow. Michigan: University of Michigan Press, 35–50.

women are not entitled to enjoy their sexuality' (Martínez 1996: 12). However, this manifestation of desire is literally presented like a commercial-sexual fantasy involving the well-known American brand Sara Lee. This brand, famous for their cakes, previously served as comfort food for Hannah after separating from her husband, but in the context of the dream they represent the promise of intimacy instead of its absence. Visually stunning in a range of pink and black colours in a modern kitchen, the cakes in this dream connect discursive and global dynamics in Mexico. Hannah dares to explore and negotiates her lesbian desire through cultural practices that embody modernity, globalization, intimacy, and even sexual commodification. In this visually playful erotic dream, *Sara Li* (represented by Sandra) is the protagonist. Lured by the smell of cakes that Sara Li is baking, Hannah enters the kitchen with an innocent face. Sara Li, clad in a black wig that defines her as a dominatrix type, explains to Hannah the different types of cakes she has to offer. The cakes, their preparation and consumption, serve as a metaphor for their sexual desire:

> Hannah: At what temperature do you bake cakes?

> Sara Li (Sandra) (bringing her mouth closer to Hannah's while she is speaking and spilling the cake mixture on Hannah's breast): Just 60 minutes at 150° ... they'll be ... spongy and ready to eat. (translated by Serna)

With these words, Sara Li 'gets Hannah ready', and approaches Hannah sexually on the table between cakes and baking utensils. The next minute, Hannah remains on the table while Sara Li takes off her robe and undresses Hannah's upper breast. Evoking the classic dynamics of activity/ passivity in the sexual act, Hannah shows signs of pleasure on her face when she sees herself literally covered by the woman who, for the first time, arouses her sexual desire.

Just two minutes into Hannah's dream, the erotic encounter is interrupted by a presence that reveals the commodified character of the sexual fantasy: Aunt Jemima, an African-American character who personifies the famous pancake syrup brand, comes into the kitchen and becomes indignant about the scene, asking in English, 'What are you doing?' This evocative scene also reveals one of the basic purposes of this work: to analyse the representation of sexual intimacy with respect to the media and global market. That is to say, in Padilla (et al.)'s words: 'How do desires, pleasures and emotions circulate as commodities in the global market place? In what ways do the economic processes characteristic of contemporary economies shape the acceptability of both public and private expressions of sexual intimacy and the ways in which sexuality is depicted and reproduced in global media?' (Padilla et al. 2007: x).

Even though this emblematic scene represents the manifestation of both women's sexual desire as well as the probability of pleasure fulfilment, the limits of this representation must be recognized. The contradictory aspect of this fantasy is that it uses traditional ways of representing the female body, and even the lesbian body. The viewers contemplate the scene through a perspective that depicts both women's entire bodies alternating with close ups towards traditionally sexualized body parts: Hannah's naked breast, Sara Li's butt and long legs. On the other hand, allowing women's pleasure on the cinematic screen may be acknowledged as a sign of the confirmation and recovery of the female body traditionally asexualized even by conservative feminist discourses. As Cherry Smith (1990) suggests in her critical reflection on pornography that responds to lesbian or bisexual desire, it is necessary to understand if traditional logics of representation still define the female and lesbian sexualities. Historically, cinematic productions –pornographic or not – systematically have perpetuated several ways of representation. Ways that perpetuate a hierarchy, a patriarchal and euro-centred order in which objectification of women's body is defined out of oppressive discursive systems: 1) the control that the gaze exerts on the body (kind of shots, body fragmentation-fetishizing/ eroticizing); 2) the lack of representation of women's pleasure that, at the most, is represented with rehearsed screams or vocal manifestations; 3) the perpetuation of an order that still privileges the representation of the racially so-called 'white' as an ideal, commodified and aesthetic model; 4) the reproduction of the dominant/ submissive, passive/ active hierarchical system that has been the basis of inequality in relationships (Smith 1990: 153).

Hannah's representation responds to these four visual principles. Thus, it is difficult to identify *Así del precipicio* as a counter-cultural feminist manifestation in which coercive practices derived from heterosexual and Eurocentric matrices are subverted. The difficulty in displacing the heterosexual norm becomes explicit by Aunt Jemima's bursting in. She prevents the fulfilment of desire, bringing Hannah's sexuality back to silence as her interruption awakes Hannah to her life 'reality'. Also, in this scene, the complexity of lesbian desire and eroticism are rendered simplistic by the dominant/submissive heterosexual dynamics – in which Sara Li (Sandra) literally takes the directive while Hannah remains motionless underneath. Since there is no irony or distance in the way dominant/submissive heterosexual practices work, the encounter further confirms asymmetric dynamics that produce and regulate power and identities. In addition to the obvious fragmentations of the female body, this scene reinforces to the utmost the ornamental, hypersexual and traditionally feminine nature associated with blonde women. This way of representation is still more coercive because it is a movie contextualized in contemporary Mexico. Despite the fact Mexico presents itself as multicultural, it still perpetuates, as the film shows, the racial neo-colonial hierarchy that excludes mestizo or indigenous, and working class Mexican viewers as participants of modernity. This Eurocentric approach also shows a power/ lack of power manifestation derived from the dynamics that organize the contours of corporeal modernity: 'Colonial/ colonized body boundaries comprise not an enduring marker of modernity/non-modernity, but a shifting topography of power and difference' (Radcliffe 2007: 29).

The ornamental representation of intimacy between Sandra and Hannah is repeated in the second part of the movie when both women have accepted their attraction and let their desire take over at Sandra's place. Even though the second encounter is not a dream, it too simplifies lesbian intimacy and makes the connection between Hannah and Sandra seem as ornamental as their fashion choices and as superficial as their whitewashed portrayal of intimacy. The viewers are excluded from a truly intimate portrayal of sexual dynamics since a love song sets the scene's atmosphere, silencing the characters' intimate dialogue. Therefore, the complexity and richness of the lesbian intimate citizenship is barely sketched by the images. Instead it is framed up on an eternal aesthetic space that prevents these characters from expressing some of the multiple discourses and directions of lesbian identity that prevail in contemporary Mexico.

Statement 4: Revealing and Hiding Cinematic Lesbian Intimate Citizenships

Even though *Así del precipicio* presents a discourse of apparent acceptance for the main character and her sexual orientation, as shown by the last scene in which Hannah appears with Sandra at Carmen's wake, it is meaningful to examine other aspects around the production of this movie to further understand the limits and contradictions inherent to this film. As mentioned above, the ornamental visual representation and the constant silencing of the intimacy dynamics between Hannah and Sandra are a way to deny the characters the power of enunciation. Moreover, several remarks made by actress Ingrid Martz during the movie advertising campaign, as well as at the time of its release, show the same contradictions about the movie since they reveal/hide the lesbian intimate citizenship of Hannah's character. Martz, although tolerated while playing the lesbian character of Hannah on the cinematic screen, must be normalized in the extra-diegetic and social spaces where the actress moves as a member of the Mexican TV and cinema star system.

Interviewed by Noemí González, Martz was delighted at playing the part of this complex character who made her come out of her comfort zone not only as an actress but as a heterosexual woman (2005: 1): 'There were months of workshops, improvisation, talks, socialization with lesbians to know what they feel. They love deeply but the difficult thing is to come out of the closet'. Martz' remark points out the possibility of a production really interested in empowering this invisible and silenced character on Mexican cinematic screens. However, the actress' own intervention is also quite revealing. Just after remarking on the risks that this performance might entail to her public image, she channelled the interview into normalizing her own sexuality (González 2005: 1): 'Yes, I kissed her (Ana Ciocceti). It was very hard. It is not the same kissing a man 50 times on a scene as kissing a woman. Teasingly, I said, "I don't want to kiss you anymore" and she said that she didn't either'. Martz' normalization as a heterosexual woman –which marks a clear distance from Hannah– was also confirmed in September 2008. Martz then posed for the magazine *H. Para Hombres* that, as indicated by its name, is geared toward heterosexual men. The magazine showed her in hypersexual pictures with captions such as 'A blonde soft spot/temptation [...] a charming blondie. You can't resist her charms'. Hence even if we emphasize that 'these are other times' in which the director and actress can represent a character that breaks with the heterosexual matrix, it is pertinent to question the limits of such representation. That is, a representation defined in a cultural environment that apparently accepts sexual diversity, but which, at the same time, makes explicit the superficial nature of such acceptance. Martz' image could not remain associated to Hannah's lesbian identity within the great modern global Mexican family that still considers heterosexuality as a synecdoche of the whole nation.

Conclusions

From the Golden Age of Mexican Cinema to the New Mexican Cinema film has embodied anxieties and tensions regarding the definition of Mexico as a modern space. Despite the fact Mexican cinema has presented refreshing and more democratic versions of gender and sexual experiences since the 80s, it is vital to recognize the boundaries and contradictions of such representations. Examining contemporary Mexican films such as *Así del precipicio*, produced and released after the political transition to democracy in 2000, reveals some of the contradictory ways in which contemporary film represents gender and sexuality in the light of the global era. This film incorporates a lesbian character as one of the protagonists. In this way, it responds to the notion of a modern Mexico that embodies global attitudes that promote diversity, tolerance, and above all, respect for individual free choice. Located in middle and upper class contexts of Mexico City, the female characters clearly explore and negotiate their intimate citizenships though the reflection on individuality, love, freedom of choice, among other values, that, interrelated with social practices and discourses, are contradictorily opening and denying discursive power for women (both lesbian and heterosexual) in contemporary Mexico. In this sense, the intimate citizenships of these characters, particularly Hannah who comes out of the closet, are clearly constituted through practices that intersect private decisions with discourses administered by public institutions such as family, media, and legal codes, among others. Hannah, one of the three protagonists in the movie, claims her lesbian identity by disidentifying herself from her heterosexual marriage and traditional family, demonstrating private negotiations with her own identity that are also related to social dynamics and definitions of gender, love, sexual orientation, and social class. Despite the fact the film depicts the contours of her lesbian intimate citizenship through the representation of her wishes, fears as well as redefinitions of love and sexual identity, it still adopts a contradictory dynamic that simultaneously reveals and hides the complexity of Hannah's intimate experiences. On the one hand, Hannah and her sexual partner in the film, Sandra, are depicted following patriarchal and neo-colonial logics of visual representation, perpetuating for these two characters an ornamental function within the film. On the other hand the film insists on using the unpronounceability of lesbian desire and identity as a discursive standpoint –

neither Hannah nor the other characters dare to pronounce the word 'lesbian'. In addition, the intimate citizenship of the lesbian characters is constantly silenced by music or other external elements, such as Aunt Jemima in Hannah's the sexual fantasy, which undermine the complexity and discursive power of lesbian representations in Mexican contemporary cinema.

In Carmen Tisnado's (2006: 278) analysis of dominant styles of representation in the Latin American imagination, she argues that, 'The stories are constructed as such that the lesbian character never fully emerges. The lesbian character is tentative in process-to be, ambivalent. In other words, she does not exist [yet]'. Therefore, we witness a process-to-be, an ambivalent rise of enunciation of lesbian intimate citizenship in the mass media. As such, several directions need to be explored in visual productions, such as cinema, since they have the power to represent, propose, and administer cultural meaning on the complexity of queer identities in contemporary global Mexico.

Bibliography

Así del precipicio (dir. Teresa Suárez, 2006).

Casi divas (dir. Issa López, 2008).

Carreño, D. 10 June 2007. *Nutren con realidad el cine.* [Online]. Available at: www.reforma.com/gente/articulo/777948/ [accessed: March 23, 2010].

Ching Chan, S. 2006. Love and Jewelry: Patriarcal Control, Conjugal Ties, and Changing Identities, in *Modern Loves. The Anthropology of Romantic Courtship and Companionate Marriage,* edited by J. Hirsch and H. Wardlow. Minneapolis: University of Michigan Press, 35–50.

Danzón (dir. María Novaro, 1991).

Duggan, L. 2003. The Trial of Alice Mitchell: Sensationalism, Sexology, and the Lesbian Subject in Turn-of-the-Century America, in *Queer Studies: An Interdisciplinary Reader*, edited by R.J. Corber and S. Valocchi. Malden: Blackwell, 73–87.

García Canclini, N. 2007. Culture and Communication in Inter-American Relations: The Current State of an Asymmetric Debate, in *When Was Latin America Modern?* edited by N. Miller and S. New York: Palgrave, 177–89.

Gutiérrez, N. 2 August 2005. *Besa Martz a Cioccetti en película.* [Online]. Available at: www.reforma.com [accessed: March 23, 2010].

H. Para Hombres 112 (2008). http://www.hparahombresusa.com [accessed: April 2, 2010].

Hernández, M. 24 November 2006. *Arrojan hoy tabúes al precipicio.* [Online]. Available at: www.reforma.com [accessed: March 25, 2010].

Hijas de su madre: Las Buenrostro (dir. Busi Cortés, 2005).

Irwin, R.M. 2003. *Mexican Masculinities.* Minneapolis: University of Minnesota Press.

López, A. 1993. Tears and Desire: Women Melodrama in the 'Old Mexican' Cinema, in *Mediating Two Worlds: Cinematic Encounters in the Americas*, edited by J. King, A. López and M. Alvarado. London: BFI, 147–63.

Padilla, M.B., Hirsch, J. et al. (eds) 2007. *Love and Globalization: Transformations of Intimacy in the Contemporary World.* Nashville: Vanderbilt University Press.

Martínez, E. 1996. *Lesbian Voices from Latin America: Breaking Ground.* New York: Garland.

Méndez, L.H. 2008. Neoliberalismo y Derechización en México (1983–2000). *El cotidiano*, 23, 5–15.

Miller, N. 2007. Interdisciplinary Approaches to Modernity in Latin America, in *When Was Latin America Modern?* edited by N. and S. Hart. New York: Palgrave, 1–17.

Monsiváis, C. 1998. Lo masculino y lo femenino al fin del milenio, in *Masculino y femenino al final de milenio*, edited by C. Monsiváis and M. Lamas. Mexico City: Díler/Apis, A.C., 7–24.

Monsiváis, C. 1978. Notas sobre cultura popular. *Latin American Perspectives*, 5(1), 98–118.

Monsiváis, C. 2003. No estamos en contra de las libertades sino de su ejercicio (Sobre la derecha en México). *Debate Feminista*, 14, 3–27.

Monsiváis, C. and Bonfil, C. 1994. *A través del espejo. El cine mexicano y su público.* México: El Milagro.

Nadie te oye: Perfume de violetas (dir. Marisa Sistach, 2001).

Ni de aquí ni de allá (dir. María Elena Velasco, 1998).

Niñas mal (dir. Fernando Sariñana, 2007).

Olesky, E.H. 2009. Citizenship Revised, in *Intimate Citizenships: Gender, Sexuality and Politics*, edited by E. Olesky. New York: Routledge, 1–15.

Olvera, V. 22 October 2006. *Reflejan dura realidad.* [Online]. Available at: www.reforma.com [accessed: March 25, 2010].

Ortiz Monasterio, J. 2004. *México eternamente: Vicente Riva Palacio ante la escritura de la historia.* México: Fondo de Cultura Económica/ Instituto de Investigaciones Dr José María Luis Mora.

Ortner, S. 2005. Subjectivity and Cultural Critique. *Anthropological Theory*, 5(1), 31–52.

Plummer, K. 2003. *Intimate Citizenship: Private Decisions and Public Dialogues.* Seattle: University of Washington Press.

Povero, D. 2006. Entrevista. Eugenio López y Teresa Suárez. Así del precipicio: El sueño hecho realidad. [Online]. Available at: www.reforma.com [accessed: March 25, 2010].

Radcliffe, S. 2007. Geographies of Modernity in Latin America: Uneven and Contested Development, in *When Was Latin America Modern?* edited by N. Miller and S. Hart. New York: Palgrave, 21–48.

Rashkin, E.J. 2001. *Women Filmmakers in Mexico. The Country of Which We Dream.* Austin: Texas University Press.

Rich, A. 1994. *Blood, Bread, and Poetry.* New York: Norton Paperback.

Rose, G. 1993. *Feminism and Geography. The Limits of Geographical Knowledge.* Minneapolis: University of Minnesota Press.

Rozado, A. 1992. *Cine y realidad social en México, una lectura de la obra de Emilio Fernández.* Guadalajara: Universidad de Guadalajara.

Sánchez-Prado, I. 2009. Narrativa, afectos y experiencia: las configuraciones ideológicas del neoliberalismo en México. *Revista de Crítica Literaria Latinoamericana*, 35(69), 115–33.

Sedwick, E.K. 2002. Epistemology of the Closet, in *Queer Theory and the Jewish Question,* edited by D. Boyarin, D. Itzkovitz and A. Pellegrini. New York: Columbia University Press, 41–63.

Smith, C. 1990. The Pleasure Threshold: Looking at Lesbian Pornography on Film. *Feminist Review*, 34, 152–59.

Tisnado, C. 2006. Do Lesbians Characters Make Lesbian Stories? The Representation of Lesbianism in four South American Short Stories', in *Desde aceras opuestas. Literatura/cultura gay y lesbiana en América Latina*, edited by D. Ingeschay. Madrid/Frankfurt: Iberoamericana/Vervuert, 267–81.

Torres, L. and Pertusa, I. (eds) 2003. *Tortilleras: Hispanic and U.S. Latina Lesbian expression.* Philadelphia: Temple University Press.

Torres Sanmartín, P. 2008. 'La recepción del cine mexicano y las construcciones de género. ¿Formación de una audiencia nacional? *Revista de estudios de género La ventana*, 3, 58–103.

Tuñón, J. 1998. *Mujeres de luz y sombra en el cine mexicano. La construcción de una imagen, 1939–1952*. Mexico City: El Colegio de México/Instituto Mexicano de Cinematografía.

Wardlow, H. and Hirsch, J.S. 2006. Introduction, in *Modern Loves. The Anthropology of Romantic Courtship and Companionate Marriage*, edited by J. Hirsch and H. Wardlow. Michigan: University of Michigan Press, 1–31.

Wittig, M. 1992. *The Straight Mind and Other Essays*. Boston: Beacon Press.

Chapter 4

Sexual Citizenship and Youth Identities: *Camino a casa. Un día en la vida de un joven mexicano* by Naief Yehya

Bladimir Ruiz

In 2005, under the collective guidance of several civil organizations, a *Cartilla Nacional de los Derechos Sexuales de los y las Jóvenes en México* [*National Declaration of the Sexual Rights of Youth in Mexico*] was published. Among those rights (13 are listed), this important document highlights: the right to make decisions about your own body and sexuality, the right to practice and enjoy your own sexuality and the right to express feelings in the public sphere.

At the core of this discussion, following the argument made by Alma Rosa Sánchez in her article on sexualities in Mexico, is the idea of a human body that is sexually controlled, repressed and subjected to the institutional mandate of dominant heterosexuality (Sánchez 2009: 103). Consequently, expressions of alternative sexualities face different discriminatory retaliations and social violence.

Recent scholarship in the social sciences and in cultural studies is now focusing on how these ideological processes intervene in the lives of young people. Similarly, Latin American literature has also examined how these tensions impact the lives of the youth in specific. *Camino a casa*, a Mexican novel by Naief Yehya (1994), focuses on the representation of processes by which identity is configured, specifically youth subjectivities. But this configuration involves much more than just the idea of youth.

The novel narrates a single day in the life of a middle-class adolescent (a Saturday), from the moment he decides to go with a friend to a popular flea-market in the Mexican capital until an evening party where he witnesses his girlfriend making out with his best friend. But although this is a day in which almost nothing really happens, we are presented with a perspective that abandons the adult-centred point of view and, with plenty of contradictions, tries to make sense of the experiences and emotions of the young protagonist. And more importantly, this deceptively 'light' narrative explores issues of sexual identity, the configuration of hegemonic masculinity, the role of music and consumerism in the configuration of youth subjectivities, and the opposition of youth- and adult-centred perspectives.

Camino a casa: **Intimate Citizenship and Hegemonic Masculinity**

This analysis of Naief Yehya's novel will focus on how it represents the construction of youth identities and the processes by which the hegemonic ideologies of gender and masculinity are appropriated and resisted. Both of these representations challenge how our society configures the legal and political status of the social actors that form it. One of the most relevant concepts related to this discussion is citizenship.

Traditionally citizenship has referred to a set of rights and responsibilities that all socially recognized individuals have, that is to say, individuals who are politically and judicially regulated. Citizenship, then, is a concept expressed within the context of the relationships between citizens and civil society. However, if the category of youth, as a social construction, has been mainly conceptualized from adult-centred positions that make invisible the agency of the social actor it describes, then a set of questions arises: Is it possible to connect citizenship with youth? If so, how can citizenship be possible for youth in a society that stigmatizes them? Or, even more to the point: is it possible to place this discussion of citizenship into the realm of intimacy and explore the intersection of youth and intimate citizenship? It is this last question constitutes the focus of this analysis.

The concept of intimate citizenship is important because it places a critique of heteronormativity at the centre of academic discussions and because it expands the notions of citizenship to include what traditionally has been conceived as the private sphere. It is almost impossible today to separate the idea of citizenship from the realm of sexual politics, or from any space in which social actors fight for the right of self-determination as sexual beings, for the freedom of expression, and for the right to control their own bodies. David Bell and John Binnie question in *The Sexual Citizen*: 'when we speak of citizenship, are we facing a legal, sociological or political category?' (Bell and Binnie 2000: 11). The answer seems obvious: citizenship includes *all* of them, but also incorporates less obvious categories such as sexuality. Thus, the main premise would be that all citizenship is sexual citizenship. It is not by chance, for example, that the concept of family built from the citizenship perspective is one that implies socially and juridically acceptable ways of living as a family and of establishing intimate relationships. Ultimately, intimate citizenship is relevant since it challenges the traditional division between the public and the private.

Ken Plummer reflects on the adjective 'intimate' and its correlative noun 'intimacy' and concludes that both of them belong to the complex sphere of the 'inmost relationships with self and others' (Plummer 2003: 13). Intimate relations, then, would include not only those close relationships with family members, friends, or lovers, but also those deep and transcendental experiences we establish with ourselves, our feelings, our bodies and identities. Intimate citizenship for this author constitutes 'the decisions people have to make on the control (or not) over one's body, feelings, relationships; access (or not) over representations, public spaces, etc.; and socially grounded choices (or not) about identities, gender experiences, erotic experiences. It does not imply one model, one pattern or one way' (Plummer 2003: 14).

All of these elements are present in *Camino a casa*, and part of the one-day journey documented in the novel deals with the actions and reflections of the young narrator who is trying to make sense out of the many ideological forces to which he is subjected. And from all of these social pressures, socially accepted sexual scripts become a source of conflict and inner turmoil that the protagonist needs to navigate and overcome. The narrative, as explained before, represents codes of behaviour and communication between contemporary urban middle class youth, which are linked to ideologies of masculinity and gender differentiation and the process by which they are appropriated and, sometimes, contested. Both of these topics are clearly connected with the concept of intimate citizenship, but from a youth perspective.

The modern view of sex is linked to a narrative of sexuality often seen as linear, casual and driven. This narrative constructs the category of sex as a 'truth' to be discovered (Attwood 80). Furthermore, the characters' interactions configure a symbolic system in which masculinity is associated with physical and verbal aggression, sexual curiosity, and female objectification. Similarly, the novel's constant mention of AIDS as a threat to health conveys a representation of a social issue that the young characters have to confront, and consequently, it creates a social context in which youth sexuality becomes an option limited by a discourse that combines elements of fear and responsibility. On the other hand, the narrative shows a clear awareness (on the part of the young characters) of living in a society in which sexual relationships must occur in consonance with a sense of responsibility regarding being 'safe'.

One cannot separate the ideologies of youth from the ideologies of gender, particularly in this novel. A sexist point of view pervades the text, one especially linked to youth's sensitivities, tastes, and values. In other words, in Yehya's novel, the development of cultural sensitivities is delineated by clear, and traditional, gender divisions. It is for this reason, for example, that our protagonist and narrator is affected emotionally by the death of Kurt Cobain, but his girlfriend is made sad by 'stupid things', like the character played by Kevin Costner in the film 'The Bodyguard'. And this brief example leads into a discussion of one of the most important topics in the narrative of *Camino a casa*: the representation of the code of conduct and communication between contemporary Mexican youth, linked to the construction and enforcement of masculinity.

The young characters' interactions in *Camino a casa* configure a symbolic system in which masculinity is associated with verbal and physical violence; with competition for trivial achievements (power manifestations on a shallow context); with the repression of emotions; with sexual curiosity; and with the configuration of women as sexual objects and of the homosexual as the abject 'other'.

Insults and vulgar and sarcastic language, a common linguistic feature in youth speech, becomes in the novel a mark of differentiation ('this is the way we young people talk') as well as a clear manifestation of the ideological power of dominant masculinity. The young characters verbally assault each other ('fucking jerk') and they relate to each other in a way that, on the surface, seems conflictive. Affection is never expressed, neither by words, nor by actions. Their constant fighting is a feature of the plot that, for the most part, has as a goal to achieve symbolic spaces that the characters perceive as powerful: who will sit in the front seat of a friend's car or who will decide which music to listen to. What is highlighted in the narrative is that these verbal and sometimes physical fights become an end in themselves and also symbolic tests that make evident a battleground where the conceptualizations of virility and hegemonic masculinity are materialized.

One way to analyse these verbal expressions is to inscribe them in the psycho-linguistic processes characteristic of youth cultures. Klaus Zimmerman states that insults should be evaluated as: 'kind of a game and a ritual in which the participants know that what has been said is not the truth. They try, then, to counter attack this insult with an equal or superior insulting expression in a quite original and innovative way ... this demonstrates the high level of creativity of youth' (Zimmerman 2003: 50). One example of this kind of youth-focused linguistic narrative in the novel illustrates this conflictive construction of competing masculinities:

> How did it go yesterday with Marcela – I asked Javier – Did you *heat it up*?
>
> Yep!
>
> Do you know that her boobs are fake?
>
> Mmm.
>
> Like your boss' [= your mother's].
>
> Go fuck yourself, dude. Fake is your wiener. (Yehya 1994: 25)

Verbal interchanges, such as the one above, should be categorized as a way of talking and of being linguistically creative. From the use of slang to the redefinition and renegotiation of concepts like fakeness, this encoding is a way for young people to express their subjectivities.

This kind of language (and the set of violent actions that often accompany them), however, should also be viewed as a power dynamic clearly linked to traditional gender divisions, especially to constructions of virility. For this reason, insults, fights, jeering, threats, abusive behaviour – just to name some of the dynamics represented in the novel – not only portray a learning process in which masculinity is *performed*, but also makes evident a power trip over young women and their male friends. In the same vein:

According this to "mystique", the values of a true man should be vigor, physical strength, indifference under physical pain, the inclination towards adventure, heterosexual ostentation, the hiding of one's feelings, the perpetual competing against others, the spirit of conquest, the act of seduction of females, and the constant enunciation of "male superiority". (Lomas 2007: 95)

The idea of masculinity, clearly intertwined with the concept of virility, is always tested and surveilled by different institutional and social mechanisms. This virility 'constitutes a structure of inter-subjective meanings translated into representation through our bodies and also defined by social interactions. This dynamic creates a concrete and significant area of recognition and power' (Alvarez Chavez 2003: 101). This hegemonic conceptualization of masculinity affects not only social and sexual scripts, but also the perception we have of ourselves and others. From a youth perspective, following the analysis of *Camino a casa*, peer pressure is the dominant mechanism of social pressure and the surveillance of masculinity, one that promotes early sexual experimentation for young men and the simultaneous objectification of women. Furthermore:

In this ideological universe, the performance of the hegemonic masculinity becomes a mechanism of oppression for both men and women. From the point of view of youth, this model, slowly learned and internalized, implies a constant dynamic where both the performance and the surveillance of that performance are updated. In this context there is no space for fear, insecurity or sadness because all of these feelings are seen as weak and therefore non-masculine (or feminine/queer). These oppressive mechanisms result in an intermittent monitoring of your own social presentations and of your peers. (Alvarez Chávez 2003: 102)

Camino a casa shows how certain elements like drugs and sexual experimentation play an important role in the daily life of the young characters. Drugs function as an invitation to fill out the space left by boredom, but also trigger emotional reactions and group tensions. The constant mention and use of drugs in the narrative is always presented as a natural and spontaneous occurrence and the constant reference to pornography must be linked to the discovery and exploration of sexuality and corporal pleasures and to a fondness for what is considered forbidden. The configuration of an acceptable masculinity requires the acceptance and internalization of these social dynamics.

The episode entitled 'Chronicle of Three Expected Fucks' ('Crónica de tres fajes anunciados') illustrates what was briefly explained about dominant masculinity and its representation on the novel. Jorge, one of the protagonist's friends, plans a party at home. He invites three girls with the sole purpose of getting laid (the narrator and another friend, Javier, complete the trio of guys looking for an easy sexual escapade). In this episode, the (male) youths' position regarding sex is represented in a clear, ideological fashion: that sex is viewed as a primordial male drive that needs to be quenched, and girls are the object/prey that make such a goal possible. In this pursuit of sexual pleasure and gratification, the three young male characters depict the three young female acquaintances as utterly disposable objects, stripped of individuality and agency, and useful only as long as they can make male orgasms a physical reality.

But this episode is much more complex (and funny) than what this summary shows. In this passage, humour, male complicity, clumsiness, and the gap between expectation and fulfilment stand out. The narrative represents with ease and candour the inexperience of the protagonist and how his need to comply with normative masculinity fails with every attempt. The narrative also highlights how this performance of dominant masculinity is theatre: in this particular case, the saddest of comedies. And the spectators – in this episode, the two male friends and the three girls – are part of this symbolic, theatrical representation in which all social actors try their best to perform the sexual scripts they have at their disposal.

The cultural analysis made by Ana Amuchástegui and Marta Rivas provides interpretive leverage for this scene. These authors consider that: 'Masculine sexual initiation compels compliance with an accepted norm of erection and penetration, often without the presence of sexual desire, leaving behind experiences of confusion and dissatisfaction that hardly can be expressed without risking mockery' (Amuchástegui and Rivas 2008: 103–4). Furthermore, these scholars argue that talking about sexual conquests between boys is a way to validate a masculinity that is always involved in some sort of masculine contest (Amuchástegui and Rivas 2008: 104). Thus, sexual expression for boys (and by extension for men) is controlled by hegemonic narratives of masculinity that are linked to what the authors term as 'narratives of what should be done'. Such narratives elaborate a list of 'do's and don'ts' that become the dominant sexual script of masculinity.

For this reason, the main character must constantly check the meaning of his speech, his appearance, and his social interactions. And this process of self-monitoring has the purpose of projecting an image that is consonant with the expectations the other characters have of him in any particular situation. Obviously, theis episode represents the young protagonist's failure of a basic test designed to define, and therefore control, notions of acceptable masculine behaviour. But what it is actually emphasized is how this hegemonic ideal of manhood is not only oppressive to women, but also to men – since in most cases men – and in particular, young boys – are unable to fulfil these 'lofty' social expectations. The failure of the protagonist in his mission becomes evident in his own evaluation of the situation: 'being there trying to design another plan of attack was like a penance, like being punished. Even more so trying to make myself believe that being rejected was not a big deal' (Yehya 1994: 38).

Another 'masculinity test' represented in the novel has a different group as witnesses and incorporates class into the process of women's sexual objectification. The protagonist goes with his mother to visit his aunt and cousins (whom he despises). During that visit his two (male) cousins invite him to see 'Leti's boobs' (Leticia being the domestic servant of the house). When the young narrator rejects the offer and states that he prefers to watch TV, the controlling eye of compulsory heterosexuality replies: "'So, do you really prefer to see soccer players rather than Leti's boobs? I think you are a fag" – José Luis almost yells at me' (Yehya 1994: 74). This homophobic challenge achieves its goal: the protagonist changes his mind. Later, when Leti asks him if he is attracted to her, he timidly replies: 'No ... I mean ... yes ... yes'. But it is relevant that while saying this, his inner reflection focuses on what he is really feeling: 'but my ears were in flames and I was sweating copiously ... so I did not have anything better to do than look at my soup and eat it as fast as I could' (75). The body, as expected, becomes the *locus* where social pressures and ideologies become visible.

The protagonist's discomfort highlights one of the main themes of this novel: how discovering and exploring sexuality can be difficult and even painful. And it is at this point that the novel contextualizes what has been said regarding hegemonic masculinity: we are facing an oppressive 'ideal' impossible to materialize in all of its manifestations. Different failed experiences are processed individually depending on factors such as race, ethnicity, social class, or, in the protagonist's case, age. Furthermore, *Camino a casa* suggests a crisis of this hegemonic model and an ambiguous emergence of alternative models of masculinity in constant conflict with the hegemonic paradigm. That is why the narrator emphasizes what he 'feels' while experiencing sexual opportunities (as opposed to experiencing sex from merely a genital perspective); he stresses his confusion through each exploration.

Youth sexuality is also represented not only as an identity that is being formed, but also defined. The apparently homosexual encounter that the protagonist experiences in a mall restroom triggers questions and reactions about an 'unknown world' that he instinctively feels he must reject. This is yet another episode that offers a 'virility test' the young character must pass, but now without witnesses. The main character's reaction to this encounter is illuminating:

> When I realized he was approaching, I felt my back turning ice cold and, without thinking about it, I left the restroom at a run and quickly went downstairs. I was such an idiot by reacting that way! Instead of running, I should have yelled at him or beat him up, but I could not understand what had happened to me. *I was very confused, between furious and agitated ... and certainly embarrassed.* I should go back and insult him. Or call the police ... What the fuck should I do? [...] I was sweating profusely and my hands were shaking ... Fucker! I am going to kill you! Poor dude, he must be really desperate [...] *I felt terribly vulnerable!* (Yehya 1994: 56; author's emphasis)

The episode stresses the fact that this experience subtly questions different socio-cultural teachings. On the one hand, the learning of a compulsory heterosexuality and of a hegemonic masculinity assumes an active resistance to *any* sign of homosexual desire, even if (perhaps especially if) you are the object of such a drive. That would explain the (expected) violent rejection to the alleged sexual proposition by a supposed homosexual in a public restroom. However, the protagonist's reaction also includes deviations from this hegemonic model by incorporating feelings of confusion, fear and vulnerability. Interestingly enough, the episode continues and the protagonist decides to return to the restroom, to act on his learned sexual script. This reaction could be analysed as an attempt to erase the transgression and re-assert 'normality': he knows he must return and beat the stranger up. The ending of this passage again challenges the dominant conceptualizations that the novel constantly and paradoxically embraces and rejects:

> An older man all dressed up entered the restroom and saw me. He wanted to take a piss and started to unzip his pants. He saw me walking from one corner of the restroom to the other and then hesitated. Never taking his eyes off of me, he finally decided to go to a stall and locked himself in it. So, not only did my reaction happen a little too late, but, on top of that, the guy acted as if *I* was the queer! (Yehya 1994: 57)

This (highly comic) inversion of perspectives makes the narrator question his own reactions and emotions, and in particular his deviation from the cultural norm – he did not physically hit the alleged homosexual and, to make matters worse, he felt vulnerable both during and after the experience. On the other hand, he experiences what is to be seen and perceived as a weirdo and a possibly gay person. Finally, he learns that not all of the reactions to encounters such as the one he had must end up in violence as a way to reinforce power and dominant masculinity: for example, the older man decided to do his own business privately and to ignore the alleged advances of a 'young homosexual' – he did not yell at him, or beat him up.

The learning of dominant masculinity by the main character, as discussed, implies contradicting forces. For this reason, for example, at the end of the novel, he is emotionally conflicted: angry, because of the discovery of his girlfriend's infidelity (with his best friend!) and at the same time, desperate, because of his need to establish a more intimate communication with Lola, the 'different' girl who rejects social categorization. It is not by chance, then, that it is with her that the protagonist is finally able to openly express emotional responses that have been repressed by peer and other social pressures: "'I know what is to feel that shit!" – she told me while caressing my head. I could no longer contain my sadness and started to cry in silence. We remained standing close to each other for a long while' (Yehya 1994: 106). Later, in the same final passage, the narrator explains that although he feels sexually aroused, he understands that 'there is something more' in Lola's communicative gesture: 'I did not think her caring way of treating me meant more than a mere act of solidarity and real friendship. But that was enough to save me from drowning' (Yehya 1994: 106). And it is at this climatic point that the novel shows the possibility of building more democratic intimate relationships. The narrative of *Camino a casa* once again challenges the dominant system of power and implies that its alienating force creates a *habitus* that young people internalize without realizing it. Thus, the narrative conclusion delineates a less hegemonic conceptualization of heterosexual relationships and of intimate gender interactions.

Yehya's novel elaborates a set of representations in which youth sexuality is centrally placed and affected by ideological constructions concerning what it means to be a man and the 'nature' of masculine desire. *Camino a casa* occasionally becomes a sort of manual for youth on how to enforce hegemonic masculinity. At the same time, by emphasizing the emotions and failures of the protagonist in the process of enforcing such rules, the novel seems to rebuke the updating of the heterosexist patriarchal dominant model. In this line of inquiry, what is most interesting about this contemporary Mexican novel is that in its conceptualization of the youth world there is a clear challenge to traditional gender models and a gesture towards alternative constructions of sexuality and social interactions. *Camino a casa* represents a process of configuration of youth sexuality in which there is a mixture of certainties and insecurities; of social pressures and individual resistance; of heterosexist ideologies and new ways of visualizing sexual and intimate relationships that are less oppressive and more egalitarian.

Camino a casa: Youth Identity and Adult-Centrism

If identity can be defined as a series of internalized cultural repertoires through which social actors mark their 'personal frontiers' and, therefore, are differentiated from other actors in a specific geographic, social, and historical context (Jiménez 2002: 38), then it is clear that the novel emphasizes the mechanisms by which this identity (in this case cultural identity) is built. Furthermore, *Camino a casa* configures a narrative field charged with conflicting ideologies. And out of all of these tensions, the one that is privileged is the battle between youth and adult-centred perspectives.

The adult-centred perspective characterizes the juvenile condition more by what it lacks than by what it has. That is to say, that given a series of elected parameters, the lack, absence or negation of such parameters constitute what could be called the essence of the young subject. The problem with such view is that 'it loses sight of the youth condition as a social construction, and that it does not take into account that behind most conceptualizations calling for a natural phenomenon there hide highly ideological discourses with a dangerous discriminatory approach' (Chaves 2005: 14). Included in these kinds of representations are the concept of the teenager as a very insecure human being (opposed to adults who would own such sense of security); the idea of youths conceptualized as beings-in-transition (opposed to adulthood, conceptualized as a final and desirable destination); adolescents as non-productive individuals; youths as incomplete human beings; adolescents as people who do not know what they really want; and even children as dangerous social actors. In short, the dominant adult-centred perspective 'locates adulthood as a point of reference for youth, in relation to what it should be, or what should be done or achieved in order to be accepted as a positive member of society (maturity, responsibility, integration to the mass market, family reproduction, civic participation, etc.)' (Duarte 2003: 63).

In clear contrast with these positions, there are a number of academic approaches that place youth identity in the category of a social construction. Lydia Alpízar and Marina Bernal, for example, consider that youth cultures should be seen as 'the way in which the social experiences of young people are expressed collectively through the construction of distinctive life-styles, which are located mainly in leisure time or in those spaces where institutional life intersects' (Alpízar and Bernal 2003: 14). This kind of research rejects the idea of a homogeneous collective that is characterized by using a predicted number of cultural stereotypes. Instead, it privileges flexible conceptualizations that are able to convey the transitory and relational character of this kind of subjectivity. Thus, one could conclude that:

> Young people cannot be labeled simplistically as a homogeneous social *corpus*, we are talking about heterogeneous social actors that are constituted while performing actions. Even more, their social practices are grouped (and dispersed) by communitarian dissidences: the ecology, sexual freedom, peace, human rights. Another group of youth prefer the anonymity, the individualistic pragmatism, the hedonistic mercantilism, the pleasure of consumption. (Reguillo Cruz 2000: 15)

In *Camino a casa*, the first-person narrative, sometimes reflexive and always full of an enchanting freshness and a sense of spontaneity, rejects the adult-centred point of view and erects a value system that gives centrality and visibility to the youth perspective. That is why, for example, the protagonist is constantly making fun of the adults and their inability to understand a *logos* different than their own. For this reason the narrator resists being evaluated as a problem that must be solved and, consequently, presents as an alternative the idea of a being trying to express, experiment with, and validate his own views.

The mother of the protagonist (and her disparaging comments on all that her son thinks and wishes) becomes the adult-centred voice, whose authority and control are constantly challenged by the youth perspective prevalent in this text. For the mother, the adult world is the point of reference used to evaluate her son's actions. She constantly judges and thus discredits the youth experience. For instance, the protagonist (and main narrator) avoids talking about the last movie he saw (the oh-so-youth-centred 'Wayne's World'): 'I had an intuition that she would start a sermon on what she calls the culture of idiocy' (Yehya 1994: 12). Sure enough, as the protagonist predicted, the mother ridicules the movie:

> ... two idiots walk around saying the least ingenious and most silly things anyone in the whole world can say. That is no real cinema, but a collection of non-funny and stupid occurrences. But these two assholes give an impression of

intellectuals, like the other ones from MTV, Beavis and Butthead. Those are the
real kings of the culture of idiocy. (Yehya 1994: 12)

It is not by chance, then, that in Mexican slang, frequently employed in the novel,
a mother's nickname is 'boss'; nor is it surprising that the narrator, jokingly,
expresses that his mother always 'adopts the tone of voice of a scolding elementary
school teacher' (Yehya 1994: 55).

The conversations between mother and son can be characterized as a battle
ground between the imposition of rules and expectations and the rejection of such
power by using a humorous and sarcastic discourse. Sarcasm in *Camino a casa* is
a tool used by the narrator to counter-attack a discourse of power that constantly
diminishes the value of the youth experience. Interestingly, though, this youth
perspective privileged in the narration not only values this specific worldview,
but also reverses occasionally the hegemonic order (adult-centred) and, therefore,
mimics its disqualifying dynamic (in this case: *everything* that comes from
the adults).

Similarly, the conversations (shall we say arguments?) between the young
protagonist and his mother are relevant because they make evident the generational
gap that is manifested not only through the language used by the characters, but
also by the cultural references through which each of them shows his/her personal
taste and cultural identifications. The young narrator constantly makes fun of his
mother's musical taste because he considers her favourites to be 'sugar-coated'
and in response she criticizes how 'gringo-oriented' her son's musical preferences
are. This particular opposition is even more relevant if we view it in terms of
a contrast between the nationalistic vs. the globalized approach to music. Also,
the novel focuses on the idea of language as a vehicle of identity. The young
man's speech, full of humorous turns of phrase and neologisms, gestures towards
a linguistic usage that accentuates novelty and spontaneity. His mother, on the
contrary, uses language as a rational tool, with more uniform tendencies.

Another process clearly linked to the construction of youth subjectivities in
Yehya's novel is the incorporation of young people within a larger framework
of cultural consumption, especially music, videogames, and clothing. The novel
shows how music (rock, reggae), films, videogames, and fashion become 'marks'
that identify the protagonist as an individual and at the same time as a member
of similarly-marked youth, with associated subcultures. In this sense, these
'marks' function not only as commercial labels, but also *cultural* labels; they are
associated with processes in which both identification and diversification play a
role in the formation of identity. As figured in the novel, there is a direct link
between consumption and identity.

Videogames, for example, function in *Camino a casa* as identity elements
connected to capitalist consumption. 'Mortal Kombat' is presented, explained,
and exemplified as an attempt to show how through cultural artefacts the young
characters not only find fun and entertainment, but also a collective sense of
belonging (through cooperative or competitive video-gaming). That is why the

protagonist frequents 'Pantylandia', a video-game saloon where he and his friends configure their spaces of socialization. Furthermore, videogames in the narrative are presented as an opportunity to enter in a more vivid reality in which the youth can exhibit a greater agency, with fewer variables. Such video games can also be viewed as cultural artefacts through which youth develop new talents and their own ways of communicating with their peers. One can actually argue, then, that videogames make possible the construction of 'ephemeral identities' that are also of great symbolic value in the complex process of formation and restructuration of youth subjectivities.

Finally, the narrative suggests a connection between videogames like 'Mortal Kombat' and the performance of a hegemonic masculinity focused on violence. It is not by chance that the episode with these videogames ends in a brawl between the protagonist and his friends against another group of youth. It must be stressed, though, that the reflection of the first-person narrative on this episode has a moralizing tone (an adult-centred position) towards these videogames that links them to the violent behaviour of youths. For this reason, the protagonist reflects: 'While walking, I imagined that I jumped on, kicked, and hit every single person who was strolling through the mall. It always happened to me that after playing these videogames for a while, my sense of reality remained altered for a while' (Yehya 1994: 54).

Just as with the video games that the narrator and his friends play, clothing and style also become tools of self-expression for the youth in the novel while simulataneously constituting mechanisms of class differentiation clearly linked to commercial brands. The narrator makes a point in saying that he is wearing 'Adidas trekking shoes, a Depeche Mode t-shirt and a pair of Guess jeans that I like a lot' (Yehya 1994: 14) and, by doing so, not only connects attire to a way to see himself as an unique self (and paradoxically similar to young people he wants to associate with), but also makes a class statement: he is separating himself from those youth who belong to an 'inferior' social-economic class and, therefore, are unable to belong to *his* group. In similar fashion, the narrator describes that 'Javier had earrings and a small tattoo on his arm [...], Jorge had a tattoo on his chest and Martin had two piercings in his nose' (Yehya 1994: 28). The piercings should be evaluated both from the perspective of individual identity-building and a more political angle. Given the frequent adult-centred power trip that results in the constant marginalization of the youth point of view, this body ornamentation can also be seen as an empowering gesture called by some researchers a 'terrorizing visibility'. It can be explained as 'a mechanism of affirmation, of rejection of devaluation, and of appropriation and gratification that is within the reach of adolescents' (Krauskopf 126). In this 'territorialization of the human body' young people (and some adults as well) create a geography of the human body closely linked with not only a personal view of aesthetics, but also a self-perception of the body as territory that can be transformed, like a page on which one inscribes a personal letter of self-affirmation.

Music, as has been mentioned, plays a special role in the identity configuration of the young protagonist.[1] From the very beginning of his narrative, he makes an effort to present the music he identifies with and the different functions that it seems to have in his life. *Rock 101* is his favourite radio station (and waking up mechanism); Kurt Cobain's death keeps him in a general state of sadness; and he and his friend have created a rock band. The music of Springsteen, Nirvana, Stone Temple Pilots and other similar groups likewise give the protagonist elements of identification and differentiation. Against these cultural marks – that function in the text as a sort of retaining wall of identity and differentiation – rock groups like the 'Dementes Apestosos' are shown in opposition (their heavy metal sensitivity is considered by the narrator a sign of 'abnormality' and excess). Similarly, José Luis and Miguel Ángel, the narrator's cousins, are considered abnormal because they do not fit into the idea of 'coolness' to which he and his friends subscribe:

> No one will be able to convince me that José Luis, who is 14 years old, and Miguel Ángel, who is 15, are normal people. They knew nothing about videogames [...], did not play soccer, but baseball! ... they did not get excited with real music, but with the same music their parents like, which is to say Barry Manilow, Ray Coniff, and other people whose names I do not want to even pronounce. They did not know what rap or techno were and never had heard of *grunge* until I explained them what it was! (Yehya 1994: 69)

His cousins, from this account, do not belong to his experience of what youth is about and, therefore, constitute a different reality of youth. Cultural consumption has differentiated and separated them into sub-groups, which reveals diversity within youth subjectivities: such consumption, then, resists and evades the homogenization imposed by an adult-centred worldview. Angeles Garcés Montoya calls this the plurality of cultural identities, a categorization that seems particularly appropriate in reference to youth cultures. Montoya emphasizes not only the heterogeneous nature of youth experiences, but also (and mainly) their permanent reconfiguration as categories that 'do not remain static and are inscribed in the dynamism of cultures' (8). In sum, music becomes an identifying mark both on the personal and collective levels:

> Music is the creative and generating force of youth cultures, because by listening and making music young people put into play their creative capabilities and at the same time elaborate ways to promote group recognition and participation. For a young social subject, music is more than a way to express ideas: it is a way of living. Thus, their affinity with certain musical genres is much more

---

1   The protagonist remains anonymous throughout the novel; perhaps this is to signify the author's wider concerns with youth-as-symbol.

than the result of personal taste or casual inclination. Music becomes for them an aesthetic force through which they discover an "us" and a "them". (Vila 2002: 33)

The episode on the 'flying papayas' deserves special mention, in part because in this passage the narrative focuses on the characterization of a mechanism of youth socialization from a Mexican middle class perspective. It is also a relevant episode because it shows, with large doses of humour and a lackadaisical air, the defiant and rebellious attitudes that young people manifest as a way of rejecting and challenging the hegemonic authority of adult-centred society. Humour in episodes such as this one is achieved through the presentation of extraordinary (and exaggerated) situations in which the characters behave in unpredictable and outrageous manners. The compact discs used as 'frisbees'; the relaxing marijuana; the flight of a papaya from an apartment balcony to a car passing by; the consequent fight between the young characters and the owner of the vehicle; and the final revenge of the young clan and their sudden scramble for safety: all of these elements create a picture that combines extremely uncommon situations with equally unique reactions. That is why it is safe to say that the humour achieved in the pages of *Camino a casa* is presented from a youth perspective. In addition, these subversive acts by the young characters should be evaluated not only as rejection of the normative control of the adults, but also as a manifestation of boredom and the lack of a concrete sense of direction. From an adult-centred perspective, one might risk a moral judgment about the social value (or lack thereof) of the youth's activities; but it is more interesting to see how these 'irresponsible' actions of the young make evident a rejection (indeed, a mockery) of the rules perceived as oppressive. In that sense, boredom and *malaise* should be seen as reactions to what youth consider an unfair imposition of values. It is not without reason, as mentioned previously, that kids called their parents 'bosses'. Another way of seeing this is to evaluate the actions of these adolescents as liberating exercises, as a statement on how to live life without limiting it by the possible consequences. If adults always plead with youth 'to think of the future', this perspective highlights a rejection of such advice: perhaps because what is ahead is no longer seen as the time of achievements – a time of professional and personal success – but a period defined, rather, by uncertainty and lack of options.

Camino a casa, by Naief Yehya, is a novel that shows the complex dynamics associated with youth relationships; with identity construction (youth, gender or sexual); with the processes by which youth negotiate with adult-centred ideologies; with the configuration and challenge of hegemonic masculinities; and, finally, with the possibility of building sexual citizenship from a youth perspective. In doing so, the narrative emphasizes the need to create symbolic spaces where the youth may engage in less repressive and more democratic processes of negotiation.

Bibliography

Álvarez Chávez, R. 2003. Significado tradicional de la sexualidad masculina: La masculinidad y la homofobia. *Avances en Ciencias Sociales*, 1, 96–106.

Alpízar, L. and Bernal, M. 2003. La construcción social de las juventudes. *Última Década*, 19, 1–20.

Amuchástegui, A. and Rivas, M. 2008. Construcción subjetiva de ciudadanía sexual en México: género, heteronormatividad y ética, in *Sexualidad, derechos humanos y ciudadanía. Diálogos sobre un proyecto en construcción*, edited by I. Sazsz and G. Salas. Mexico City: El Colegio de México, 57–136.

Attwood, F. 2006. Sexed Up: Theorizing the Sexualization of Culture. *Sexualities*, 9(1), 77–94.

Bell, D. and Binnie, J. 2000. *The Sexual Citizen. Queer Politics and Beyond.* Cambridge: Polity Press.

Chaves, M. 2005. Juventud negada y negativizada: Representaciones y formaciones discursivas vigentes en la Argentina contemporánea. *Ultima Década*, 13(23), 9–32.

Duarte, K. 2003. ¿Juventud o Juventudes? Acerca de cómo mirar y remirar a las juventudes de nuestro continente. *Última Década*, 13, 59–77.

Garcés Montoya, A. (n.d.) *Nos-Otros los jóvenes: Pistas para su reconocimiento.* [Online]. Available at: http://www.portalcomunicacion.com/dialeg/paper/pdf/ 71_garces.pdf [accessed: 10 July 2013].

Jiménez, G. 2002. Paradigmas de la identidad, in *Sociología de la identidad*, edited by A. Chihu Amparan. Mexico City: Universidad Autónoma Metropolitana, Iztapalapa-Ediciones Porrúa, 35–62.

Krauskopf, D. (n.d.) *Dimensiones críticas en la participación social de las juventudes.* [Online]. Available at: www.inau.gub.uy/bilioteca/adole/DinaK1. pdf [accessed: 10 July 2013].

Lomas, C. 2007. ¿La escuela es un infierno? Violencia escolar y construcción cultural de la masculinidad. *Revista de Educación*, 342, 83–101.

Lozano Urbieta, M.I. 2003. Nociones de Juventud. *Última Década*, 18, 1–19.

Plummer, K. 2003. *Intimate Citizenhip. Private Decisions and Public Dialogue.* Seattle: University of Washington Press.

Reguillo Cruz, R. 2000. *Estrategias del desencanto: Emergencia de cultura juvenil.* Bogotá: Grupo Editorial Norma.

Sánchez, A.R. 2009. Cuerpo y sexualidad, un derecho: avatares para su construcción en la diversidad sexual. *Sociológica*, 24(69), 101–22.

Vila, P. 2002. Música e identidad: La capacidad interpeladora y narrativa de los sonidos, in *Cuadernos de nación: Músicas en transición*, edited by Ministerio de Cultura. Bogotá: Ministerio de Cultura, 15–44.

Yehya, N. 1994. *Camino a casa. Un día en la vida de un joven mexicano.* Mexico City: Planeta.

Zimmerman, K. 2003. Constitución de la identidad y anti-cortesía verbal entre jóvenes masculinos hablantes del español, in *Primer Coloquio del Programa del EDICE*, edited by D. Bravo. Stockholm: EDICE, 47–59.

Chapter 5

Men and Conjugal Life in Mexico: Change and Persistence

Olga Rojas

Taking into account the advances in social research undertaken in Mexico on the transformations in the organization of family life, gender relations and the meanings given to sexuality, this chapter uses a gender perspective to analyse male attitudes and practices regarding their lives in the marital context. Additionally, this chapter takes into account the particularities of the Mexican context, which has been characterized by persistent and extremely deep gender, ethnic and socioeconomic inequalities at the same time as it has experienced intensely modernizing social, economic and cultural transformations within a relatively short period.

Our interest lies in the detection of possible changes in certain dimensions of male identity related to conjugal life, bearing in mind the fact that these changes may vary depending on the persistent socio-economic inequality in the country. We initially analyse the meanings and values of male sexual practices within the context of the marital union. The limited research on the subject indicates that for Mexican men, sexuality is one of the main forms of representing and asserting masculinity.

Against this background, we analyse the extent to which new gender relations in family life and marriage are emerging, relations in which a couple share an interest in moving towards a more intimate, egalitarian relationship. At the centre of our analysis are men and the possible redefinition of their identity, not only based on their role as economic providers and the exercise of compulsive sexuality, but on the construction of new forms of an intimate, loving relationship with their spouses, based on trust, equity and communication.

Mexico: A Scenario of Significant Although Not Widespread Social and Cultural Changes

In recent decades, Mexico, like the entire Latin American region, underwent extremely intense economic and social changes within a relatively short period. As a result of this process of modernization, Mexico swiftly transitioned from an eminently rural to a predominantly urban, industrialized society. Moreover, in a very short time, substantial progress was made in the population's educational achievement and mass access to health services and family planning. All this resulted in a significant decline in fertility and a major increase in female participation in the labour market.

These changes were compounded by the existence of a significant process of social and cultural change, fed by secularization and modernization, as well as participation in the globalization of culture. Drawn from the discourse on equality and freedom, these forces offer different patterns and ideas about what marriage, family, sexual practices and parenting should look like. They are all mainly accessible to the urban population with high educational attainment.[1]

It is important to draw attention to the relativity of these changes in Mexican society. Regarding sexual and reproductive issues, religious discourse still coexists with scientific information disseminated in schools, population policies, the media and intensive family planning and HIV/AIDS campaigns. As a result, conceptions of sexuality and sexual practices in the country are acquiring new, different meanings, especially among the young population and in urban settings. That is why some academics (Salles 1995, Amuchástegui 2001, Nehring 2005) assert that the Mexican cultural context is currently considered heterogeneous, complex and 'hybrid'.

This set of social, economic and cultural changes has significantly affected the structure and functioning of Mexican families, while it has helped change the meanings of sexual and reproductive behaviour for the population and, therefore, certain dimensions of gender relations and identities. Social researchers in the country (Oliveira 1998, Ariza and Oliveira 2004, García and Oliveira 2005, 2006) note that certain social sectors are experiencing the redefinition of social images concerning femininity and masculinity.

In the particular context of Mexico, the constitution of gender relations must be understood from the consideration of modernization and cultural globalization and the interpenetration of heterogeneous cultural elements from internal and external sources. Thus, gender relations in Mexico, especially since the early 1980s, have become much more complex, since certain patriarchal patterns coexist with new alternatives, available to the Mexican population, in terms of beliefs and practices (Nehring 2005).

The 1980s in Mexico were a watershed that marked the beginning of a systematic increase in women's incorporation into the labour market.[2] This has had significant consequences for the functioning of families, since the conditions have been created for a change in the structure of roles between men and women. Indeed, Mexican married women's economic activity outside the home facilitated

---

1   It is very likely that with this increased access to cultural discourses and assets, the middle class population will construct its individual identity in a more reflexive manner and its group identity with more egalitarian, libertarian discourses and repertoires than the rest of the population (Esteinou 2008).

2   Female participation in the labour force was 17 per cent in the 1970s. By the mid-1990s, it had increased to 30 per cent and now totals 39 per cent.

a more equitable division of family labour, which translated into increased male participation in domestic work and childcare (Esteinou 2008).

It should be added that women who combine home and work are predominantly middle class. For these women, work represents a choice of personal development rather than a pressing economic need, which implies an expansion of their symbolic horizons. It is now possible for them to imagine, choose and implement life projects that clearly differ from the patriarchal trajectories oriented towards entering marriage at a certain age, followed by motherhood and confinement to domestic life. Women today have the possibility of access to higher education and the labour market, and even the single life. This has relativized the meaning of the traditional roles of wife, mother and housewife, central elements in defining the identity of women of previous generations (Nehring 2005, Esteinou 2008).

Increasing female participation in the labour market has had a significant impact on the thinking of women, especially middle-class ones, because their social position and identity are no longer tied to marriage and procreation. For them, having a job is as important as marrying and having a family. This is leading to a redefinition of roles and, therefore, processes of negotiation between spouses that result in tensions and conflicts that can lead to the dissolution of marriages (Esteinou 2008).

Indeed, the foundations of marriage are changing, since people are more likely to evaluate their marriages and lives as a couple in terms of the emotional and affective satisfaction they provide. Thus the influence of the family as a group, relatives and religious norms become less important. Previously held ideas about the family as the institution for reproducing the species, which ignored the pursuit of sexual pleasure and happiness in married life, came into question. Such questioning reflects the greater freedom couples have to define what works for them, and men and women can decide more freely than before to end a marriage.[3] However, it should be noted that divorce in Mexico is more common in urban areas and among the younger generations, which points toward individuation processes related to major cultural changes recorded in these social sectors (Esteinou 2008).

Marriage was previously experienced as a union involving cooperation and efforts to meet every day needs. A union in which men and women were obliged

---

3   Conjugal unions in Mexico have been characterized by their marked stability over time, since there have always been low levels of divorce and separation, especially when compared with the experience of other countries, even in the Latin American region. However, they have increased, since in the 1950s the divorce rate was 4.4 per cent, whereas by 2007, 13 per cent of marriages ended in divorce, the present rate being approximately 14.5 per cent. These data are relevant if one considers that the country's life expectancy has substantially increased, meaning that couples stay together longer before conjugal unions end as a result of the death of one of the partners. Overall, the low divorce rate suggests that in broad sectors of Mexican society, the institution of marriage (both religious and civil) continues to exert a considerable influence (Ojeda 1989, García and Rojas 2004, López and Salles 2006, Esteinou 2008).

to identify with their gender roles, with men as the sole economic providers while women were tasked with childcare and housework. On the basis of these rules and definition of roles, relationships between spouses and between parents and children were marked by a strong hierarchy (Esteinou 2008).

Today, largely because of their increased participation in the workforce, some Mexican women have begun to question their submissive role in relation to men and attempted to establish more equal gender relations in the marital sphere. Female resistance to the structures of roles and authority occur more often in younger, better-educated, salaried women, who control more resources and assume a greater commitment to work outside the home (García and Oliveira 1994, Oliveira 1998).

However, these changes have not spread throughout Mexican society. They are mainly restricted to the social sectors with better living conditions and higher educational attainment who often live in urban areas. There are also gaps and tensions between macro structural changes and those occurring in the forms of coexistence between men and women. Recent social research has discovered that working-class, popular, rural and indigenous social sectors resist changes in family and married life, since extremely unequal relations prevail, especially as regards the sexual division of labour and the sphere of sexuality (García and Oliveira 1994, Oliveira 1998, Ariza and Oliveira 2004).

In these social sectors, many women and men have not yet incorporated female paid employment into their imaginary world of possibilities, meaning that there continues to be a reaffirmation of traditional gender roles with the man as provider and the woman dedicated exclusively to the home and her children. In these contexts, the idea that the family as a group takes precedence over individual decisions is still deeply entrenched. The influence of relatives in the lives of couples and families restricts the development of individual freedom and helps to reproduce gender inequalities arising from rigid hierarchies that structure people's lives and kinship relations (Esteinou 2008).

For the men in these social groups, being a provider and therefore the head and authority in their families remains a fundamental aspect of their identity. That is why they disagree with their spouses' incorporation into the labour market and do not give their consent because in their opinion, this would entail the neglect of their children and homes. Thus, despite the high levels of poverty and the growing need for female economic participation in the labour force, women in these social contexts still have to ask for permission from their husbands to work. This reflects the subordination and obedience in which they still live, since they cannot ignore the authority of their husbands as heads of the household and breadwinners. Paid employment for these women is perceived by their husbands as social evidence of their inability to fulfil their role as providers (García and Oliveira 1994, Rojas 2008a).

What we have reviewed so far shows that while Mexican society has undergone a process of modernization and profound cultural diversification, these changes have failed to change the gender structures in all social groups. Instead, this differentiated scope in social and cultural transformations has produced greater complexity and a multiplicity of forms of family functioning.

In light of these recent transformations in marital and family relationships, we now turn our discussion to the implications of these changes in male roles as fathers and husbands. The following section examines whether these recent developments in intimate relationships have contributed to men building closer relationships with their children and spouses and also identifies what aspects of male identity are still anchored in male roles and therefore express resistance to change.

Men and Conjugal Sexuality

The work of some researchers (Szasz 1998a, Amuchástegui 2001, Hernández-Rosete 2006, Jiménez 2007) about the cultural meanings and sexual behaviour of the Mexican population have described the existence of a double standard of sexual morality that regulates the sexuality of men and women differently. On the one hand, it pressures men to have a variety of partners and sexual experiences that help prove their manhood and, on the other hand, it drives women towards modesty, passivity and the denial of their sexual desires.[4]

Sexuality among many Mexican men is one of the main forms of representation and assertion of their masculine identity, since male power is expressed, measured, or limited by it. Belonging to the male world must be constantly reaffirmed and demonstrated and one of the main ways of proving this is through sexual prowess. Men perceive a prescriptive mandate to engage in sexual relations with multiple partners and fear that their masculinity will be called into question if they fail to prove their experience. These mandates are exercised through discourse, surveillance and social control, and end up being internalized (Szasz 1998a).

Within this cultural context, specifically within the area of sexuality, masculinity is closely related to activity, while femininity is linked to passivity. Hence the split image of femininity: on the one hand there are decent women who behave modestly and do not express their sexual desires,[5] and on the other, there are promiscuous women who are eroticized and actively express their sexual desires. These two images of women are difficult to reconcile in men's experience. Closely related to this split view of femininity, some Mexican men express their sexuality in two areas: one linked to married life, with restricted practices subject to controls

---

4   For many Mexican women, sexual practices are restricted to the formation of married couples, the marital union and the aim of procreating children. In certain sectors of society, there are still rules which, through social sanctions, brand them as promiscuous or unreliable women if they express desire or pleasure, particularly if they do so outside the context of marriage and reproduction (Amuchástegui 2001).

5   These women are viewed by men as respectable and reliable, with whom they can form a couple because they do not threaten the reputation of their manhood (Núñez 2007).

and limits, and one outside married life with women regarded as promiscuous, commercial sex workers and even other men (Szasz 1998a).

For this reason, in conjugal sexuality, male fears are linked to the possibility that the woman will demonstrate an active, eager, non-procreative attitude to sex, implying the possibility of wanting other men and, therefore, of being unfaithful. Men therefore seek to control female sexual activity through restriction, procreation and placing limits on female mobility outside the home. Conversely, for some Mexican men, sexuality is a biological need they cannot resist and therefore they succumb, and when it occurs in the conjugal sphere it is linked to exchange and kinship, whereas when it occurs outside marriage, it constitutes a sphere of transgression and prohibition (Szasz 1998a, 1998b, Fernández 2006, Hernández-Rosete 2006).

Data from the few national surveys on sexuality suggest that most female sexual activity is still restricted to marital relationships and that a small proportion extends to courtship prior to the marriage. In contrast, Mexican men report having had a greater number of sexual partners prior to married life while a significant proportion report having concurrent relationships with more than one sexual partner during married life.[6] These distinct sexual practices between men and women are correlated by the cultural valuations people have of their sexuality. It is therefore not unusual to find in these same polls that significant proportions of Mexican women still believe that sex is more important to men because they need it more and it is therefore up to them to decide when to engage in sexual relations. In practice, according to these data, it is usually men who take the initiative to have sex in married life and, in some cases, a wife's refusal to have sex may result in insults or violence.. This gender inequality in sexual practices and valuations in the context of marital life in Mexico is more pronounced in low-income social strata and among the older generations (Szasz 2008).

Among some Mexican men, especially among the older generation, prevail extremely conservative standards regarding gender and sexuality. Their wives never initiated intimate encounters and the men never knew whether their wives experienced sexual pleasure. In the opinion of these men, they have sexual needs that women must meet due to the marriage bond and because they fully comply with their obligations as responsible husbands. In this context, women's sexual attention is a form of recognition and a reward for their manliness and the fact that they are men who meet their obligations as breadwinners. The marital bond is therefore maintained by the exchange of work by the spouses: men engage in the work of supporting the household while their wives must attend to them. This exchange creates sharp gender inequalities in the exercise of sexuality (Núñez 2007).

---

6   Nearly 25 per cent of the men in conjugal unions interviewed in the Reproductive Health Survey on Members of the Mexican Social Security Institute (IMSS) 1998 (ENSARE-1998) reported having had sex with other women while they were married (Szasz, Rojas and Castrejón 2008).

By contrast, among the population of the higher social strata, both partners are more likely to take the lead in initiating sex and there is a higher proportion of women with a greater capacity for decision-making than among women from low income groups, at least in the sense that they can refuse to engage in sex when they do not want to, without suffering insults, scolding or violence (Szasz 2008).

As regards male sexual practices in the extramarital field, research in Mexico is extremely scarce. The few recent studies (Fernández 2006, Hernández-Rosete 2006, Jiménez 2007, Rojas, Córdoba and Nehring 2009) have found that male infidelity is a sexual conduct structured by gender norms. It is regarded as an unquestionable form of male sexual life since it is an expression of virility; therefore, it is a widely tolerated, extremely common practice among the Mexican male population, regardless of their socioeconomic status.

Some Mexican males commonly argue that although they can establish sexual links with several women, they maintain total social and emotional commitment to just one woman, with whom they have chosen to procreate their children and raise a family. This practice reflects the idea of sexual desire being a natural force that is uncontrollable and irresistible because it goes beyond their conscious and rational control. For them, sexuality practiced outside the marital sphere is amply justified by a routine married life, full of obligations and pressures, but without satisfactions. Sexual infidelity is conceived as an escape route from boredom and, above all, as a form of relief from the lack of marital sexual satisfaction. Ironically, extramarital sex ends up becoming an important factor of stability in their marriages, insofar as it is considered a complement that helps preserve the marriage bond and enables men to put up with everything that this implies, since it provides a sense of satisfaction they fail to obtain from their wives. They therefore develop complicated strategies for denying these practices to their spouses (Fernández 2006, Rojas, Córdoba and Nehring 2009).

However, dissatisfaction, marital problems and male infidelity do not necessarily lead to the breakdown of marital unions. Although wives are sometimes aware of these extramarital male sexual practices, some of them may not see the need for separation or divorce to terminate the marriage, preferring to tolerate their husbands as long as they fulfil their role as providers and their parental responsibilities. These concepts are complemented by the male consideration that extramarital affairs must always be temporary and should not involve the establishment of loving bonds or financial obligations through the existence of children (Rojas, Córdoba and Nehring 2009).

In this respect, the possibility of having extramarital sexual encounters is a reason often wielded by men to be sterilized by vasectomy, since this reduces the risk of impregnating women who are not their wives, while avoiding potential economic responsibilities outside marriage.[7] Thus, in the context of

---

7   It is worth recalling that this type of sexuality is conceived and carried out by men separately from reproduction, so it is very likely that the use of male birth control is not related to the regulation of their fertility in the conjugal sphere, since this responsibility

marital infidelity, for some Mexican men vasectomy becomes an opportunity to engage in extramarital sex without 'regrettable consequences' (Córdoba 2005, Fernández 2006).

The coexistence of strong, apparently stable marital ties with widely tolerated extramarital sexual practices constitutes a central node in the cultural organization of intimacy in contemporary Mexico that makes both forms of intimate male relations deeply ambiguous. It is therefore suggested that male infidelity, in addition to being understood as a social and cultural construction that confirms masculinity and as an escape route in the absence of sexual satisfaction in the marital context, should also be understood as a central factor that may be contributing to the persistence and stability of marital unions in Mexico (Jiménez 2007, Rojas, Córdoba and Nehring 2009).

At the same time, it is important to note there are currently different cultural and normative systems regarding sexualities in Mexico. Ideas and evaluations based on more conservative standards regarding kinship and marriage overlap with scientific ideas and arguments regarding people's sexuality and modern ideas about personal and sexual life spread by the media. Moreover, the processes of secularization and mass education, experienced by the country during most of the last century, have contributed to the weakening of the influence of religious institutions that promote explicit principles regarding intimate practices. This coexistence of conflicting arguments about the regulation of sexuality has been called 'cultural hybridization' by some researchers (Amuchástegui 2001, Nehring 2005, Szasz 2008).

Modern ideas about sexuality from scientific discourses and messages in the media have contributed to the reinterpretation of hegemonic conservative norms regarding sexuality and to the creation of individual thought processes as well as new forms of negotiation with sexual partners, especially among the urban population, the middle classes and the younger generations. The evidence suggests the emergence of multiple cultural models that significantly diverge from traditional patterns, which reflect significant generational differences in the rules concerning gender and sexuality. However, it should be remembered that even if these generational changes in the dominant ideas about married life and sexualities are considered, socioeconomic differences continue to prevail (Amuchástegui 2001, Szasz 2008).

Among the younger population in urban areas from the affluent socioeconomic strata, the bond with one's partner no longer seems to depend on an unequal exchange of obligations, but rather on ideas concerning romantic love and intimate well-being. Interpersonal relationships rely increasingly on a certain degree of individuality for both partners, as well as greater, clearer negotiation of sexual practices. This has transformed expectations about marital fidelity, as young women are demanding reciprocal treatment in order to achieve more satisfying

---

falls almost always on wives, but rather on the exercise of their sexuality in extramarital contexts (Szasz 1998a).

sex as well as the sexual exclusivity of both partners, basing their faithfulness on love rather than marital obligation. Men and women are attempting to construct new, more progressive, open and rational forms of conjugal relations, free of the constraints experienced by their parents. The meaning of sexuality tends to lie in the experience of intimacy and mutual satisfaction rather than reproduction and women's obligation to satisfy their husbands as part of the marriage agreement. As a consequence, reproductive practices have also been modified, since the first pregnancy after marriage is beginning to be delayed, allowing couples to enjoy each other's company and seek the stability of the relationship, while planning to have a small number of children (Amuchástegui 2001, Szasz 2001, Rojas 2008b).

There are indications that the sexual practices of the younger generation of Mexican men are beginning to be associated more with individual decisions than with socially prescribed rules. This may be indicative of a transformation towards a lower demand for sexual performance by men and the establishment of greater emotional links in male sexual exchanges (Amuchástegui 2001).

This younger generation of men regards male fidelity as important and thinks that both spouses are responsible for mutual sexual satisfaction, with an emphasis on communication between partners. They are trying to establish new forms of relationship with their wives, based on a genuine sexual and intimate bond. Thus, marriage and sex life are acquiring another meaning, which leads them to question the need for parallel or extramarital relationships (Szasz 2008, Rojas, Córdoba and Nehring 2009).

And even though they still believe that men's sexual impulses are impossible to resist, these men are moving away from the traditional model of male sexuality. They no longer seem to make a distinction between good and bad women, nor do they establish a clear opposition between established forms of intimacy with their wives and potential sexual partners outside marriage (Szasz 2008, Rojas, Córdoba and Nehring 2009).

This new type of marital relationship not only entails knowledge and mutual understanding of the other, but also a deeper degree of empathy or emotional understanding.[8] This provides greater scope for sexuality and female sexuality in particular becomes less of an obligation to the husband than the pursuit of pleasure for women. Couple relationships therefore tend to be more satisfactory but also more negotiated, and therefore more fragile. Women are changing their attitude towards their husbands since they question and are less tolerant of male infidelity. These women no longer accept the sexual double standard that has prevailed in Mexican society (Esteinou 2008).

---

8   As the scope for love and the development of a satisfactory sexuality is expanded and the importance of the reproduction of the specie is reduced in these new conjugal contexts, the nuclear family as an institution becomes less important and begins to be replaced by the importance attached to the achievement of individual happiness (Esteinou 2008).

Discussion and Final Considerations

In our analysis of the changes in intimate life in contemporary Mexican families, we have noticed that Mexican women have been at the forefront of these changes since they have won greater autonomy and freedom. Their growing educational attainment and their mass incorporation into the labour market, coupled with the possibilities they now have to choose their partners, use contraception and, therefore reduce their fertility, are elements that have contributed to creating reflexive processes in them and reshaping their individual identity. These conditions are essential for the democratization of private life, family and marital relationships, and ultimately, personal life.

These transformations have involved the major social and cultural changes that have taken place in Mexico in recent decades, which have been nurtured by secularization, modernization and participation in the globalization of culture. This has contributed to the emergence of cultural models that diverge from traditional patterns, which were organized by gender, the Church and kinship, and provide new assessments of sexual, marital and family life. These new cultural repertoires are primarily available to the younger generation, since it is young people who are incorporating new notions of personal and sexual life that lead them to reinterpret the traditional rules that governed the lives of their parents at the individual and family levels. However, it should be noted that in the Mexican context, the process of modernization and transformation of private life has been uneven and is giving way to the coexistence of different regulatory regimes. The new concepts have not spread throughout society in a generalized or uniform fashion, nor are they clearly integrated individually, since the new cultural repertoires combine with certain notions acquired throughout a person's life.

One should therefore realize that these changes in intimate life cannot be generalized to the whole of Mexican society. They are mainly restricted to the social sectors with better living conditions and higher educational attainment typically residing in urban areas. This leads us to posit that in Mexico, family, parental and marital relations are registering clear generational transformations nuanced by social class.

Material living conditions and educational attainment as well as city life apparently condition the possibilities of men and women's personal autonomy as well as the resistance to gender mandates and access to new types of relations between parents and children and between spouses. Among the younger generations of the urban middle classes there appears to be a predominance of ideas about romantic love and emotional well-being, based on satisfactory sexual intimacy, which enables the formation of conjugal unions in which there is greater potential for autonomy among women and negotiation between both members of the couple.

In these sectors of society, young men and women have begun to question the traditional roles involving the sexual division of labour and intimate relationships. There are clear signs of the expansion and modification of men's role as spouses.

New forms of intimacy in family relationships among the middle classes in Mexico entail greater flexibility of roles not only in terms of the division of labour, since women are increasingly involved in activities outside the home, while men participate more actively in the care and upbringing of their children, but also in the structure of authority, since women have gained more spaces and scope for freedom and autonomy. Moreover, since affective relations are more intense, more expressive, more communicative and more reflective, they may involve greater conflict than before. In this new type of relationship, there is greater equity because the margins for negotiation between men and women now are broader, with couple relationships tending to operate between equals. This is made possible by the increasingly pronounced presence of individualistic patterns, since through their employment outside the home and a monetary income women have acquired greater scope for action and autonomy from their partners.

However, the acute social and economic inequality prevailing in Mexico and the resulting poverty and segregation of a large part of the population, which lives mainly in indigenous, rural and marginalized urban contexts, has contributed to maintaining traditional cultural patterns and marked expressions of gender inequality. In these social sectors, people's lives and family and marital coexistence continue to be defined by social structures and institutions such as the Church and kinship relations, which set clearly differentiated standards for men and women regarding the sexual division of labour and sexuality.

In these impoverished, marginalized populations, intimate relations in marriage are still characterized by the couple's lack of agreement on the desire to have sex. These disagreements are based on traditional cultural conceptions regarding the needs and erotic possibilities of men and women bound by marriage. These conceptions attribute erotic desires exclusively to males and exclude female sexual desire from the sphere of marital life, assigning women the obligation to satisfy their husbands sexually. This lack of communication between spouses, together with the lack of intimate contact and sexual understanding in married life, inevitably leads to dissatisfaction, frustration and the emergence of claims and conflicts that men often resolve in the sphere of extramarital relations. The persistence of family and marital ties, in these social contexts, is based on the offspring and the exchange of obligations between spouses. While men are economic providers and protect their families, women are responsible for reproductive work and meeting their husbands' needs.

As we can see, in contemporary Mexico, everyday life and social relations in couples and families are moving towards a new, albeit partial, intimacy mainly involving the most privileged sectors of society and excluding broad sectors of the population who are economically and socially disadvantaged.

Bibliography

Amuchástegui, A. 2001. *Virginidad e iniciación sexual en México. Experiencias y significados*. Mexico City: The Population Council/EDAMEX.

Ariza, M. and Oliveira, O. 2004. Universo familiar y procesos demográficos, in *Imágenes de la familia en el cambio del siglo*, edited by M. Ariza and O. de Oliveira. Mexico City: Universidad Nacional Autónoma de México, 9–45.

Córdoba, D. 2005. *Ellos y la vasectomía: temores, precauciones, deseos y mitos de la sexualidad masculina*. Unpublished doctoral thesis. Mexico City: Escuela Nacional de Antropología e Historia.

Esteinou, R. 2008. *La familia nuclear en México: lecturas de su modernidad. Siglos XVI al XX*. Mexico City: CIESAS/Porrúa.

Fernández, A. 2006. Masculinidades frente a la vasectomía: la gestación de una brecha, in *Mujeres y hombres frente a las instituciones de salud*, edited by L. Melgar. Mexico City: El Colegio de México, 77–138.

García, B. and Rojas, O. 2004. Las uniones conyugales en América Latina: transformaciones en un marco de desigualdad social y de género. *Notas de Población*, 78, 65–96.

García, B. and Oliveira, O. 1994. *Trabajo femenino y vida familiar en México*. Mexico City: El Colegio de México.

García, B. and Oliveira, O. 2005. Las transformaciones de la vida familiar en el México urbano contemporáneo, in *Familia y vida privada ¿Transformaciones, tensiones, resistencias o nuevos sentidos?* edited by X. Valdés and T. Valdés. Santiago: FLACSO, 77–106.

García, B. and Oliveira, O. 2006. *Las familias en el México metropolitano: visiones femeninas y masculinas*. Mexico City: El Colegio de México.

Hernández-Rosete, D. 2006. La vida extramarital masculina en tiempos de VIH/Sida. Usos y prácticas entre algunos varones con profesiones ligadas a las ciencias sociales, in *Ser padres, esposos e hijos: prácticas y valoraciones de varones mexicanos*, edited by J.G. Figueroa, L. Jiménez and O. Tena. Mexico City: El Colegio de México, 195–217.

Jiménez, L. 2007. Sexualidad, vida conyugal y relaciones de pareja. Experiencias de algunos varones de sectores medio y alto de la Ciudad de México, in *Sucede que me canso de ser hombre ... Relatos y reflexiones sobre hombres y masculinidades en México*, edited by A. Amuchástegui and I. Szasz. Mexico City: El Colegio de México, 185–240.

López, M. and Salles, V. 2006. Los vaivenes de la conyugalidad, in *Fortalezas y desafíos de las familias en dos contextos: Estados Unidos de América y México*, edited by R. Esteinou. Mexico City: CIESAS, 385–435.

Nehring, D. 2005. Reflexiones sobre la construcción cultural de las relaciones de género en México. *Papeles de Población*, 11(45), 221–45.

Núñez, G. 2007. Vínculo de pareja y hombría: 'Atender y mantener' en adultos mayores del Río Sonora, México, in *Sucede que me canso de ser hombre ...*

Relatos y reflexiones sobre hombres y masculinidades en México, edited by A. Amuchástegui and I. Szasz. Mexico City: El Colegio de México, 141–84.

Ojeda, N. 1989. *El curso de vida familiar de las mujeres mexicanas; un análisis sociodemográfico*. Mexico City: UNAM/CRIM.

Oliveira, O. 1998. Familia y relaciones de género en México, in *Familias y relaciones de género en transformación. Cambios trascendentales en América Latina y el Caribe*, edited by B. Schmukler. Mexico City: The Population Council/EDAMEX, 23–52.

Rojas, O. 2008a. *Paternidad y vida familiar en la Ciudad de México*. Mexico City: El Colegio de México.

Rojas, O. 2008b. Reproducción masculina y desigualdad social en México, in *Salud reproductiva y condiciones de vida en México*, edited by S. Lerner and I. Szasz. Mexico City: El Colegio de México, 95–137.

Rojas, O., Córdoba, D. and Nehring, D. 2009. Gentlemen have no memory. Some considerations about male infidelity in Mexico, in *Sociology in a Changing World: Challenges and Perspectives*, edited by Gregory Katsas. Athens: Athens Institute for Education and Research (ATINER), 349–62.

Salles, V. 1995. Familia y sexualidad. *Reflexiones. Sexualidad, salud y reproducción*, 1(4), 7–8.

Schmukler, B. 1998. Comentarios finales, in *Familias y relaciones de género en transformación. Cambios trascendentales en América Latina y el Caribe*, edited by B. Schmukler. Mexico City: The Population Council/EDAMEX, 541–52.

Szasz, I. 1998a. Los hombres y la sexualidad: aportes de la perspectiva feminista y primeros acercamientos a su estudio en México, in *Varones, sexualidad y reproducción*, edited by S. Lerner. Mexico City: El Colegio de México/ SOMEDE, 137–62.

Szasz, I. 1998b. Sexualidad y género: algunas experiencias de investigación en México. *Debate feminista*, 9(18), 77–104.

Szasz, I. 2001. La investigación sobre sexualidad y el debate sobre los derechos reproductivos en México, in *La población de México. Tendencias y perspectivas sociodemográficas hacia el siglo XXI*, edited by J. Gómez de León and C. Rabell. Mexico City: CONAPO/FCE, 365–97.

Szasz, I. 2008. Relaciones de género y desigualdad socioeconómica en la construcción social de las normas sobre la sexualidad en México, in *Salud reproductiva y condiciones de vida en México*, edited by S. Lerner and I. Szasz. Mexico City: El Colegio de México, 429–73.

Szasz, I., Rojas, O. and Castrejón, J.L. 2008. Desigualdad de género en las relaciones conyugales y prácticas sexuales de los hombres mexicanos. *Estudios Demográficos y Urbanos*, 23(2), 205–32.

Chapter 6

Love Matters: Couple Relationships among Young Female Professionals from Mexico City

Daniel Nehring

In this chapter, I will explore narratives of couple relationships, love and intimate attachment among young female professionals from Mexico City. Since the early 1980s, Mexican society has been profoundly transformed by a string of economic crises, neoliberal programmes of structural adjustment and privatization, political dynamics which brought about the end of the continuous 70-year rule of the Institutional Revolutionary Party, and the weakening of public security and social and political institutions through violent conflicts between the state and organized crime (González de la Rocha 2000, Landau 2005, Muller 2013, Wise 2006). At the same time, research on contemporary patterns of intimate life has highlighted the weakening of traditional patriarchal power relations and a trend towards love-based companionate relationships (Hirsch 2003, Hirsch 2004, Ariza and de Oliveira 2004). The consequences of these changes for the personal lives of young, urban, middle-class women have so far hardly been explored. Therefore, my first objective in this chapter is to document in depth how such young women understand and experience their everyday intimate lives. Second, I will consider what these understandings and experiences reveal about the scope and limits of intimate citizenship among young middle-class women.

This study is built on qualitative case study research on cultural dynamics of intimate life among young professionals in Mexico City. In particular, in the mid to late 2000s, I conducted 21 life story interviews with young women employed in a variety of white-collar professional occupations. Some of them were married and living with their partner and, in a few cases, had children. Others were involved in more or less casual dating relationships, and some were not in a relationship at all. In our conversations, we discussed the role which love, intimate attachment, and couple relationships played in their lives, and we spoke about the ways in which they made choices about their intimate relationships and their life plans at large.

Exploring these themes, I point to 'negotiated familism' as the principle around which my participants' intimate lives were organized. I use this concept to highlight the complex ways in which the women I interviewed negotiated attachment and allegiance to their families, while at the same time making strong claims to autonomous choices about their intimate lives. In their narratives, family consistently appeared as an essential source of social and individual stability, as well as personal fulfilment. In an everyday environment which many of them described as chaotic and unsafe, the idea of family, as well as their ties to their actual families, provided them with a sense of belonging and constancy. At the same time, they viewed themselves as free from direct paternalistic control over their personal lives. In the interviews, they spoke about the self-directed choices they made about intimate relationships and family ties, in the context of broader reflexive life plans built around the pursuit of self-fulfilment.

The Decline of Patriarchy in Contemporary Mexico

Over the past 30 years, Mexicans' intimate lives have undergone profound changes. The socio-economic and political underpinnings of these changes have been extensively discussed elsewhere (e.g. Ariza and de Oliveira 2004, Chant and Craske 2003, García and de Oliveira 1994, García and de Oliveira 2005), and there is no need to re-examine them here. Instead, it is my intention to consider shifts in the culturally situated beliefs, norms, and values through which Mexicans organise their everyday experiences and practices of family life, couple relationships, and sexuality.

Until approximately the early 1980s, Mexicans' gender and intimate relationships in Mexico were organized through hegemonic patriarchal norms, values and beliefs closely associated with Catholic morality.[1] Arguably, in the decades since, Mexican patriarchy has both been transformed and weakened by an array of fundamental structural transformations. These include the decline and eventual demise of authoritarian one-party rule, a string of prolonged economic crises, the consequent remaking of Mexican economy and society according to neoliberal blueprints, women's large-scale entry into the labour force, a notable decline in fertility rates, and, particularly since the mid-2000s, a continual decline of public security in ways that has left women particularly at risk (Ariza and de Oliveira 2004, Chant and Craske 2003, de Oliveira 1998, Ensalaco 2006, Talcott 2011).

In the context of these transformative developments, patriarchal narratives of what intimate relationships are and should be, have lost much of their compelling force. In other words, the past three decades have witnessed a decline of patriarchal familism. The term 'familism' is used in academic debates in a frequently rather schematic manner to differentiate 'collectivist' from 'individualistic' understandings of family and intimate life. Instead I use familism as a descriptive term that characterises specific discourses and practices of intimate life throughout Mexican history.

---

1   As historical formations of Mexican patriarchy have been discussed extensively elsewhere, I will not review them in detail in this chapter. In this context, see Amuchástegui (2001), Olcott, Vaughan and Cano (2006), and Rivas (1998).

The decline of patriarchal familism has led to a contradictory pluralization of both large-scale discourses and personal experiences and practices of intimacy. By this I mean that a range of competing and often contradictory discourses of intimate life have come to be pervasive in Mexican society. A notable pluralization of norms, values, and beliefs about topics such as couple relationships, love, sex, family life has taken place, giving Mexicans a broader range of socially acceptable choices on how to conduct their intimate lives (Gutmann 2007, Amuchástegui Herrera 2001, Carrillo 1999, Carrillo 2002, González-López 2005). The legalization of abortion and same-sex civil unions[2] in Mexico City are two notable examples in this regard (Maier 2012). Recent research (Hirsch 2003, Hirsch 2004) has also pointed to the growing importance of companionate, love-based couple relationships, while drawing attention to the ways in which the possibility of experiencing such relationships is modulated by a variety of institutional and socio-economic factors. Gloria González-López (2005) has proposed the term 'regional patriarchies' to distinguish such divergences in Mexicans' culturally situated understandings and practices of sexuality. The extensive work of Orlandina de Oliveira and Brígida García (1995, 1997, 1994, 2005) likewise highlights the diversity on socio-economic patterns of family life in Mexico according to variables such as social class, educational levels, and geographical location.

Notably, these developments highlight a significant widening of intimate citizenship in Mexico.[3] Analyzing the legalization of same-sex unions in Buenos Aires and Mexico City, Jordi Díez argues that social movements with broad support among the political class and in wider society were instrumental in creating the political conditions that would allow the respective laws to be passed:

> The two cases exhibit several key, and striking, similarities. In both processes, well-organized and well-resourced activists were able to establish important alliances to place their proposal on the public agenda, and they began the debate by equipping themselves with a series of frames that they thought would help them win the debate and apply pressure on their respective targeted governments. In what framing scholars refer to as "frame alignment", in these two cases, the policy advocates sought to win support for their initiative through the elaboration of arguments that would resonate with the population and

---

2   In this context, also see Irwin, Nasser and McCaughan (2003) on the historical exclusion of same-sex intimate relationships from legitimate public debates and attention.

3   The concept of intimate citizenship has been proposed relatively recently (Plummer 2003) as a means of exploring the social, economic, cultural, political, and technological practices that circumscribe the legitimacy of forms of intimate life. Intimate citizenship thus concerns the interplay between social-structural conditions and the problems of recognition and choice that individuals come to face when negotiating sex, love, intimate attachment, childbearing, and so forth. Intimate citizenship draws attention to respective public debates, struggles, and conflicts, and it emphasizes the embedding of these struggles in globalization and modernization.

politicians themselves, that is, to seek a resonance of one's frame within a larger "master frame". (Diez 2012: 223–4)

Nevertheless, the opposition of the conservative federal government, the Catholic Church, and the media and the public in many states highlight the persistent importance of narrow patriarchal sexual norms, as well as notable regional discrepancies in the scope of legitimate practices of intimate life (Associated Press 2006, Avilés 2008a, Avilés 2008b, Cuenca 2007, Rodríguez 2005). Writing about the politics of abortion in the wake of its legalization in Mexico City in 2007, Elizabeth Maier (2012) goes so far as to argue that a culture war is diving Mexican society. While in Mexico City abortion was legalized, Maier explains, conservative politicians, social movements and the Catholic Church cooperated to ensure the passage of strict anti-abortion laws in 17 of Mexico's 32 states:

> Since their passage, doctors and nurses in public hospitals have been obligated to inform police of suspected abortions. Many women have been jailed for ending unwanted pregnancies. A rough, unofficial estimate indicates that more than 300 young low-income women have been incarcerated in nine states for offenses related to these laws. (Maier 2012: 157)

Maier attributes these divergent trends in abortion politics to a broader conflict between secular-cosmopolitan and conservative discourses about the meaning of family, church-state relationships, and state intervention into citizens' intimate lives (Maier 2012: 163). Moreover, she points to significant discrepancies between the progressive politics and relatively secular culture of Mexico City and moral discourses about intimate life in other regions of the country. Her findings in this sense support the argument that a contradictory pluralization of public discourses and practices of intimate life has been taking place in Mexico, which has given public legitimacy to alternative understandings and practices of intimate life in some sectors and regions of Mexican society while simultaneously reinforcing patriarchal-religious discourses in others.

Intimate Life and Social Change among Mexico's Middle Class

Within this panorama, what has become of couple relationships and family life among the urban middle class? There has been very little research about patterns and dynamics of personal life among the Mexican middle class, much of which is now outdated (e.g. Careaga 1984, Careaga 1997). At the same time, there have been few detailed studies of the Mexican social structure, none of which are recent.[4] These problems notwithstanding, extant research does suggest that Mexicans'

---

4 The most notable discussions of this issue can be found in Portes and Hoffman (2003) and Davis (2004).

understandings, experiences and practices of personal life are differentiated in important ways by variables such as occupation, education, and income. Based on these variables, researchers often differentiate between different 'classes' or 'sectors' of Mexican society.

Drawing on definitions used in previous research (e.g. García and de Oliveira 2005, Rojas Martínez 2008, Portes and Hoffman 2003, Esteinou 1996), the Mexican middle class can be defined – provisionally and in an approximate way – in terms of, first, its relatively elevated academic capital, characterized by high levels of schooling and frequent access to university education, second, specific occupational positions ranging from the ownership of small businesses to middle-level white-collar employment in public administration, academia, and private enterprise, and, third, typical patterns of residence, variable but commonly strong access to property and consumer goods, and intermediate income levels sufficient to afford the outlined way of life.[5] Within this overall pattern, variations in terms of the outlined indicators may differentiate a range of subgroups within the middle class.

Extant research is concerned with the socio-economic underpinnings of domestic relations of power and production among the middle class. The already mentioned work of Orlandina de Oliveira and Brígida García (1995, 1997, 1994, 2005) is of particular note in this context. Their findings in the 1990s and early 2000s indicate a general trend towards relatively egalitarian relationships among middle-class couples, but they also highlight the persistence, particularly among older couples, of a clear division of labour between a male breadwinner and a female housewife, as well as a tendency for men to have the 'final say' in important household decisions. Likewise, in her study on men's experiences of couple relationships, sex, and family life in Mexico City, Olga Rojas (2008) finds that younger men, men whose spouses permanently participate in extra-domestic labour, and men belonging to the middle class and thus having higher educational levels are more likely than others to openly discuss decisions about sexuality and childcare with their spouses. These studies point to a partial departure from patriarchal understandings and practices in earlier decades, characterised by a lack of open communication between spouses, fathers' focus on their role as providers, and notable emotional distance between them and their children (Careaga 1984).

My research builds on these earlier studies by exploring in depth culturally situated understandings and experiences of intimate life among young middle-class women who have grown up in the outlined period of socio-cultural change since

---

5   In a recent article, Flores and Telles (2012) discuss ethnicity and skin colour as central dimensions of social stratification in Mexico. A comprehensive analysis of patterns of social stratification in Mexico would indeed need to account for these issues. However, ethnicity and skin colour did not emerge as significant topics during the interviews I conducted for the present case study. Therefore I will not consider them in this chapter. Understandings and experiences of ethnicity and social stratification among the Mexican middle class are, however, important topics that deserve greater attention in future research.

the early 1980s. In previous publications (e.g. Nehring 2009b, Nehring 2009a), I have argued that young urban middle-class people today are exposed to a wide variety of values, norms, and beliefs about intimate life, for instance through their exposure to global mass media. These narratives include, on the one hand, patriarchal-religious accounts focused on the safeguarding of traditional families built around the religiously sanctioned marriage of a heterosexual couple. On the other hand, they involve highly individualistic secular accounts centred on the ideal of love-based companionate relationships pursued for the purpose of finding lasting happiness and individual fulfilment.

My argument is based on 20 life story interviews I conducted between 2004 and 2009 with young middle-class women in Mexico City. All my participants had earned a college degree and were, at the time of our interview, employed in a range of white-collar professional occupations, for instance in public administration, higher education, or private business. Some were also pursuing postgraduate studies alongside their work. Their age ranged from 25 to 34, and their relationship status varied. Some were married and had children, while others were involved in more or less serious dating relationships or unattached. They all described themselves as heterosexual.

Contact with my participants had come about through chain referral sampling (Biernacki and Waldorf 1981), using contacts in various universities and companies as a starting point. I conducted the interviews in several stages between 2004 and 2009. They usually took place in a public place, such as a café or restaurant, or in participants' homes. Interview topics included their understandings and experiences of family life, couple relationships, and sexuality in the context of their broader biographical development and future plans.

Coping with Everyday Life in Mexico City

During my fieldwork, one of the most noteworthy problems I encountered was my prospective participants' lack of time. I met many young women who were interested in the topic of my research and would, in principle, have liked to take part in an interview. However, they were generally far too busy to easily accommodate an extended meeting in their schedules. On average, those who did take part worked 10 hours per day, often including weekend work. Quite a few of them also combined their employment with full-time or part-time studies, often in the evenings, in order to enhance their competitiveness in the labour market. Moreover, they faced long hours commuting back and forth, due to the perpetual congestion of Mexico City's roads and highways and the typically considerable distance between their homes and their workplaces in one of the world's largest cities by land area.

In my interview guide, I had included questions about the best and worst aspects of living in Mexico City. When we discussed these questions – and sometimes without me even raising them – the impact which traffic and long distances had on their lives became readily apparent. Across my participants' narratives, I noticed a pervasive sense of everyday life in Mexico City being so chaotic that it curtailed their plans and activities in significant ways. Sandra, a 30-year-old teacher working at a private university on the city's outskirts, described her experiences of urban life as follows:

Q: And the greatest disadvantages [of living in Mexico City]?

S: I think it's the traffic. Distances are very large sometimes, depending on where you have to go, and even if they are not large, they become large because there is so much traffic. So you could be stuck on a major avenue for two hours to get somewhere, when normally it would take you thirty minutes to arrive. [...].

Q: And what do you do to deal with those problems?

S: Well, look, when I can, I use the underground [...] and I don't drive. If I have to drive, well, I take it with a lot of calm and, in a way, I mentally prepare myself. I try to go out at times that are not so problematic, and I tell myself: "Well, I know that it will take a long time". So I take along a good CD or two or three or as many as I need, and I mentally prepare myself, to know that I will be stuck in traffic for hours. [...] So I don't make appointments. I mean, if I know that I have to cross the city, it is: "I will call you when I arrive because I don't know when this will be" [...]. (Extract 1, author's translation)

Sandra's account makes it clear that her everyday life, as far as extra-domestic activities were concerned, was very difficult to organize and extremely time-consuming, to the point of her giving up on making appointments. My participants' sense of urban life bordering on the unmanageable was compounded by a perceived lack of basic safety and the ever-present danger of becoming a victim of serious crime. Particularly from the mid-2000s onwards, violent crime in Mexico has escalated, with women being particularly at risk (Olivera 2006). While measures have been taken to improve public security in certain areas of the city (Bayon and Saravi 2012, Becker and Muller 2012), this has done little to alleviate the concerns of young middle-class people such as my participants. A number of them had been victims of crime, usually muggings and assaults, and all of them were afraid of becoming victims in the future. For instance, Rosario, a 27-year-old lawyer, explained that nobody in Mexico City felt safe and described the collective state of mind as a 'delirium of persecution'. At the same time that they were afraid, my participants' held little hope that the security situation would be improved. Karina, a public relations professional, described this sentiment as follows:

We are very afraid, we feel helpless and frustrated. [...] I have just been a victim of robbery. Outside our house, our car has been ransacked thrice. It is a situation that makes us feel very angry and very helpless [...]. (Extract 2, author's translation)

Later, she added that, in spite of all precautions she and her husband could take, in the end they had to 'leave things to God [*encomendarte a Dios*]', as there really was no other solution to the problem.

These feelings of fear and helplessness had very direct consequences for my participants' personal lives, as they often led them to limit as much as possible the amount of time they spent outside their homes. Just a few months before our interview, Mayra, a young lawyer who was still living with her parents, had caught a thief breaking into her house at night. After this experience, she felt such fear that she did not even want to go to work anymore. Claudia, a 31-year-old public relations professional who had lived in Europe for an extended period, argued that her personal life had been strongly affected by her feeling of being unsafe in Mexico City. She told me:

> The security situation in the city also makes it very difficult. I mean, I cannot go out with a lot of confidence, and so I prefer, for the time being, to stay at home. And this means that you cannot meet so many people. I mean, you do not talk to so many people – you never know. I mean, you go out with a lot of care. (Extract 3, author's translation)

Claudia's statement that 'you never know' what might happen in encounters with others is particularly telling, as it highlights the pervasive lack of trust which my participants experienced regarding public life in the city.

Life Plans, Love and the Pursuit of Happiness

My participants' experiences of urban space had a direct impact on their personal lives. To begin with, the fact that they spent most of their time away from home and busy, working or studying, is significant. All of them were educated at least to degree level, and they had built on their education to develop careers in a range of white-collar professional occupations. Through these experiences on their own and away from home, they generally had come to develop a strong sense of personal autonomy. This theme figured very strongly in all the interview conversations. The young women I interviewed were strongly concerned with achieving goals and fulfilling ambitions that had defined for themselves according to a voluntaristic life plan. In our conversations, they expressed clear hierarchies of priorities for their lives, which were guided by their wish for happiness and self-fulfilment.

Patricia, an academic in her mid-30s, highlighted her pursuit of happiness numerous times in our interview. Being happy, she told me, has been a driving force of her life plan as an adult:

When I was 16, with my first boyfriend my goal in life was to become a housewife and marry while still a virgin. Fortunately, I lost this objective quickly, and afterwards everything took shape when I was 25. Then, I was in Europe, and I discovered that happiness can be achieved. I mean [...], for me happiness has been something like a path, right? Because I experience very intense moments of happiness, and this is what I need. And at that moment, when I was 25 [...], I had broken free from my family, I felt completely free [...], I felt fulfilled in many ways. I was working as a waitress, I had learned French very well, I had done many things that had allowed me to discover myself as a person. [...] Being in Paris helped me [...] to really define that I wanted to do a PhD, define what I wanted to do with my life, define that in my intimate life – I want to keep working [...] – I want a relatively equal division between work and all this, right? (Extract 4, author's translation)

Patricia's account here is as much the coming-of-age story of someone finding her place in the world as it is about transcending patriarchal norms that, for a long time, have defined young women's lives. Her expectations in her youth – marriage, life as a housewife, no sex before marriage – seem built around central elements of the patriarchal cultural models dominant between the end of the Mexican Revolution and the 1980s.[6] In contrast, Patricia's life as an early adult is characterized by a clear break with these cultural models, with her moving abroad, learning to get by on her own, and making plans for a future that would involve her own professional projects as much as intimate attachment to another person. Her achievement of happiness and her sense of self-fulfilment seem to follow directly from her experience of being 'completely free' and living in a self-directed manner. The life plans of the other participants in part differed notably from Patricia's. Nonetheless, the notions that happiness and personal fulfilment are central to life and that they follow from one's ability to autonomously define a plan for one's life were present in all of them in by and large the same way.

Within such ways of experiencing one's personal development, couple relationships become important in so far as they act as a source of happiness.

---

6   According to Carlos Monsiváis (2006), a 'patriarchal contract' was an important element of post-revolutionary politics. The new Mexican state emphasized the image of the patriarchal family as primary source of social stability and prosperity. This patriarchal family was built around the marriage between a heterosexual couple, the exclusive legitimacy of sex in marriage, a clear gendered division of labour, in which women's primary duty lay in motherhood and the upkeep of the home. At the same time, however, women in this period experienced enhanced opportunities in the labour market, particularly in occupations that had traditionally been regarded as 'female'. Monsiváis (2006) in this context discusses the co-optation of a significant part of the feminist movement by the post-revolutionary state and its reorientation from a struggle for political rights to demands regarding domestic issues in line with the regime's political projects. Only in response to this acquiescence, Monsiváis argues, the patriarchal state finally conceded women the right to vote in national elections in 1953.

Genuine experiences of love, intimate attachment, companionship, and mutual understanding thus dominated in the interview narratives, instead of ideas about marriage as a pre-ordained, mandatory step in one's gendered life path. Thus, for instance, Patricia later went on to live with her boyfriend in Paris, discovering later on that their relationship was serious and meaningful enough for them to marry. Others I met had chosen to remain single until they met the right person. Rosa, for instance, told me that she would like to have a long-term relationship, but had recently broken up with her boyfriend because their feelings for each other just had not been strong enough. Aged 31, Rosa was working for a large transnational corporation in Mexico City and had gone on to live by herself after the end of her relationship. When I asked her how important being in relationship was to her, she answered:

> It is very important. At the moment, I do not have [a relationship]. About nine months ago, I broke up with one of my boyfriends. It definitely is important. I would definitely like to have a relationship, and it was peculiar, because the reason that I am not with him anymore – it was by mutual decision – where are we going, what do we want, and if we are not interested, then why are we still together, why are we not better just friends, and there it ends [ahí muere]. [...] The right moment will come, in the right place, right? It is an important part of life, and, for me personally, sharing, giving to and receiving from a loved one is important, and I would like to have a new relationship, right? I am convinced of this. (Extract 5, author's translation)

Ideas about marriage, founding a family, and having children as mandatory steps to be taken at a certain time in one's life do not figure into Rosa's story at all here. Being in a relationship is important and highly desirable, but only because of the experience of deep and intimate involvement with another it may carry with it. Therefore, Rosa's relationship with her ex-boyfriend had lost its meaning and could not last, and therefore, in a later part of our conversation, Rosa told me that she would not mind at all living by herself if she did not find the right partner. For her, finding the right person to be with, as an outcome of purely emotional experiences, is something to be hoped for, but it is not something that can be planned.

Rosa's views were widely shared among the women I interviewed. Their understandings of couple relationships were shaped by strongly held ideals of romantic love. This is to some extent visible in Rosa's narrative as quoted above. The most eloquent account of romantic love, however, was given by Laura, a financial analyst working for a government ministry. At the time of our interview, Laura was living with her boyfriend in their apartment in a quiet, centric neighbourhood of Mexico City, an arrangement which she enjoyed immensely. She told me that she had grown up in a conservative family and received a somewhat restrictive education concerning issues of sex and intimate life. She had come to reject her parents' values and experimented freely with her sexuality, having numerous intimate relationships before finally meeting her boyfriend. When I met Laura, she had settled into her relationship and was looking forward to being with her boyfriend long-term. When I asked her about the meaning of love, she replied:

> It's tied to sex, but it's also about feelings and mutual identification. Love emerges when one speaks about oneself – about what one is – with complete honesty – opening yourself completely – everything you are and want to be, and the other person listens to you, experiences with you what you are, and you hear everything the other person is, feels, thinks and has experienced. And in this convergence of histories and in daily life together, what love is about emerges – accepting each other as one is, touching each other, sharing bodies, souls, ideas, sensations. Through this […] love is constructed little by little […]. (Extract 6, author's translation)

Laura's explanation of love weaves together many observations in a complex form. She describes love as a multi-layered experience that combines sexual affinity with a shared understanding of one's way of being, achieved through the ability to communicate in particularly profound ways, to the point of far-reaching mutual identification. In spite of this description of love as an almost mythical total mutual understanding, Laura also states that 'love is constructed little by little'. In other parts of our conversation she explained this further by highlighting the need to continuously work on her relationship with her partner by spending time together and sharing experiences. Thus, while love has a unique emotional quality, it also needs to be grounded in the realities of everyday life together. While most of the other women I interviewed found it more difficult to put their understandings of love into words, they generally shared Laura's views. On the one hand, they described it as a unique and special kind of understanding with another person, while, on the other hand, they emphasized that such an understanding could not be taken for granted and had to be achieved by dedicating time and attention to one's partner, staying involved in each other's lives, and maintaining a high level of communication.

However, in spite of the importance they gave to romantic love, my participants equally pointed out that being in a relationship needed to be balanced against their need for individual autonomy and the ability to develop their personal and professional plans as freely as possible. For instance, Karen, a 29-year-old public relations professional, thus argued that her ideal relationship would mean that 'each one was self-sufficient, that there was absolute trust, that the other's personality could make oneself grow, that they complemented each other, that there weren't things like pushing, like "don't grow anymore" or "don't do this", because of the insecurity of the other' (Extract 7, author's translation). Karen's views underline the great importance which the ability to make self-directed choices about their lives had for my participants. In her view, and in that of all the others I interviewed, being in a long-term relationship was highly desirable, but not something to be achieved at the cost of her professional development and the ability to make her own plans for her life.

Negotiated Familism

As I have described them on the preceding pages, my participants' ways of making plans and choices for their intimate lives seem highly individualistic. Nonetheless, their life stories cannot simply be described as narratives of individualization. Instead they were structured by a 'negotiated familism', in which their autonomous pursuit of self-fulfilment is deeply embedded in their relationships with long-term intimate partners and family members. Negotiated familism can be explained through Neil Gross' (2005) differentiation of regulative and meaning constitutive tradition. The young women I interviewed by and large were not exposed to patriarchal traditions that directly regulated their lives through control over their bodies and their actions. By and large, they did not have to struggle with attempts on the part of family members and others to control their lives and impose a particular way of life. However, their own emphasis on family and lifelong attachment to an intimate partner as sources of personal stability and happiness provided my participants with a horizon of cultural meaning in terms of which they organized, with some notable variations, their understandings and experiences of personal life. At the same time, in their narratives, they reorganized this traditional meaning system so as to make it compatible with notions of self-determination and personal fulfilment, which, throughout large parts of Mexican history, had remained largely unintelligible and overshadowed by religiously inspired discourses of familial duty and female obedience (González Ruiz 1998).

In this sense, traditional familism played an important role in my participants' lives, but was adapted to and merged with an individualistic cultural logic[7] of personal autonomy and self-fulfilment. Familism is rendered soft and malleable, so that its central propositions about family and lasting intimate attachment can continue to be provide a framework for my participants' concrete experiences of personal life without contradicting their desire for and ability to pursue other activities central to their sense of autonomy and fulfilment. Stable attachment to family was a welcome source of security for my participants, who, at the same time, rejected the curtailment of their autonomy as a consequence of such an attachment.

This model of intimate attachment is visible, first of all, in my participants' expectations of couple relationships. As I have suggested in the preceding section, they all described being in a long-term, stable and loving relationship as an essential part of their lives. At the same time, they all pointed out that a relationship should not limit their ability to make plans and pursue their own life plans. Karen's arguments in extract 7 are emblematic of this attitude.

---

7   I use the concept of cultural logic in the sense proposed by Swidler (2001).

When we discussed their relationships with their families of origin, they professed similar views. The great majority of my participants described their relationship with their families and parents as always having been unproblematic. As they told me, their parents had been supportive of their education, had encouraged their professional development, and had let them make their own choices and plans. A few, however, had faced complex and prolonged negotiations with their parents to be able to pursue their life projects as they desired. Lourdes, for example, described her family as 'absolutely traditional'. In her youth, they encouraged her to study, but made it clear that they expected her to marry soon and dedicate herself primarily to her domestic life. In our interview, Lourdes depicted them as controlling her early life to a considerable degree:

> So they were very narrow-minded, and things were difficult, because my parents decided what I could do and what I had to leave. I mean, for everything I had to ask for permission, and I had to let them know about everything I did. [...] I mean, they imposed rules with which I often did not agree. (Extract 8, author's translation)

In the end, Lourdes defied her parents and decided to move to Mexico City, living on her own and pursuing a degree course she liked. When I met her, she had recently married and begun a successful career in media. Importantly, she and her parents had reconstructed their relationship, with her parents coming to accept the choices she had made for herself. When I asked her what her family now meant to her, she told me:

> Well, I think that it is the most important thing in my life. They are the most important people in my life. My parents are everything, right? I have learned a lot from them. I mean, I don't know, we also have had some – not everything has been wonderful, right? We have had bad experiences, but, well, in the end I have learned from this, and I think that what I am grateful for is all the support they have given me. Maybe they didn't know how to be perfect parents, but they did try, right? (Extract 9, author's translation)

Asserting her autonomy, Lourdes thus had managed to renegotiate her relationship with her family, overcoming her parents' attempts to control her and turning their relationship into a source of identification and personal wellbeing. In similar ways, all my participants described their relationships with their families as playing a central role in their lives. One important way of expressing and maintaining this attachment lay in regular family visits. Even though my participants had little free time and were often keen to spend it with their intimate partners, many of them dedicated their weekends to visiting their parents and other family members. Equally, many of them told me that they regularly shared important developments in their lives with their parents and maintained close communication.

In this sense, my participants were able to pursue their individual life projects free from external control. At the same time, precisely due to their independence, they were also faced with the task of organizing their long-term plans and making sense of their everyday experiences. Close attachment to their families and, where present, intimate partners served as important cognitive and emotional anchors in this endeavour. Patriarchal familism did not have any compelling force in their lives, but it functioned as a source of meaningful stability.

Conclusion: Building Companionate Relationships, Negotiating Intimate Citizenship

My participants' narratives seem deeply embedded in the structure of life in Mexico City. In our conversations, my participants highlighted the extent to which they spent their lives at work and away from home. Throughout their waking time, their efforts mostly had to be focused on their professional success, and they did not have a chance to spend much time with their families and intimate partners. Moreover, they found themselves exposed to the danger and disorder of urban life for prolonged periods of time. This might help to explain the duality of individualism and familism which prevailed in their interview accounts. Systems of cultural meaning come to organize experience and practice to the extent to which they resonate with the institutional arrangements actors encounter and have to come to terms with in everyday life (Swidler 2001). Therefore, a highly individualistic approach to everyday life, focused on personal success and fulfilment, might have allowed my participants to better cope with the demands of challenging professional settings they had to confront alone. At the same time, in an urban environment they experienced as precarious and unpredictable, strong bonds with an intimate partner and their families of origin provided them with a crucial sense of lasting personal stability.

Negotiated familism is meaningful in my participants' lives because it resonates with both traditional, widely accepted forms of family life and notions of self-fulfilment that enhance life in a competitive and challenging, but also comparatively open and tolerant, urban environment (Maier 2012). My participants' idealization of love shows at least some affinity with portrayals of romance in Mexican popular culture throughout the twentieth century (de la Mora 2006). Likewise, their ideals of self-directed, love-based partner choice and companionate relationships allowed them to engage with the complexities of their everyday intimate lives in an urban setting in which traditional mechanisms of social control and guidance are in retreat. Likewise, negotiated familism enables my participants to reject patriarchal mechanisms of control over women's lives, while allowing them to express their desire for strong intimate bonds.

In this sense, negotiated familism points to a widening in the range of intimate citizenship, as experienced by my participants in Mexico City in comparison with previous generations of women. In our conversations, it became evident that they felt in control of their intimate lives and able to make the respective choices as they desired. Equally, the narratives documented on the preceding pages point to greater social acceptance of choices about intimate life that would have been unacceptable among older generations. For example, neither Rosa's decision not to marry and keep dating men well into her thirties nor Laura's choice to cohabit with her boyfriend without marrying would have been easily feasible for women in their parents' or grandparents' generation. Likewise, they might entail greater challenges in smaller towns. In spite of occasional tensions and conflicts, such as Lourdes' struggle with her parents during her youth, my participants found their personal choices recognized and accepted by their families and significant others in their everyday lives in Mexico City. Due to this acceptance, they were able to pursue their life projects largely as they chose.

Negotiated familism constitutes a hybrid system of cultural meaning. It has, to a significant degree, divorced from the patriarchal social structures that have organized family ties throughout much of Mexican history. At the same time, it retains many of the core meanings of attachment to family. In their narratives, my participants incorporated familism into an individualistic mode of intimate life grounded in ideals of romantic love and personal fulfilment. Negotiated familism therefore might be understood to bridge historically established forms of intimate life in Mexico with the institutional arrangements of modern urban life.

Negotiated familism thus points to an individualization of intimate life among young middle-class women, such as my participants. However, my participants' individualism does not coincide widely with narratives of individualization that have been put forward by scholars elsewhere in the West. The popular and widely cited works of theorists such as Ulrich Beck and Elisabeth Beck-Gernsheim (2010), Zygmunt Bauman (Bauman 2003), and Eva Illouz (Illouz 2007, Illouz 2012) emphasize the fragmentation and precarization of intimate bonds in the context of the neoliberal project of globalization. In this sense, they suggest a wide-ranging convergence of cultural understandings and experiences of couple relationships and family across societies.

In contrast, the trend towards individualization I noticed among my participants is deeply embedded in forms of family life particular to Mexican society. Just as Mexican and Latin American modernities both participate in global processes of modernisation and are shaped by locally contingent socio-historical dynamics. (Whitehead 2006) Negotiated familism simultaneously forms part of a global trend towards companionate relationships (Hirsch and Wardlow 2006) and locally grounded cultural forms of personal life. Negotiated family is both my participants' response to the specific challenges and demands of their life in Mexico City and part of a broader, transnational cultural trend.

Bibliography

Amuchástegui Herrera, A. 2001. *Virginidad e iniciación sexual, experiencias y significados*. México D.F.: EDAMEX.

Ariza, M. and de Oliveira, O. (eds) 2004. *Imágenes de la familia en el cambio del siglo*. México D.F.: Universidad Nacional Autónoma de México, Instituto de Investigaciones Sociales.

Associated Press. 2006. Aplauden uniones gay en México. *El Universal*, November 22, 2006.

Avilés, C. 2008a. Avizoran que el proyecto diga no al aborto en el DF. *El Universal*, August 15, 2008, Online Edition.

Avilés, C. 2008b. El paladín de los antiabortistas. *El Universal*, August 25, 2008.

Bauman, Z. 2003. *Liquid Love: On the Frailty of Human Bonds*. Cambridge: Polity Press.

Bayon, M.C. and Saravi, G.A. 2012. The Cultural Dimensions of Urban Fragmentation: Segregation, Sociability, and Inequality in Mexico City. *Latin American Perspectives*, 40(2), 35–52.

Beck, U. and Beck-Gernsheim, E. 2010. Foreword: Varieties of Individualization, in *iChina: The Rise of the Individual in Modern Chinese Society*, edited by Hansen, M.H. and Svarverud, R. Copenhagen: Nordic Institute of Asian Studies, xiii–xx.

Becker, A. and Muller, M.M. 2012. The Securitization of Urban Space and the 'Rescue' of Downtown Mexico City: Vision and Practice. *Latin American Perspectives*, 40(2), 77–94.

Biernacki, P. and Waldorf, D. 1981. Snowball Sampling: Problems and Techniques of Chain Referral Sampling. *Sociological Methods and Research*, 10, 141–63.

Careaga, G. 1984. *Mitos y fantasías de la clase media en México*. México D.F.: Ediciones Océano.

Careaga, G. 1997. *Biografía de un joven de la clase media*. México D.F.: Aguilar, León y Cal Editores.

Carrillo, H. 1999. Cultural change, hybridity and male homosexuality in Mexico. *Culture, Health & Sexuality*, 1(3), 223–38.

Carrillo, H. 2002. *The Night is Young: Sexuality in Mexico in the Time of AIDS*. Chicago: The University of Chicago Press.

Chant, S. and Craske, N. 2003. Gender in Latin America. London: Latin American Bureau.

Cuenca, A. 2007. Legalizan aborto en la ciudad. *El Universal*, April 25, 2007, Online Edition.

Davis, D.E. 2004. *Discipline and Development: Middle Classes and Prosperity in East Asia and Latin America*. Cambridge: Cambridge University Press.

de la Mora, S. 2006. *Cinemachismo: Masculinities and Sexuality in Mexican Film*. Austin: University of Texas Press.

de Oliveira, O. 1998. Familia y relaciones de género en México, in *Familia y relaciones de género en transformación*, edited by Schmukler, B. México D.F.: EDAMEX, 23–52.

Diez, J. 2012. Explaining Policy Outcomes: The Adoption of Same-Sex Unions in Buenos Aires and Mexico City. *Comparative Political Studies*, 46(2), 212–35.

Ensalaco, M. 2006. Murder in Ciudad Juarez: A parable of women's struggle for human rights. *Violence Against Women*, 12(5), 417–40.

Esteinou, R. 1996. *Familias de sectores medios, perfiles organizativos y socioculturales*. México D.F.: CIESAS.

Flores, R. and Telles, E. 2012. Social Stratification in Mexico : Disentangling Color, Ethnicity, and Class. *American Sociological Review*, 77(3), 486–94.

García, B. and de Oliveira, O. 1994. *Trabajo femenino y vida familiar en México*. México D.F.: El Colegio de México.

García, B. and de Oliveira, O. 1995. Gender Relations in Urban Middle-Class and Working-Class Households in Mexico, in *Engendering Wealth and Well-Being: Empowerment for Global Change*, edited by Blumberg, R.L. and et al. Boulder: Westview Press, 195–210.

García, B. and de Oliveira, O. 1997. Motherhood and Extradomestic Work in Urban Mexico. *Bulletin of Latin American Research*, 16, 367–84.

García, B. and de Oliveira, O. 2005. *Dinámica Intrafamiliar en el México Metropolitano*. México D.F.: El Colegio de México.

González-López, G. 2005. *Erotic Journeys: Mexican Immigrants and Their Sex Lives*. Berkeley: University of California Press.

González de la Rocha, M. 2000. *Private Adjustments: Household Responses to the Erosion of Work*. New York: Social Development and Poverty Elimination Division (SEPED), United Nations.

González Ruiz, E. 1998. Conservadurismo y sexualidad en México, in *Sexualidades en México, Algunas aproximaciones desde la perspectiva de las ciencias sociales*, edited by Szasz, I. and Lerner, S. México D.F.: El Colegio de México, 281–305.

Gross, N. 2005. The Detraditionalization of Intimacy Reconsidered. *Sociological Theory*, 23(3), 286–311.

Gutmann, M. 2007. *Fixing Men: Sex, Birth Control, and AIDS in Mexico*. Berkeley: University of California Press.

Hirsch, J. 2003. *A Courtship After Marriage: Sexuality and Love in Mexican Transnational Families*. Berkeley: University of California Press.

Hirsch, J. and Wardlow, H. (eds) 2006. *Modern Loves: The Anthropology of Romantic Courtship and Companionate Marriage*. Ann Arbor: University of Michigan Press.

Hirsch, J.S. 2004. 'Un noviazgo después de ser casados': Companionate Marriage, Sexual Intimacy, and the Modern Mexican Family. *Categories and Contexts*, 249–76.

Illouz, E. 2007. *Cold Intimacies: The Making of Emotional Capitalism*. Cambridge: Polity Press.

Illouz, E. 2012. *Why Love Hurts: A Sociological Explanation*. Cambridge: Polity.

Irwin, R.M., Nasser, M.R. and McCaughan, E. (eds) 2003. *The Famous 41: Sexuality and Social Control in Mexico, 1901*. New York: Palgrave Macmillan.

Landau, S. 2005. Globalization,Maquilas, NAFTA, and the State: Mexican Labor and 'The New World Order'. *Journal of Developing Societies*, 21(3–4), 357–68.

Maier, E. 2012. Documenting Mexico's Culture War. *Latin American Perspectives*, 39(6), 155–64.

Monsiváis, C. 2006. When Gender Can't Be Seen amid the Symbols: Women and the Mexican Revolution, in *Sex in Revolution: Gender, Politics, and Power in Modern Mexico*, edited by Olcott, J., Vaughan, M.K. and Cano, G. Durham: Duke University Press, 1–20.

Muller, M.M. 2013. Penal Statecraft in the Latin American City: Assessing Mexico City's Punitive Urban Democracy. *Social & Legal Studies*, 22(4), 441–63.

Nehring, D. 2009a. Cultural models of intimate life in contemporary urban Mexico: A review of self-help texts. *Delaware Review of Latin American Studies*, 10(2).

Nehring, D. 2009b. Modernity with limits: The narrative construction of intimacies, sex and social change in Carlos Cuauhtémoc Sánchez's Juventud en Éxtasis. *Sexualities*, 11(5), 33–59.

Olcott, J., Vaughan, M.K. and Cano, G. (eds) 2006. *Sex in Revolution: Gender, Politics, and Power in Modern Mexico*. Durham: Duke University Press.

Olivera, M. 2006. Violencia Femicida: Violence Against Women and Mexico's Structural Crisis. *Latin American Perspectives*, 33(2), 104–14.

Plummer, K. 2003. *Intimate Citizenship: Private Decisions and Public Dialogues*. Seattle: University of Washington Press.

Portes, A. and Hoffman, K. 2003. Latin American Class Structures: Their Composition and Change during the Neoliberal Era. *Latin American Research Review*, 38(1), 41–82.

Rivas Zivy, M. 1998. Valores, creencias y significaciones de la sexualidad femenina. Una reflexión indispensable para la comprensión de las prácticas sexuales, in *Sexualidades en México: Algunas aproximaciones desde la perspectiva de las ciencias sociales*, edited by Szasz, I. and Lerner, S. México D.F.: El Colegio de México, 137–55.

Rodríguez, G. 2005. Las trincheras del conservadurismo en la educación sexual, in *Los rostros del conservadurismo mexicano*, edited by de la Torre, R., García Ugarte, M. E. and Ramírez Saíz, J. M. México D.F.: CIESAS, 289–308.

Rodríguez, S. 2010. Son pobres las 300 mujeres procesadas por aborto. [Online]. Available at: http://lajornadaaguascalientes.com.mx/index.php?option=com_content&view=article&id=14485:son-pobres-las-300-mujeres-procesadas-por-casos-de-aborto&catid=5:sociedad-y-justicia&Itemid=11 [accessed: June 9, 2013].

Rojas Martínez, O.L. 2008. *Paternidad y vida familiar en la Ciudad de México: Un estudio del desempeño masculino en los procesos reproductivos y en la vida doméstica*. México D.F.: El Colegio de México.

Swidler, A. 2001. *Talk of Love: How Culture Matters*. Chicago: University of Chicago Press.

Talcott, M. 2011. Terrorizing Women: Feminicide in the Americas. *Contemporary Sociology: A Journal of Reviews*, 40(5), 586–88.

Whitehead, L. 2006. *Latin America: A New Interpretation*. New York: Palgrave Macmillan.

Wise, R.D. 2006. Migration and Imperialism: The Mexican Workforce in the Context of NAFTA. *Latin American Perspectives*, 33(2), 33–45.

Chapter 7

Experiences and Understandings of Intimate Life in Tehuitzingo: Courtship, Marriage and the Dissolution of Relationships[1]

Dubravka Mindek

The concept of intimacy in sociology has various connotations which are not necessarily exclusive: it can refer to a close and deep relationship based on mutual understanding or alternatively, a space that remains out of sight of strangers or of other people. Finally, it can mean a social sphere in which personal relationships of different types develop, such as courtship, marriage, or post-marital relationships (Guevara Ruiseñor 2005: 860–62). This chapter explores this last connotation of the concept of intimacy. Specifically, it examines courtship, marriage, and marriage breakdown among the inhabitants of a small town in central Mexico. Ultimately, this chapter aims to contribute to discussions of intimacy and modernity in rural Mexico, seeking to answer the following question on the basis of a case study: To what extent, in this town and others like it, does the irruption of modernity and individualization in the sphere of intimacy make love and compatible companionship key factors in the formation and sustainability of conjugal relationships? In other words, is love becoming increasingly important to the lives of the inhabitants of rural Mexico?

The location in question is Tehuitzingo, situated in the southern part of the State of Puebla. According to the Eighth Population and Housing Census carried out in 2010, the town has 4,739 inhabitants. It forms part of the Mixteca, an area that was governed and occupied in large part by the Mixtec people before the Spanish Conquest. Today, Tehuitzingo is a modernized, post-indigenous place, whose

---

1 This chapter is based on an unpublished doctoral thesis in anthropology entitled *Patterns in the Dissolution of Relationships in Tehuitzingo, Puebla*, presented at the National School of Anthropology and History in Mexico City in 2009. The data on which it is based were collected through observation, interviews and revision of the records of the municipal justice department, known locally as the justice of the peace. I conducted formal and informal interviews on different topics with about 50 people from the town. I have compared my data with those of other researchers who have explored the same topics during the same period in other rural areas (both mestizo and indigenous). Most of these other rural areas included in similar studies are also in the State of Puebla and in other parts of central Mexico.

inhabitants have lost the language of their ancestors, even while they maintain and recreate some of their traditions. It is located in a rural area; nonetheless the majority of the population does not depend on an agrarian lifestyle. Instead, they work in construction, trade or service activities, making a living in the informal as well as the formal economy. A proportion of the inhabitants have tried their luck looking for work outside the town or outside the country, and a proportion of homes and families depend for their everyday living on remittances from the United States. On the basis of these characteristics, Tehuitzingo is representative of a range of rural settlements in central Mexico that have passed through similar processes in the construction of a new rurality.[2]

Courtship in Tehuitzingo in the Past and Present:
From 'Just Looking at Each Other', to Embracing and Kissing in Public

In a path breaking book on courtship and dating among young people in rural areas in Mexico entitled *Night-time is meant for men: Sexuality in the process of courtship among young campesinas and campesinos*, published for the first time in 2002, authors Gabriela Rodriguez and Beno de Keijzer (2002: 42) define courtship as a social relation explicitly agreed upon by two people to accompany each other in social and recreational activities filled with emotional and romantic sentiments that are expressed through words and physical contact.[3] In turn, the dictionary of the Spanish Royal Academy defines courtship as a romantic relationship maintained between two people without the intention of getting married and without living together. Both definitions correspond with the concept of courtship as understood in modern day western societies. Nevertheless, it has not always been like this in the West, far less in rural Mexico.

In the West, the modern concept of courting has an interesting and relatively short history. It appears approximately 90 years ago (in the 1920s and 1930s) as a state of transition between bachelorhood and marriage. It was closely related to the latter of these, to the extent that being someone's sweetheart meant the same as being their betrothed. The institutionalization of courting in the United States is associated with industrialization and the incorporation of women into the factory workforce on a mass scale. It is also associated with the development of public education, and lastly also with the mass production of cars. All of these contributed to a closer interaction between men and women without the constant supervision of

---

2   One can speak of a new rurality in relation to localities traditionally associated with agriculture but which now encompass a diversity of activities and social relations that are closely linked to urban centres, industrial activities and services. Referring to the new rurality, researchers point out that in the present day in rural areas, non-agricultural income from industry or services is more important than that derived from agriculture (Arias 1992, Reardon et al. 2001).

3   *Campesinas* and *campesinos* are female and male small farmers.

their elders. Cars allowed middle-class couples to spend time together away from the home, a social space where men had previously come to visit women under careful parental watch and guidance. Getting out of the house and away from the surveillance of the woman's family allowed couples to experiment gradually with a greater physical and emotional closeness. Nevertheless, in spite of the growing intimacy of couples, it was not until the seventies that courting was no longer necessarily considered as the prelude to marriage. This situation changed with the sexual revolution, and the mass availability of contraception. With this, courting became less formal, more intimate and eroticized, and was no longer necessarily linked to marriage (Schwartz and Scott 2010).

In the context of rural Mexico, the history of courtship as we know it today is even shorter, and did not exist until a few decades ago. Researchers point out that in the past young couples contracted to marry without passing through a courtship phase. Marriages tended to result from a negotiation carried out by the young people's parents. Or in the best of cases, a young man would choose the girl he wished to marry and then ask his parents to make the necessary approaches to obtain the consent of the parents and/or the girl (González Montes 1999, Ávalos Aguilar et al. 2010). In the case of women, researchers highlight the passive role of being chosen, or at best, having agency to the extent of being able to accept or reject suitors according to her own will (Hirsch 2003, Mindek 2009).

For around two or three decades such practices have been diminishing in rural communities, principally those in which schooling, migration and mass media have allowed young people to become aware of other models, symbols and values. This has permitted them to live different realities to those of their parents and grandparents: to court, to establish emotional bonds, and in some cases, to experience sexuality as a constitutive element of courtship (Ávalos Aguilar et al. 2010, Hirsch 2003, Rodríguez and Keijzer 2002, D'Aubeterre Buznego 2000, González López 2009).

Despite its own nuances and particularities, Tehuitzingo generally fits this pattern. In contrast to the observations of the authors already cited, as far as people can remember in this town, choice of spouse has been a private matter, principally concerning the couple involved. According to informant testimonies, single people in the town have always chosen their romantic companions freely and on their own, without parents imposing. What has changed slowly is the character and content of courtship.

In the past, courtship was generally understood as a preparation for marriage, and lasted a long time, up to several years. It was characterized by secrecy, fleeting encounters, furtive glances and the sending of notes that were passed on by mutual friends. Just as in other parts of the Mexican Republic, courting among the inhabitants of Tehuitzingo in past times, or what was considered as such, was characterized by zero or very limited personal interaction and intimacy, and was carried out in a fraught atmosphere with frequent chastisements or punishments.[4] This is illustrated by the experience of a 60 year old informant who told me that her courtship to her now-deceased husband lasted six years. During that time, she hardly saw him more than once a month on the street just right outside her house. She would watch him from the window without exchanging a single word, although occasionally he would send her a note. When the father of this informant was away and her mother in bed, they could converse 'sticking close to the window'; even so the young man was 'desperate to avoid being found out'. In the past, men feared being discovered by the parents of their girlfriends when loitering around their house, and they were ready to scurry off at the first sign that they might be seen by the parents. The reason was that this interaction was considered inappropriate before the formalization of the union. In other words, until the final decades of the twentieth century, courtship in a post-indigenous and rural Mexican setting was characterized by distance and supervision.

Nowadays, courtship is seen as a phase of life for young people, for enjoyment above all, and something that offers the possibility of couples getting to know each other as friends. This would have been difficult to imagine in the courtships of their grandparents, described as consisting of 'no more than looking at each other', of 'not even talking to one another'. Today, couples live with much greater liberty, openness, expression of emotions and interaction. A combination of cultural and structural changes have contributed to the disappearance of hidden courtship. At the same time, they have created the possibility of getting to know the other person, and allowing more time and greater space for romance, closeness as well as for sexual intimacy. For women, the passage of time has increased the number of possible and permitted boyfriends at the same time as weakening the connection between courtship and marriage (Rodríguez and Keijzer 2002). While older women talk of having a single boyfriend, and of courtship as being a preliminary to marriage, young men and women from the 1990s onwards have started to have a succession of relationships which are not necessarily linked to marriage.

In contrast to previous periods, there are now more pretexts to be out of the house. To begin with, the majority of teenage boys and girls (especially girls) attend school for longer than they did in the past. School has become one of the main sources of information about the lives and social relations of young people, including courtship. Furthermore, in school they spend several hours of the day in close contact with their peers from the opposite sex and receive information about different kinds of social relationships including friendship and romantic involvement. School plays an important role as a space for socialization and for the consolidation of young people's identity in a rural environment. It is the main place that boys and girls start to get to know each other. During break-time in

---

4   For similar descriptions of courtships in past times in rural areas in central Mexico, see D'Aubeterre Buznego 2000, Hirsch 2003, Rodríguez and Keijzer 2002, among others.

the playground of the local secondary school, one sees couples holding hands, embracing or kissing each other in view of everyone, including teachers.

Those who go to school or to work outside Tehuitzingo, where there is less chance of being seen or recognized by a relative or neighbour, have greater freedom over what to do with their time. Furthermore, they have roughly a couple of hours more to socialize with their peers from the opposite sex: an hour by bus on the way to or back from Izúcar de Matamoros or Acatlán de Osorio, the two main places where young people work or study if they don't do so in the town.

Even when young people don't go to school or work outside the home, they spend more time in the street than their parents did, and much more than their grandparents did in their respective youths. This has to do with the fact that the inhabitants use the shops and services of the town on a daily basis, and young people are often sent by their elders to buy a something needed for the home, make a payment or for some other task. This is colloquially referred to as *running an errand*, and provides a space in which boys and girls can see others, be seen themselves, and socialize with their current or intended boyfriend or girlfriend.

In addition, because more services are readily available in town and because of the decline in agricultural activities in the area, young people have more free time for leisure than previous generations did. These changes have thus expanded the space and time available for courting and, at the same time, intensified possible interaction between individuals in courting relationships.

On par with the changes mentioned in the previous paragraph, young people have begun to interact more with their peer group of both sexes, and to construct a youth identity, characterised by free time and enjoyment. Typical spaces for this are dance-halls, basketball courts or the central square of the town. There is also one disco in town. Young and single men and women go dancing without the escort of an adult. In the same way, they go for walks in the centre of town or sit on a bench to eat ice cream, providing the opportunity to be approached by suitors, or by boyfriends or girlfriends.

These days some parents know that their sons and daughters have girlfriends or boyfriends, while others ignore the fact. Couples can be seen embracing or walking hand and hand in the street, something which provokes comment but nothing more. People note that couples today are seen and express themselves with greater freedom in public places, and don't care that they are seen. Some inhabitants disapprove of 'such confidence' and exhibitionist behaviour by young people, and comment that in their day people were more shy and kept out of sight. Others observe things more philosophically and say that young people need to get to know each other and have fun.[5]

---

5   Authors describe similar attitudes to what happened in the past in other study areas. That is, that young people were more obedient and modest then than today (Fagetti 2006: 56–8, Rodríguez and Keijzer 2002). In Degollado, Jalisco, Hirsch (2003: 96) found the same reproachful attitude towards open manifestations of erotic love and exhibitionism. The inhabitants told her repeatedly that couples had lost their modesty

There are no strict rules or cultural norms about how to undertake a courtship in Tehuitzingo. Everything suggests that the way a courtship unfolds currently depends on the character and personality of the sons and daughters and parents, how open they are, and how much closeness and trust there is between them. Within one family, I met two very different girls who related to their parents in different ways. One was very outgoing and knew how to manipulate her parents to get what she wanted and to get their permission for everything, including going out with her boyfriend. The other didn't tell them or ask them anything. They didn't even know whether she had a boyfriend or not. The mother of these girls said that the former is not discreet at all: 'there she is, dancing around' with her boyfriend. As seen in the footnote number five, researchers have recorded similar comments in other parts of rural Mexico.

In contrast to what Schwartz and Scott (2010) describe as the displacement of courtship in the West from the house to the street, this has never been common in Tehuitzingo. Nor is it common for couples to visit each other's homes, or at least not openly or with the consent of their respective parents. Even so, I am aware of at least one case of parents who accepted their daughter having a boyfriend and allowed him to visit the house (and vice versa) so that they could carry on their relationship freely and openly, even if this raised eyebrows among the neighbours. A female teacher who lived near the parents of this young woman told me 'the issue is that now you don't know if she's a Mrs or a Miss'.

The availability of modern technology in Tehuitzingo has also allowed courtship to continue between people living in the town and those who have migrated. A quarter of the homes have a private telephone; furthermore, there is more than one public telephone in each part of the town. While only 6 per cent of homes have internet access, there is at least one internet café in the town. As a result, partners who are physically separated for reasons of work, study or residence have the possibility of staying in contact by phone or *Skype*. This allows much greater continuity and fluidity in their relationships than would be the case if they had to depend only on visits and meetings within the town.

The growing availability of vehicles also allows the young population of Tehuitzingo more freedom to engage in courtship. According to the 2010 Census of Population and Housing, 26 per cent of the population of the municipality had a vehicle.[6] Currently, at sunset or at night one can observe cars or pick-ups parked on the banks or in the dried-out bed of the river that passes through Tehuitzingo. Sometimes the lights are off, sometimes on. However, if the occupants notice someone coming they switch the lights off. Many of these vehicles have United

---

and kissed each other in sight of everyone. Rodríguez and Keijzer (2002: 99) document similar comments about couples embracing and kissing in open view in the area where they carried out their research.

6   Figures for the town (as opposed to the municipality as a whole) are not available. Nonetheless, it can generally be expected that the figures for the town, as the municipal centre, are at least equal to if not greater than the municipal average.

States number plates, indicating that they belong to or have been brought to the town by migrants.

In the same vein, increased accessibility to the mass media has been influential in informing courtship practices . Eighty per cent of homes in Tehuitzingo have TV sets, and watch soap operas and films that provide examples of intimacy based on emotional and physical closeness. Various authors speak of the role of television in the formation of youth identity in rural environments (Ávalos Aguilar et al. 2010, Rodríguez 1999, Feixa and González 2006). Inhabitants of a Zapotec village in Oaxaca interviewed by Feixa and González (2006: 181) viewed television as having a negative influence on young people, teaching them 'to have a boyfriend or girlfriend and then to split up with them, to get married and then to get divorced'. In a similar fashion, those interviewed by Rodríguez and Keijzer (2002: 106) said that one learns everything from films and television, 'including how to give yourself to someone' (in the sexual sense).

Increased physical intimacy is also part of the changing nature of rural courtship. When Hirsch (2003: 108) mentions qualitative changes in courtship in current day Degollado, Jalisco, she notes that physical intimacy has come from being an exception (or at least, she says with prudence, everyone claims it was an exception in the past), to being the rule. I didn't discuss this issue explicitly in Tehuitzingo. However, I can say that premarital sexual relationships do occur even though they are not openly discussed. I met and had cases mentioned to me of young women who had engaged in sexual relationships before marriage, and with more than one partner. Rodríguez and Keijzer (2002) examine in more detail the theme of physical intimacy in their research on courtship and pre-marital relationships in a rural location in the same region as Tehuitzingo. They found that sexual relations were a constitutive element of courtship for young people in the rural area they studied.

Love, Trust and Respect in Marriage as a Life Project

It has been said that with modernity and individualization, social actors gain new spaces for action and possibilities for choosing (Beck-Gernsheim 2011: 85). In this sense, some opt for a career and being single, while others choose family life. For those who form families there are a vast range of models and structures for living together: nuclear families, single parent families, living without children or without sharing a home, late marriage, legal or common law marriage. This is the case in the West, and is gradually emerging in Mexican cities. It is not the case however in rural areas.

In rural Mexico these days, it is still imperative for young people to form a married couple because the status of adulthood and advancement to the social category of *señor* and *señora* is closely linked to being married (D'Aubeterre

Buznego 2000: 101, Good 2003: 159, Mindek 2009: 149, Fagetti 2006).[7] According to Antonella Fagetti's book (2006), *Anomalous Women*, based on a study of a Nahua farming community also located in the State of Puebla, those who chose not to be in a marital relationship are considered an anomaly.

Tehuitzingo follows the same pattern. Among its inhabitants, marriage is not considered as just one option for life and adulthood, but as the only viable option. Being single is not something that is chosen so much as something that unfortunately happens to them. Neither do they choose not to have children. Young single people aspire to find a partner and have children with him or her. Their aim in life consists of forming a family, which they consider as the main medium for personal realization and for finding happiness. However, this does not mean that they accept or choose the first candidate that they bump into. Instead, it means that they wait and hope to find a partner who shares their interests and affections.

Nonetheless, love is not the only or principal motive for forming a marital partnership in every case in Tehuitzingo. In fact, I have heard testimonies from women who not only do not talk of love as a motivation for starting married life, but say that on the contrary, it was absent. The women who stated that they did not get married for love did highlight its importance, as if they wanted to say that the right thing would have been to do so.[8] In this light, I offer the testimony of a 31 years old woman who formed a free union with a man when both were in the United States. This informant admitted that at first she didn't like the man or love him, but allowed him to court her, and moved in with him because she felt lonely and abandoned. Nonetheless, with time she had come 'to love him too much'.

In her book, *A Courtship after Marriage*, Hirsch (2003) examines sexuality and love among transnational families in Degollado, a mestizo town in the State of Jalisco. In particular, Hirsch analyses the role of women in being chosen or choosing a partner. On the basis of interviews with 20 informants living with a partner, including mothers and daughters from different generations, the author identifies two characteristic patterns of choice in the area. The author links each pattern to an understanding of marriage that is distinct to each generation. According to her research, up until the 1960s, marriage was conceived as a mechanism for social reproduction. At that time, couples understood it as a responsibility which required respect for and dedication to the gender roles of the man as the provider and the woman as a house wife. Women of this generation speak of marriage in terms of destiny rather than the result of choice or personal decision. As a result, it was less important for them to be actively involved in the choice of husband than it was to know how to put up with whatever married life might involve (Hirsch 2003: 87, Hirsch 2007). In contrast, those who got married from the middle of the 1980s onwards view mutual trust as the basis for a good marriage, with this translating

---

7   *Señor* and *Señora* are Mister and Mrs.

8   For further discussion of the expression and importance of love, attraction and romance in courtship and indecisions to marry in rural areas in central Mexico, see Fagetti 2006, D'Aubeterre Buznego 2000, Hirsch 2003, among others.

into making decisions jointly, gradual advances toward a more equitable division of house work, and the importance of giving time to family activities. Younger women hoped to find in their husband a partner who shared their interests, affections and happiness. As a result, they played a much more active role in choosing an appropriate match (Hirsch 2003: 92–3).

In similar terms to Hirsch, Rabell Romero and Murillo López (2009: 295–6) speak of the transition from the model of the hierarchical family to one of the relational family. They do not refer specifically to rural families, but to Mexican families in general. All of these authors characterize the first type of family for its reproductive aims, and note that within it gender roles are very distinct, with little space for negotiation. In these families, satisfaction and ultimately, happiness, are achieved when each member fulfils the gender role assigned to them. In turn, Romero and Lopez define the relational family as one whose principal aims are happiness and love in its own right. In this new model, they assert that women participate in decision-making, work full or part time, have the right to say what they think, and look for emotional closeness. Men in this model also want emotional closeness, even if they don't want to give up power. The authors mentioned coincide with the view of Rosario Esteinou (2012: 265) that younger families with fewer children incline more towards the relational model.

Marriages in Tehuitzingo fall in a midpoint between hierarchical and relational marriages, between being founded on respect and being founded on trust. To begin with, marriage is not just one option for adults in rural areas. Rather, when referring to a civil status, it is the only and best option, and in this sense it is practically a destiny. However, it is a destiny which is helped along with agency since practices of courtship allow for individual choice and a relationship to build and develop over time.

Even though marriage is still closely bound up with reproduction, for several decades it has not been the case that people in Tehuitzingo simply 'have the children that God sends them'.[9] Instead, couples have two or three children before using some form of contraception on a permanent basis. They do not plan the number of children or the intervals between them in the strict sense of the word, but they do limit them. They prefer small families. Both partners earn an income, whether in the formal or informal economy. They accept that a single income is not enough for the family budget, and that the contribution of both is fundamental for the family to get by, at the same time as saying that women help men with

---

9   In what I consider a thought-provoking reflection on intimacy and modernity in Mexico, Guevara Ruiseñor (2005: 859) notes that in our country in general the family is focused on bringing up children and social reproduction rather than emotional satisfaction among partners. She reviews data that reveal Mexico as a conventional society in which homes with a male head of family are very much prevalent, and in which common law marriages often have more to do with factors other than the free choice of the couple. She concludes that Mexico has entered modernity adopting some new practices, but within an old system of values (Guevara Ruiseñor 2005: 874).

the budget. In many cases spouses in the town take part in the same paid work, complementing and supporting each other. They cooperate to work and manage family businesses, shops or restaurants: while one serves clients the other works with supplies or merchandise.

According to most of my male and female informants, women look after and manage the family's earnings. In the majority of cases, their male partners hand over their whole earnings, or if the source of income is not from a permanent job, the latest money that they made. Most of the male participants in the study believed that women had the right to spend their earnings on what they want, but in practice they spent mostly on home and family.

Again according to my informants, husband and wife make decisions together. The wife may suggest how to get money to pay off a debt, what it is wise to invest in, whether to sow or not, and whether it makes sense for the man to go and work in the United States. On occasion, the woman's opinion has more weight in decisions than that of the man. One informant told me that some years ago her family lived in Mexico City; her husband wanted to stay there, but she didn't like it and wanted to return to the town. She worked to convince her husband until she was able to persuade him that they should sell the house in the capital and go back to live in Tehuitzingo. Another told me that at one point her husband had the urge to buy the latest model of a car; she didn't agree with a purchase of this kind and told him it would be better not to, that what they needed more was their own house, as they were living in a rented one. They ended up buying the house rather than the car. A third interviewee told me that she had been living with her husband in the United States, and that it was she that decided that the time had come to move back to Mexico. He accepted this and they duly returned.

Some informants prefer to leave it to their husband to have the last word in making decisions, more for their own comfort than out of a supposed respect for the hierarchical order of things. Their reasoning is that the husband will have all the responsibility for the success or failure or for getting things right or wrong. The wife of a migrant stated that they 'always discuss things but ultimately he takes the decision. It's better that way, so if things go wrong it's his responsibility'.

A similar logic can be observed in parenting. When children want to do or buy something, they ask both their parents to approve it. However, the majority of women with whom I have spoken prefer that their husband have the last word: 'Men are stricter: he only has to talk to them and they pay attention; they don't pay attention to me, for example if they want to get away with something'. Wives of migrants themselves say that they assume the role of both father and mother towards their children when their husbands are away. They know they are not able to communicate with their husband every time their children want to go out dancing or every time they do something wrong. However, in the periods when their husbands are at home, the wives of migrants prefer to delegate some of the work of parenting to their husbands: 'To the extent that you battle with them when your husband isn't there, there's less point in doing so when he is.'

The wives of migrants I have talked with say that they prefer their husband to be with them rather than away. The main reason they wish their partners to be at home is for the children: female informants prefer to share the work of child rearing with the men. At the same time, they admit that in many cases they are complicit (*a go-between*) with their children and defend or cover up for them, argue on their behalf to their husbands. 'The thing is, even though you get annoyed, you're also more consenting.' Reading between the lines, this suggests a form of parenting that is more democratic than authoritarian.

When asked about their own freedoms or restrictions, women assert that they don't ask permission from their husbands to go out, but rather let them know when they are thinking of going somewhere. Asking for permission does not seem to be used literally in daily life, as Hirsch (2003: 116) also observes in Degollado, Jalisco. In relation to this, a 36-year-old interviewee said: 'I go where I want and when I want, the idea that I'm held subject, that I'm forced to ask for permission, that doesn't happen. We trust each other.'

Most of the women interviewed in the present study were felt enough trust in their relationship for them to confront their husbands in public spaces as much as private ones: to go and bring them back from cantinas or other masculine spaces where their husbands spend time drinking with their peers; to demand fidelity and to defend the right to conjugal exclusivity when they suspect or know that their husbands have other lovers; or to mark the calendar with a big red marker those days when their husbands come home drunk, among other things.

Most wives in the study also reported a sense of agency in dealing with their husband's illegitimate children or those from a previous marriage/relationship. In many instances, men would have to see or help their non-marital children discreetly, taking steps to ensure their current wife did not find out. Some wives even took steps to limit the access which illegitimate children, or those from previous marriages, could have with their husbands.

In spite of wives gaining some agency in some aspects, the study also revealed the persistence of certain cultural forms of *machismo* (male dominance in heterosexual relationships).

The most extreme manifestation of *machismo* were acts of violence committed against women. According to interviewees in the present study, women in Tehuitzingo did denounce domestic violence to the local judge. To investigate their complaints the judge will generally arrange a hearing with the aggressor. The men defend themselves against the accusations of their wives when they appear before the judge, but do not deny having assaulted them, instead presenting their version of events and trying to justify themselves with a discourse 'focused on maintaining their authority, rights and prerogatives as men' (García Peña 2006: 100). Some men would try to convince the judge that they acted within their rights, and that their wife provoked them and provided cause for the aggression. They justified themselves, calling on cultural norms about behaviour and the appropriate roles of spouses.

In light of the contradictory dynamics present in contemporary marriages in the rural town of Tehuitzingo, we turn back to the original question of the present study: what role does companionate love play in marital relationships and in decisions made in favour of or against maintaining or ending the marriage? In an effort to address this, Javiera Cienfuegos Illanes (2011) argues that the concept of married life has two analytical dimensions: the intimate, which refers strictly to the couple relationship, and the organizational, which links the couple with the family unit. At the empirical level, these two dimensions need to be assessed within a specific context. In a rural environment, existing cultural practices subordinate the intimate dimension to the organizational one. That is to say, while women aspire to having a partner who is a companion that supports, loves and respects them, the lack of these characteristics alone is not sufficient or predominant enough for women to leave their spouse. By privileging the organizational dimension of family, factors like family stability, income security, and the continuity of a traditional two-parent household come to the foreground. As a result, in Tehuitzingo the absence of love may not, by itself, be reason enough to end a marriage.

Because of this reason, the mother in law of the informant who said that at first she hadn't loved her (now ex-) husband, but that with time she had come to love him 'too much', had tried to convince the daughter to change her mind and go back to her son, for the sake of their children. However, the informant didn't agree with this argument and replied: 'In that case what I think doesn't matter, because I believe couples should stay together for love'. According to her own testimony, she had separated from this man, who was a good provider for the family, when she found out that he had a parallel relationship with another woman, which prevented him from fulfilling her need for a relationship based on companionship and affection. She was the only one out of 12 informants who talked to me about the dissolution of her marriage and who constantly emphasized the role of affection in marriage and the importance of being able to satisfy individual needs and expectations.

Final Reflections

Processes of individualization, and the discourse and practices of intimacy which belong to modernity are becoming apparent in couples relationships among the inhabitants of Tehuitzingo and the rural world of central Mexico. Their adoption by a part of the population is a result of cultural and structural changes brought about by national and transnational migration, the growing influence of mass media and the almost universal access of the younger population to formal education. These changes have brought an increasing purchasing power to the population, growing contact with a range of different cultural models, and greater access to information.

Currently, new models of intimacy, particular to modernity, can be seen to a greater extent in courtship and the choice of spouse than in representations of marriage, the day-to-day practice of marital relationships or in decisions to maintain, repair or break-up relationships. In other words, in Tehuitzingo couples are formed today on the basis of romantic sentiment and of attraction, both of which are socially constructed. However, the same sentiments are not the predominant reason for maintaining unions; neither is the absence of love necessarily a sufficient motive to end a marriage. This is understandable given the importance of marriage in gaining the status of respectable adulthood in rural localities, where there is not much room for single adults.[10] It is likely that this is the reason that men rarely separate or get divorced of their own accord, without having already begun a new relationship. Furthermore, when they themselves are abandoned, in the majority of cases they quickly find another partner.

In the case of women, in addition to the importance of marriage in the acquisition of respectable adulthood, it is also more difficult for them to find work or income in rural areas sufficient to support themselves and their children. For women, living as couple is the best means to obtain economic as well as symbolic security. For this reason, single mothers in rural areas, to whom maternity 'happens' aim to form what they describe in their own words as 'a normal family' and to have a partner at their side. This contrasts with women in different environments, principally urban ones, who deliberately decide to become single mothers. It is also for this reason that even though they get married for love and wish for a marriage based on companionship, women may give up these ideals more easily than they can give up a man who helps them achieve their instrumental needs and the need for social and family stability. In addition, they are less likely to end a marriage, even if it no longer provides affection and companionship, and are more likely to be the ones who seek a reconciliation and try to repair a damaged marital relationship.

Bibliography

Arias, P. 1992. *Nueva rusticidad Mexicana.* México: CONACULTA.

Ávalos Aguilar, S.R., Ramírez Valverde, B., Ramírez Juarez, J., et al. 2010. La configuración de culturas juveniles en comunidades rurales indígenas de la Sierra Norte de Puebla. *Culturales,* 6(12), 117–46.

Beck-Gernsheim, E. 2011. *La reinvención de la familia. En busca de nuevas formas de convivencia.* Madrid: Paidós.

Cienfuegos Illanes, J. 2011. Desafíos y continuidades en la conyugalidad a distancia. *Revista latinoamericana de estudios de familia,* 3, 146–73.

D'Aubeterre Buznego, M.E. 2000. *El pago de la novia. Matrimonio, vida conyugal y prácticas transnacionales en San Miguel Acuexcomac, Puebla.* Mexico City: BUAP and El Colegio de Michoacán.

Esteinou, R. 2012. Relaciones familiares e intimidad en la sociedad mexicana del siglo XX, in *La nueva generación social de familias. Tecnologías de*

---

10   I refer here to adulthood in the biological sense.

reproducción asistida y temas contemporaneous, edited by R. Esteinou. Mexico City: CIESAS, 257–84.

Fagetti, A. 2006. *Mujeres anómalas. Del cuerpo simbolizado a la sexualidad constreñida.* Puebla: Benemérita Universidad Autónoma de Puebla and Instituto Poblano de la Mujer.

Feixa, C. and González, Y. 2006. Territorios baldíos: identidades juveniles indígenas y rurales en América Latina. *Revista de Sociología*, 79, 171–93.

García Peña, A.L. 2006. *El fracaso del amor. Género e individualismo en el siglo XIX mexicano.* México: COLMEX/UAEMEX.

Good Eshelman, C. 2003. Relaciones de intercambio en el matrimonio mesoamericano. El caso de los nahuas del Alto Balsas en Guerrero, in *El matrimonio en Mesoamérica ayer y hoy. Unas miradas antropológicas*, edited by D. Robichaux. Mexico City: Universidad Iberoamericana, 157–84.

González López, G. 2009. *Travesías eróticas. La vida sexual de mujeres y hombres migrantes de México.* Mexico City: Miguel Ángel Porrúa and Instituto de Migración.

González Montes, S. 1999. Las 'costumbres' de matrimonio en el México indígena contemporáneo, in *México diverso y desigual. Enfoques sociodemográficos*, edited by B. Figueroa Campos. Mexico City: COLMEX y SOMEDE, 87–105.

Guevara Ruiseñor, E.S. 2005. Intimidad y modernidad. Precisiones conceptuales y su pertinencia para el caso de México. *Estudios sociológicos*, 23(69), 857–77.

Hirsch, J.S. 2003. *A Courtship after Marriage. Sexuality and Love in Mexican Transnational Families.* Berkeley: University of California Press.

Hirsch, S.J. 2007. Loves makes a family. Globalization, Companionate Marriage and the modernization of gender inequality, in *Love and Globalization. Transformations of Intimacy in the Contemporary World*, edited by M.B. Padilla et al. Nashville: Vanderbilt University Press, 93–106.

Mindek, D. 2009. *Patrones de disolución de pareja en Tehuitzingo, Puebla.* Unpublished doctoral thesis. Mexico City: Escuela Nacional de Antropología e Historia.

Rabell Romero, C. and Murillo López, S. 2009. El respeto y la confianza: prácticas y percepciones de las familias numerosas y pequeñas, in *Tramas familiares en el México contemporáneo. Una perspectiva sociodemográfica*, edited by C. Rabell Romero. Mexico City: COLMEX and UNAM, 293–352.

Reardon, T., Berdegué, J. and Escobar, G. 2001. Rural Nonfarm Employment and Incomes in Latin America: Overview and Policy Implications. *World Development*, 29(3), 395–409.

Rodríguez, G. 1999. Entre jaulas de oro y entregas por amor. Las transformaciones del cortejo en una comunidad rural en Puebla. *JÓVENes. Revista de Estudios sobre Juventud*, 3(9), 52–69.

Rodríguez, G. and de Keijzer, B. 2002. *La noche se hizo para los hombres. Sexualidad en los procesos de cortejo entre jóvenes campesinas y campesinos.* Mexico City: EDAMEX and Population Council.

Schwartz, M.A. and Scott, B.M. 2010. *Marriages and Families: Diversity and Change*. Upper Saddle River: Prentice Hall.

Wardlow, H. and Hirsch, J.S. 2006. Introduction, in *Modern Loves. The Anthropology of Romantic Courtship y Companionate Marriage*, edited by H. Wardlow and J. S. Hirsch. Ann Arbor: University of Michigan Press, 1–31.

Wardlow, H. and Hirsch, J.S. 2006. *Modern Loves. The Anthropology of Romantic Courtship and Companionate Marriage*. Ann Arbor: University of Michigan Press.

Chapter 8

Intimate Space, Assimilation and Divergence: An Analysis of the Reproductive Decisions of Contemporary Mexican American Women

Emmanuel Alvarado

The present chapter addresses current debates on intimate citizenship, cultural change, and globalization through empirical research on the reproductive decisions of college-educated Mexican American women in the area of South Texas. Plummer's (2003) account of a waning of grand narratives of intimate life in the context of rapid cultural and technological changes and globalization implies a 'contradictory pluralization' and fragmentation of discourses on couple relationships and sexual and reproductive choices. Research on contemporary patterns of intimate life has highlighted the weakening of traditional patriarchal power relations and a trend towards love-based companionate relationships (Hirsch 2003, Ariza and de Oliveira 2004). Such transformations have occurred since the 1970s in Mexico, and in locations in the United States with a strong Mexican American presence, amid cultural commonalities, tensions, and contradictions between emerging egalitarian logics and established male-dominated patriarchic relationship schemas. In this chapter, the reproductive decisions of college educated Mexican American women are analysed under the scope of a gradual decline of previously hegemonic patriarchic relationship discourses and tensions brought about by competing academic narratives supporting either the divergence (continued growth) or the assimilation (gradual decline) of Mexican American fertility.

The reproductive choices of US-born, college-educated Mexican American women are of growing national sociopolitical and sociocultural significance. The most recent estimates from the 2010 Census show that roughly one-sixth of the US population is now of Hispanic origin[1] and that this population is growing rapidly

---

1 The term 'Hispanic' or 'Hispanic American' usually refers to persons who trace their origin to Spanish speaking Latin American countries. The term 'Latino' refers to persons who trace their ancestry to Latin American countries, including non-Spanish speaking countries such as Haiti or Brazil (Oquendo 1995). Nonetheless, the two terms have been lumped together in US Census reporting since the year 2000 and are used

as a result of immigration and high fertility rates (Westoff and Marshall 2010). Most of the growth of the Hispanic population in the US has been led by Mexican Americans.[2] This notable increase in the Mexican American population brings to the foreground the fertility of Mexican American women as this segment of the US population increasingly impacts and shapes multiple facets of American public life with visible manifestations in popular culture, electoral competition, and business leadership.

In particular, an analysis of the reproductive choices of US-born, college-educated Mexican American women is of salient interest for three reasons. First, the reproductive experience of US-born Mexican American women may differ meaningfully from those of immigrant Hispanic women due to mitigating factors related to migration such as legal status, age while immigrating, rural or urban point of origin, etc. As a result, a restricted examination of reproductive choices which centres exclusively on US-born Mexican American women is necessary to exclude the multidimensional confluence of immigration and fertility choices. Second, the uniqueness of this subset of the Mexican American population allows the researcher to analyse reproductive choices in light of some of the benefits and expectations of college graduates such as better labour market opportunities, generally higher income levels, and career advancement prospects. Third, an examination of the reproductive choices of college-educated Mexican American women also sheds light on the cultural dynamics of reproduction which are likely to become ever more relevant as a broader proportion of the Mexican American population reaches and completes higher levels of education.

The primary focal point of the present study is the role which cultural models, especially cultural understandings of family life, play in the reproductive choices of US-born, college-educated Mexican American women.[3] The present study analysed this cultural context through a series of in-depth interviews conducted over South Texas in September–October 2010. Previous quantitative studies based on standardized questions from national surveys have examined the role of education, income, family schemas, and religion in Hispanic women's fertility choices through multivariate analysis (Hayford and Morgan 2008, Parrado and Morgan 2008, Westoff and Marshall 2010). However, these studies have been based on Likert scale surveys which do not allow for deeper analysis on how

---

interchangeably here, for simplicity, to mean the population in the US who trace their origin to Latin America. The term 'Mexican American' in the present text specifically applies to the US born population who trace their origins to Mexico.

2   Within the Hispanic population, the highest birth rates are among those of Mexican origin and the lowest among Cuban Americans (Landale and Oropesa 2007).

3   A cultural model is a broad schema that explains, interprets, and orders knowledge and experience about social and cultural phenomena (Lakoff 2008). Lakoff further argues that cultural models 'create a conceptual framework, a language, imagery and an appropriate emotional tone' by which we approach social and political issues, understand differences, and, ultimately, shape social positions and actions (42).

cultural models about family schemas, tradition, and religion are interpreted, acted upon, and, most importantly, reinforced when women make fertility choices. Additionally, some of these studies have approached 'Hispanic' or 'Latino' fertility as if all individuals of Hispanic heritage in the United States composed a monolithic group. Lumping all US Latinos into one unit of analysis conceals vast differences in socioeconomic status, educational attainment, and first-generation pathways to legal immigration status. It also obscures important fertility level differentials among the various national origin groups and between the foreign-born and US-born.[4]

In examining the reproductive choices of college-educated Mexican American women, the study looks beyond the theoretical paradigms of 'assimilation' and 'divergence' prevalent in the academic literature. The chapter begins with a discussion of these two counterpoised perspectives on the future patterns of Latino birth rates in America. Next, the methodology used in the study is described. Lastly, the main and recurring cultural themes found within the research interviews are presented, discussed, and analysed.

Assimilation or Divergence? Hispanic Fertility in the United States

Existing literature on the fertility behaviour of Hispanic Americans is largely influenced by two counterpoised theoretical approaches. For simplicity, they are identified here as the assimilationist and the divergence perspectives.

The Assimilationist Perspective

According to the assimilationist perspective, changes in fertility behaviour are expected to occur as part of the general process of immigrant adaptation and assimilation. Alba and Nee have defined assimilation as 'the decline of an ethnic distinction and its corollary cultural and social differences' (2005: 11). In this process, ethnic distinctions tend to fade and increasingly involve fewer domains of social life. This is not the result of a conscious effort on the part of individuals to 'assimilate', but is the by-product of purposive actions by immigrants and their children to adapt to social life and improve their life chances in the host country within human capital, social network, and institutional constraints (Parrado and Morgan 2008). Assimilation may happen on two levels: through changes in the individual, as he or she spends more time in the host society, and through changes across generations (Alba and Nee 2005). Assimilation is a multifaceted concept, however, and can proceed unevenly across various dimensions. For instance, one

---

4 For instance, Latinos of Mexican origin in the United States have considerably higher total fertility rates (3.0) than those of Cuban origin (1.9), while Puerto Ricans fall in between (2.2). Moreover, Hispanics who are US-born generally have fewer children than those who are foreign-born (Landale and Oropesa 2007).

can distinguish between structural assimilation, that is, interpersonal contact across ethnic lines; socioeconomic assimilation, or convergence in education, wages, and occupational attainment; and cultural assimilation or acculturation, expressed through language use, modes of dress, and social behaviours (Arias 2001, Gordon 1964). Immigrant assimilation in one dimension may enhance the likelihood of assimilation in another, but it does not guarantee it. For instance, a group can be relatively acculturated with respect to cultural values and practices and still not reach socioeconomic parity with the majority. Conversely, a group can achieve socioeconomic success but retain a distinctive culture and/or continue to reside in segregated communities.

Modern assimilationist scholars consider values and beliefs about family life, such as ideal family size, appropriate timing of marriage, and desirable household composition, as important aspects of immigrant assimilation (Abma and Krivo 1991, Amaro 1988, Arias 2001). These values and beliefs reflect the level of cultural assimilation and may affect the possibilities for socioeconomic assimilation and mobility. For example, successful completion of a college education may entail the postponement of marriage and childbearing, and for women in particular, upward occupational mobility is often incompatible with having a large number of children (Rindfuss, Morgan, and Offutt 1996). Thus, the modern assimilation perspective suggests that the quest for social mobility encourages Hispanic immigrants and their descendants to discard attitudes and behaviours that limit their chances of success in the United States and adopt those that promote them, including smaller families (Alba and Nee 1997). Figure 8.1 summarizes some of the factors that proponents of the assimilation perspective believe may lead toward a gradual decline in the fertility of Mexican American women and to its eventual convergence with the fertility levels of non-Hispanic American women.

Additionally, authors like Leo Chavez (2004) and Elena Gutierrez (2008) have strongly criticized theoretical approaches that stress the divergence between white and Latina women in terms of sexual and reproductive behaviour. These authors argue that popular media and academic representations of Hispanic women as hypersexual and overly fertile are unrealistic exaggerations that serve to advance a 'Latino threat' narrative. Chavez further argues that such a narrative feeds fears with regard to the 'Latinization of America' and the purported overuse of medical and social services by immigrants. This narrative, Chavez adds, is inconsistent with the striking similarities between the fertility behaviour of Anglo and Latina women found in his analysis of data from Orange County, California (2008).

The Divergence Perspective

Contesting the assimilationist perspective, proponents of the divergence perspective contend that the fertility behaviour of some ethnic groups in the United States may remain distinct from that of white Americans. As shown in Figure 8.2, they point to familism, religious involvement, lack of social mobility,

Figure 8.1   The assimilationist perspective on Mexican American women's fertility

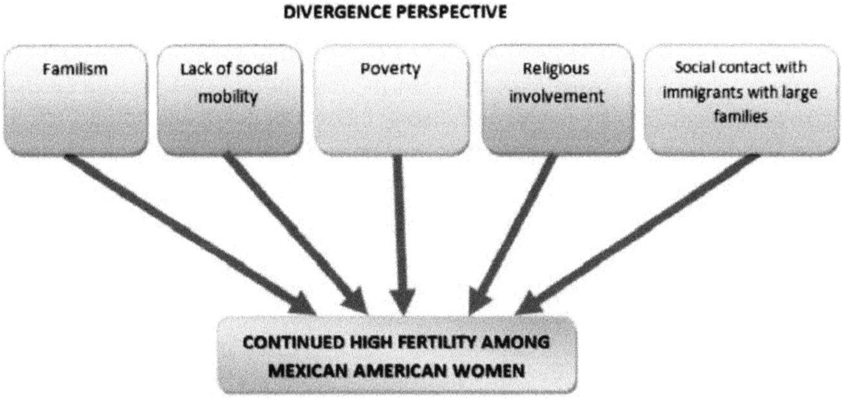

Figure 8.2   The divergence perspective on Mexican American women's fertility

poverty, and the continuous influx of large immigrant families as factors that encourage Hispanic Americans to maintain higher fertility rates over time rather than converging with the fertility behaviour of non-Hispanic Americans. For instance, Vega (1995) has argued that familism, or a strong commitment to family life, is qualitatively different among US Hispanics than among non-Hispanic whites. According to this view, because so much of Hispanic life revolves around the immediate and extended family, cultural familism plays an informative role for multiple dimensions of family life, including family structure and family size (Landale and Oropesa 2007). Westoff and Marshall (2010) and Amaro (1988) have suggested that because Latinos in the United States are generally more religious than non-Latinos and because religious narratives regarding family, abortion, and childbearing favour higher fertility, then it would follow that Christian religiosity among US Hispanics encourages large families.[5]

Some proponents of the divergence thesis have criticized the emphasis that assimilation scholars place on social mobility as an engine of cultural assimilation. For instance, Parrado and Morgan have argued that 'the assimilation paradigm is inappropriate for the current wave of immigrants, who as non-whites face barriers that earlier waves of immigrants did not' (2008: 652). Moreover, the economic context that immigrants face has changed dramatically, with an hourglass labor market structure that offers few avenues for upward mobility through blue-collar work (Portes and Rumbaut 2006). Under this scope, widespread poverty and limited labor market opportunities may also serve to diminish the opportunity costs of large families for Hispanic women.[6] Additionally, the continuous influx of new immigrants with large families reinforces preferences for higher fertility, undermining fertility convergence across immigrant generations (Lichter and Landale 1995, Portes and Rumbaut 2006).

Central to both the assimilationist and divergence perspectives is the hypothesized effect that cultural assimilation (or lack thereof), education, and upward social mobility have on the reproductive behaviour of Hispanic Americans. In order to close knowledge gaps and contribute to the academic debate on the future of Hispanic fertility, the present chapter focuses on the sociocultural context of fertility decisions of Mexican American women. More specifically, the present study examines the cultural models that inform fertility choices among college-educated women of Mexican heritage in South Texas.

Methodological Considerations

Site Selection

South Texas constitutes an area of interest for this study for several reasons. As noted in Combs's (2008) demographic report on South Texas, Corpus Christi and its surrounding towns, such as Robstown, Alice, and Kingsville, hold large second and third-generation Mexican American populations. In other words, the vast majority of Hispanics in these locations are US-born Mexican Americans. In

---

5   Empirical evidence for this argument is mixed. For instance, Westoff and Marshall (2010) found that religiosity had only a mild independent effect on fertility rates among Hispanic Americans once differences in income and education were considered.

6   The idea behind this argument is that the added responsibilities and time taken off work associated with childbearing may entail higher opportunity costs for career-minded, middle-class, professional women than for lower-income, blue-collar women whose employment prospects would not change dramatically with the addition of more children.

addition, South Texas is also home to numerous middle-class, college-educated Mexican American women.

Sample and Data Collection

A total of 36 interviews were conducted in the South Texas cities of Alice, Kingsville, Robstown, and Corpus Christi during the months of September and October 2010. Fliers inviting women to participate in the study were distributed through local chambers of commerce, academic conferences, and city fairs. Twenty-seven women meeting the requested criteria responded to the invitation to participate. These participants introduced the researcher to an additional nine women who met the criteria, and they were interviewed as well. Compensation for participation was $25, and the interviews lasted from 30 to 45 minutes.

Given that the focus of the study was on the completed fertility of college-educated Mexican American women, potential candidates had to meet certain criteria to be eligible to participate in the present study. First, they had to self-identify as Mexican American.[7] The second requirement was to have been born and raised in the United States. The third requirement was a completed fertility cycle.[8] All participants indicated that they had no plans for future pregnancies, and most were beyond the prime childbearing years.[9] Fourth, given that the focus of the study was on educated women, all participants had to possess a bachelor's degree or higher at the time of the interview.

All study participants were informed about the purpose, nature, and context of the study. It was also clearly indicated to all interviewees, both orally and in writing, that their participation was strictly voluntary and that they were free to end the interview at any point. The sampled population was interviewed on three basic topics: immediate and extended family relations, professional work life and career prospects, and reproductive choices. The responses to the questions were coded and analysed in an effort to identify emergent and recurring themes (Rubin and Rubin 2005). Although the interviews were semi-structured, follow-up questions were asked either to clarify responses or to arrive at a better understanding of participants' views.

---

7   A few of the interview participants did not have Hispanic last names but did identify themselves as Mexican American. Because ethnicity is a matter of self-identification, no additional efforts were made to ascertain the details of the participants' ethnic or family backgrounds.

8   In the academic literature on fertility a distinction is made between completed fertility and expected or intended fertility. Because the latter is a fluid concept that is subject to changing circumstances, completed fertility is believed to be a better measure of fertility behaviour.

9   A few participants were in their late thirties at the time of the interview, but the majority were between 40 and 58 years old, making future pregnancies unlikely.

Relevant demographic information was obtained in the course of the interview, including age, number of children, occupation, marital status, and place of origin. These data were gathered for informational purposes only and were not used to seek correlations with other variables through quantitative analysis. The data show that the sample reflected the diversity of educated Mexican American women in the United States with respect to age, immigrant generation, socioeconomic class, Spanish proficiency level, and number of children.

The age of the participants ranged from 36 to 58. Twenty-two of the 36 women had received their bachelor's degrees from local colleges and universities in South Texas, while the rest had earned their degrees from institutions in other parts of Texas or out of state. Nineteen of the participants had at least one parent who was born in Mexico; the rest had two US-born parents. The interviewees worked in various fields such as education, law, accounting, sales, and nursing. Marital status varied: 18 of the 36 women had married only once and remained married, 10 were on their second or third marriage, and eight were divorced at the time when the interview was done. The number of children also varied considerably, ranging from zero to seven, with a sample average of 2.65 per woman.

Factors Affecting Reproductive Choices: Emergent and Recurring Themes

The interviews were transcribed and coded for concepts and emergent themes (Bogdan and Biklen 1992; Rubin and Rubin 2005). Some of the themes explicitly address the motivations and cultural influences that shape the reproductive choices of educated Mexican American female professionals. The themes were grouped into three major categories that will be examined in turn: patriarchal/egalitarian relationships, familism, and professional success and ambition.

Patriarchal vs. Egalitarian Relationships

One of the recurring themes in the interviews was the distinction between patriarchal and egalitarian relationships. The interviews indicated that the reproductive choices and expectations of educated Mexican American women are enmeshed with the opposing cultural principles embedded in patriarchal and egalitarian relationship narratives.

In contextualizing the difference between their own reproductive decisions and those of their parents, most participants characterized their parents' relationship as male-dominated and rigidly patriarchal. For instance, one woman recalled, 'The number of kids which my mother had or was going to have was never up for discussion. That number was always set by my father's desires, mood and choice of using birth control or not. Because of this, they ended up having far more kids than I would ever choose to have'.

Such comments are highly consistent with the cultural organization of romantic relationships in Mexican history. For much of Mexico's history, until the transformational period of the 1980s, cultural narratives of love, sexuality, and intimate attachment were dominated by patriarchal norms and beliefs that had deep roots in Catholic morality. The family – nuclear or extended – was generally held to be central to social stability, and it was understood as the exclusive space within which intimate relationships could legitimately take place (Tuñón Pablós 1987, Villafuerte García 1998). The family was to be organized hierarchically, with a male head at its top and a clear gendered division of labour between its male and female members. While the former would engage in extradomestic economic activity and represent the family in public life, the latter's duties lay in housework, childcare, and the maintenance of a harmonious domestic environment (Tuñón Pablós 1987). In accordance with the family's needs, individuals' intimate lives were to be organized in a strict sequence of steps, leading from courtship of a suitable partner at a suitable age to lifelong marriage (Nehring 2005). Historical research (e.g. Stern 2005) has suggested that considerable variations existed in actual practices of intimate life in different sectors of Mexican society. Nonetheless, women's experiences of reproduction were enmeshed in a very narrow framework of public discourses and moral narratives.

The crisis of Mexican society that began in the early 1980s did much to change the cultural organization of intimate relationships. Especially in urban Mexico, the outlined traditional norms of intimate life have lost much of their compelling force (Nehring 2005, García and de Oliveira 2005). Recent research (Hirsch 2003, González-López 2005) points to substantial variations in the cultural organization of intimate relationships and to a trend towards love-based companionate relationships. At the same time, patriarchal norms and values still play an important role in Mexican society, as recent struggles about issues such as abortion and lesbian and gay civil unions have shown.

Two factors are noteworthy here. First, the data collected from the interviews point to a prevalence of patriarchal relationships among the parents of many Mexican American women, particularly those parents who originally came from or were raised in smaller Mexican towns. Second, elements of traditional patriarchal relationships were influential in fertility choices among Mexican American women who claimed to be religiously involved, especially those who were members of Protestant evangelical congregations. For instance, one of these informants said:

> For the most part, I listen to my husband on major decisions. Because of my faith, I believe he is the spiritual leader of our family and trust that God has enlightened his decisions [...] My husband always wanted a larger family. He was raised in a Christian home and believes that children are blessings from God, and the more children you get, the more blessed your household becomes.

However, most of the actual study participants viewed their own romantic relationships as mainly egalitarian, in that major decisions were discussed, negotiated, and mutually agreed by the couple. The majority of those interviewed stated that their own reproductive desires and expectations were respected and considered in both their current and past relationships. And while marriage remained a desirable goal, it was no longer mandatory; one could attain a fulfilling relationship and even successfully bear and raise children without marrying. For all these reasons, the majority of respondents perceived their own relationships to be qualitatively unlike the rigid patriarchal relationships of their parents and other older relatives.

Familism

Another recurrent theme throughout the interviews was familism. Although the concept has been used in different ways in the academic literature, there is general agreement that it entails a subordination of individual interests to those of the family group (National Research Council 2006). Familism may include a strong attachment to the nuclear and extended family, a sense of family loyalty and solidarity, frequent family contact, mutual assistance among family members, economic sharing of resources, and a preference for larger families (Steidel and Contreras 2003, Valenzuela and Dornbusch 1994). The overwhelming majority of the women interviewed as part of this study expressed a strong connection to their nuclear and extended family as a source of social support and as a formative part of their identity. One woman said, 'My family is the source of my inspiration and hope. Although we fight and disagree like any other family, my family members are my closest friends and advisors.'

The interviews reveal that familism contributes to reproduction patterns among Mexican American women in two important ways. First, the cultural centrality of family life fosters a strong desire for reproduction and family formation. Indeed, many study participants noted that their own experience of family life, shaped by close ties with the extended family, frequent family gatherings, and solidarity among family members, served to inspire and reinforce a desire for childbearing. For instance, one participant said: 'As I remembered the joy of growing up close to my parents, grandparents, uncles, and cousins, I began to think about the importance of having children of my own who would also get to experience a rich family life, as I did.'

The second way in which familism had a notable role in reproductive choices involved the presence of an extensive family network willing to help with childrearing. Most interviewees mentioned that their families and in-laws helped raise their children, by frequently taking care of them or otherwise being actively involved in their lives. In some cases families even provided financial support toward children's upbringing. Support from the family network was of particular importance for those women who had their first child at a young age. In some cases, the presence of family support was the crucial factor in the decision to bear and raise the child rather than resorting to other options, such as abortion or adoption: 'I had my first child at the age of 19 and the father had decided to be uninvolved. Truthfully, the only reason I decided to go on to have it was because

I knew that my family was always going to be there to help me.' In another case, family support for childrearing allowed a woman to complete college:

> I had my first child when I was twenty-three. I was a senior in college and about a year away from completing my degree in electrical engineering. I don't know what I would have done without my family. After I stopped working, my parents rented a small apartment for me and my grandmother. She moved in for a year to help me take care of my baby so that I could finish my bachelor's degree. To this day I am thankful that they helped to make the best out of such a difficult situation.

Professional Success and Ambition

Most study participants acknowledged that their desire for children (or more children) coexisted with an aspiration to succeed professionally. A large proportion said they were subject to strong family expectations of educational and professional success as they were growing up. This perception was most pronounced among those women whose parents were foreign born. These women in particular felt that their parents vehemently transferred their hopes for attaining the 'American dream' onto them.

In relation to this, the interviews used for the present study also suggest that familism and professional ambition constitute two competing cultural influences on reproductive choices among college-educated Mexican American women. While familism may emphasize the centrality of procreation, professional ambition and the desire to achieve career goals can motivate decisions to postpone childbearing and have fewer children. One informant stated:

> Throughout my career I sought promotion after promotion. And with each promotion came more work and responsibility. It got to the point where my husband was desperate for children and yet we kept on postponing because of my job. […] The situation almost cost me my marriage. In the end, we had our first and only child when I was thirty-four, although we would have liked more.

Many interviewees also admitted that their strong desire to become educated, independent, and professional women had a notable impact on their sexual choices during early adulthood. In some cases, the aspiration for a thriving career led to rigorous contraceptive use and to a cautious selection of romantic and sexual partners as a way to avoid unwanted pregnancies and relationships that might hinder professional success. In sum, the college-educated Mexican American women in our sample experienced a tension between career success and family procreation to the point that, more often than not, one came at the expense of the other.

In addition to professional ambition, another source of concern was how a larger family would affect the family's overall economic prospects. Among some respondents, the desire for more children ran up against the constraints of modern economic life. One respondent noted: 'Although we wanted more children, we realized that another child could easily pull us down well below a middle-class standard of living. And then I thought, "I did not go to college for six years to have such a limited quality of life". So we ended up stopping after two.'

While indirectly related to reproductive choices, the study also identified tension between the demand for labour mobility in professional life and the desire to remain geographically close to immediate and extended family. For some women, this conflict began, or was exacerbated, when they acquired more responsibilities or better positions in their workplace that required extensive travel or even relocation. Most of the respondents who faced this conflict decided to reject the relocation or avoid work travel in order to remain in their hometowns, even if it meant passing up an opportunity or eventually having to find a new job. As one woman stated: 'I turned down a better job that would have paid me nearly three times as much as what I was making but required me to move out of state. I didn't feel that the extra money would compensate for the absence of my parents and sisters.'

Discussion

Our findings signal two important problematics in current debates on Mexican American women's intimate lives and reproductive choices. One the one hand, the interviews suggest a partial waning among Mexican Americans of traditional narratives of family life, sexuality, and childbearing that are built around the religiously grounded notion of motherhood as women's central task in life. On the other hand, our participants' stories also contrast with the accounts of individualization and increasing brittleness of interpersonal relationships, associated with the overwhelming demands of the neoliberal labor market, that are dominant in the mainline sociology of personal life in the United States (Hochschild 1997, 2003, Illouz 2007, Sennett 2006).

Additionally, the overwhelming majority of the women who participated in this study conceptualized their own intimate relationships as vastly different from the patriarchal relationships of their forebears in twentieth-century Mexico. They voiced a sense of greater agency in the distribution of household roles and selection of sexual partners, and they were clear about the declining importance of marriage as a central pillar of family life and essential base for reproductive choices. Nonetheless, their narratives also suggest that traditional models continue to exert some influence on the procreation decisions of some college-educated Mexican American women, predominantly among those with strong religious involvement and, in particular, among evangelical Christians.

This finding is in line with previous scholarship pointing to the importance of religion in shaping life and family schemas, which in turn influence reproductive behaviour (Hayford and Morgan 2008, McQuillan 2004). Although study participants who claimed greater religious involvement did not report considerably higher birth rates than those who were less religiously involved, the context in which religiously involved women made reproductive choices was strikingly different from those who were not religious.[10] Religiously involved women in our sample believed childbearing should occur within the context of a religiously sanctioned marriage, and they were willing to leave the number of children up to God's will. Referencing passages from the Old Testament and the Gospels, they argued that their own procreation was determined by God's plan for their lives. Additionally, our findings suggest that traditional Catholic doctrine opposing contraception and supporting procreation within a religiously sanctioned marriage has been recast in the family values and pro-life stances of evangelical Protestantism, thus allowing old and new cultural narratives to complement one another and remain meaningful among the more religiously inclined Mexican American women.

Our findings also suggest that educated Mexican American women face an amalgamation of cultural influences where languages, consciousness, life goals, and subjectivities are constantly 'juggled'. Renowned Chicana writer Gloria Anzaldúa addresses this very issue in her conceptualization of the new mestiza – a term Anzaldúa uses to describe the mixed identity and consciousness of contemporary Mexican American women in the US. In Anzaldúa's writings, the conceptualization of the new mestiza grants value and cultural agency to a mixed and fluctuating consciousness (Amado 449). In the following passage, Anzaldúa elaborates on the notion of the mestiza:

> Una lucha de fronteras/A struggle of Borders
> Because I, mestiza,
> Continually walk out of one culture
> And into another,
> Because I am in all cultures at the same time,
> Alma entre dos mundos, tres, cuatro, me zumba la cabeza con lo contradictorio.
> Estoy norteada por todas las voces que me hablan
> Simultaneamente. (Anzaldúa 1987: 77)

Here, Anzaldúa uses English and Spanish to describe the multidimensional identity of the mestiza as well as her ability to continuously negotiate between American and Mexican culture. Additionally, the passage serves as a poetic and illustrative depiction of the various, and at times contradictory, intercultural confluences which constitute and 'speak' to the new mestiza.

In this sense, our findings highlight the cultural dynamics that underpin our participants' understandings of reproduction, childbearing, and family life more broadly. In line with the divergence perspective on the future of Hispanic birth rates in the United States, the present study suggests that familism and a desire to

---

10   This finding contrasts somewhat with the results of Westoff and Marshall (2010) on the link between religiosity and fertility.

perpetuate strong and socially meaningful family ties remain culturally informative in reproductive choices among educated, professional Mexican American women. As noted here, there are many instances in which such devotion and attachment to extended family inspires a distinct cultural preference for reproduction and expansion of family size. Moreover, a close relationship to extended family provides an extensive support network of relatives willing to be involved in childcare, thus alleviating some of the burden associated with reproduction and childrearing.

Nonetheless, our findings also highlight the extent to which educated Mexican American women are burdened by demands for professional mobility and flexibility in the context of a neoliberal socioeconomic regime. In an age of ever-diminishing returns for the efforts of the aspirational middle class, it is unsurprising that some of our younger participants would experience difficulties in reconciling the need for professional achievement with their desire for children. To the extent that this motivates decisions to postpone childbearing, our results are, to a degree, consistent with findings on contemporary tensions between work and family life in mainstream sociology and in assimilationist literature on the future of Hispanic fertility (Abma and Krivo 1991, Alba and Nee 1997, Amaro 1988, Arias 2001).

At the same time, it would be misleading to use such similarities as a basis for generalizations about the cultural assimilation of Mexican Americans. Our findings point to a need for mainstream sociological inquiry to take into account the diversity of experiences that exist in contemporary American society, especially when considering the cultural and economic tensions between work and family life. Over the past decades there has been a consistent trend toward a segregation of 'ethnic studies', including relatively recent fields such as Latino studies or Asian American studies, from mainline sociology. This has enabled mainstream sociologists of personal life to continue to focus their inquiry on the experiences of the white middle class and to disregard, at least to some extent, the increasing diversity of American life.

In contrast, 'area studies' have often shown a greater conceptual sensitivity toward the varied experiences of intimate life in a globalized world.[11] Latino studies scholars, in particular, have generally been attentive to the intrinsic hybridity of the personal experiences of this sizeable and growing sector of the US population. Our research seeks to contribute to this project and to the debunking of popular myths about the intimate relationships and reproductive behaviour of Mexican Americans (Chavez 2004). The observations outlined in this chapter complicate both assimilationist and divergence perspectives on Mexican American women's reproduction. The findings presented here suggest that family size choices among Mexican American women result from the dynamic interaction between

---

11   This corresponds to a notable 'global turn' among anthropologists and sociologists in 'area' or 'ethnic' studies in recent years (e.g., Hirsch and Wardlow 2006, Jankowiak 2008, Padilla et al. 2007).

socioeconomic and cultural assimilation, on the one hand, and the history and cultural traditions of Mexican Americans, on the other.

In fact, the binary opposition of 'assimilation' to 'tradition' may be something of a red herring, stemming, perhaps, from the linear view of modernization and social change in positivistic social science as classically expressed by Rostow (1960, 1971). A wealth of recent research has shown how belief systems, technologies, institutional arrangements, and everyday practices intertwine to produce complex social wholes that are simultaneously old and new, traditional and modern. Jolane Culhane (2006) uses the concept of 'cultural amalgamation' to reflect on these complexities. Surveying the history of Hispanic cultures in the United States, she points to a multitude of facets of popular culture, from cuisine to rock 'n' roll, that express a hybridization of cultural forms rather than simple assimilation or substitution. In this spirit, transnational migration and its many possible aftermaths are best understood as sites of open-ended possibility, in which beliefs, values, emotions, and forms of everyday experience may collide, mix, repel each other, and form new wholes in ways that are not easily mapped through the bounded and static concepts of classic social science.

The experiences documented in this chapter further substantiate this point. In making and justifying important life choices, individuals are most likely to draw on cultural models that fit the institutional contexts in which they live (Swidler 2001). Our participants' lives are characterized by their simultaneous exposure to persistent traditions of Mexican familism and to the competing demands for mobility, flexibility, and constant availability of the neoliberal labour market. The women interviewed did not respond to these institutional contexts by insisting on 'divergent' cultural traditions or by letting themselves be passively assimilated into the hegemonic culture of white middle-class America. Rather, their narratives speak of the effort to construct reflexive life projects that would allow them to maintain cherished familial bonds while pursuing demanding careers of their own. Their narratives attest to hybridity and difference – the cultural processes informing their choices are not simply Mexican, not simply middle-class American, and certainly not simply 'divergent' or 'assimilationist'.

To truly understand the reproductive choices that Mexican American women make, it is necessary to further elucidate the complexity and hybridity of their lives in the liminal spaces of American culture. This points to the need for further in-depth ethnographic explorations of the understandings, motivations, and feelings that underpin Mexican American women's choices about sexuality and childbearing in the context of, on the one hand, the strains and exigencies of the US labour market, and on the other, an ethnic culture that keenly upholds the preservation and expansion of family ties as central to a meaningful social life.

Bibliography

Abma, J.C. and Krivo, L.J. 1991. The Ethnic Context of Mexican American Fertility. *Sociological Perspectives* 34(2), 145–64.

Alba, R.D. and Nee, V. 1997. 'Rethinking Assimilation Theory for a New Era of Immigration'. *International Migration Review* 31(4), 826–74.

Alba, R.D. and Nee, V. 2005. *Remaking the American Mainstream: Assimilation and Contemporary Immigration.* Cambridge, MA: Harvard University Press.

Amaro, H. 1988. Women in the Mexican-American Community: Religion, Culture, and Reproductive Attitudes and Experiences, *Journal of Community Psychology* 16, 6–20.

Anzaldúa, G. 1987. *Borderlands: The new mestiza = La frontera.* San Francisco: Spinsters/Aunt Lute.

Arias, E. 2001. Change in Nuptiality Patterns among Cuban Americans: Evidence of Cultural and Structural Assimilation? *International Migration Review* 35(2), 525–56.

Ariza, M. and de Oliveira, O. (eds) 2004. *Imágenes de la familia en el cambio del siglo.* Mexico City: Universidad Nacional Autónoma de México, Instituto de Investigaciones Sociales.

Bogdan, R. and Biklen, S.K. 1992. *Qualitative Research for Education: An Introduction to Theory and Methods.* Needham Heights: Allyn and Bacon.

Chant, S. and Craske, N. 2003. *Gender in Latin America.* London: Latin American Bureau.

Chavez, L.R. 2004. A Glass Half Empty: Latina Reproduction and Public Discourse. *Human Organization* 63(2), 173–88.

Chavez, L.R. 2008. *The Latino threat: Constructing Immigrants, Citizens, and the Nation.* Stanford: Stanford University Press.

Combs, S. 2008. *Texas in Focus: South Texas.* Austin: Texas Comptroller of Public Accounts.

García, B. and de Oliveira, O. 2005. *Dinámica intrafamiliar en el México metropolitano.* Mexico City: Colegio de México.

González-López, G. 2005. *Erotic Journeys: Mexican Immigrants and Their Sex Lives.* Berkeley: University of California Press.

González Ruiz, E. 2002. *La sexualidad prohibida: Intolerancia, sexismo y represión.* Mexico City: Plaza y Janés.

Gordon, M.M. 1964. *Assimilation in American Life: The Role of Race, Religion, and National Origins.* New York: Oxford University Press.

Gutiérrez, E.R. 2008. *Fertile Matters: The Politics of Mexican-Origin Women's Reproduction.* Austin: University of Texas Press.

Hayford, S.R., and Morgan, S.P. 2008. Religiosity and Fertility in the United States: The Role of Fertility Intentions. *Social Forces* 86(3), 1163–88.

Hirsch, J.S. 2003. *A Courtship after Marriage: Sexuality and Love in Mexican Transnational Families.* Berkeley: University of California Press.

Hirsch, J.S. and Wardlow, H. (eds) 2006. *Modern Loves: The Anthropology of Romantic Courtship and Companionate Marriage*. Ann Arbor: University of Michigan Press.

Hochschild, A.R. 1997. *The Time Bind: When Work Becomes Home and Home Becomes Work*. New York: Henry Holt.

Hochschild, A.R. 2003. *The Commercialization of Intimate Life: Notes from Home and Work*. Berkeley: University of California Press.

Human Rights Watch. 2006. *The Second Assault: Obstructing Access to Legal Abortion after Rape in Mexico*. New York: Human Rights Watch.

Jolane, C. 2006. Minority to Mainstream: The Amalgamation of Hispanic Customs and Traditions into American Popular Culture. *International Area Review* 9(1), 3–14.

Jankowiak, W.R. (ed.) 2008. *Intimacies: Love and Sex across Cultures*. New York: Columbia University Press.

Lakoff, G. 2008. *The Political Mind: Why You Can't Understand 21st-Century Politics with an 18th-Century Brain*. New York: Viking.

Landale, N.S. and Oropesa, R.S. 2007. Hispanic Families: Stability and Change. *Annual Review of Sociology* 33, 381–405.

Lichter, D.T. and Landale, N.S. 1995. 'Parental Work, Family Structure, and Poverty among Latino Children'. *Journal of Marriage and the Family* 57, 346–54.

McQuillan, K. 2004. When Does Religion Influence Fertility? *Sage Urban Studies Abstracts* 32, 4.

National Center for Health Statistics. 2004. *Teenagers in the United States: Sexual Activity, Contraceptive Use, and Childbearing, 2002*. Vital and Health Statistics, Series 23, No. 24. Hyattsville: US Department of Health and Human Services, Centers for Disease Control and Prevention.

National Research Council. 2006. *Hispanics and the Future of America*. Washington, DC: National Academies Press.

Nehring, D. 2005. Lo mismo, pero diferente: Reflexiones sobre el estudio del aspecto cultural de las relaciones de género. *Papeles de Población* 45, 221–46.

Oquendo, A.R. 1995. Re-Imagining the Latino/a Race, *12 Harvard BlackLetter Law Journal* 93, 96–7.

Padilla, M.B., Hirsch, J.S., Muñoz-Laboy, M., et al. (eds) 2007. *Love and Globalization: Transformations of Intimacy in the Contemporary World*. Nashville: Vanderbilt University Press.

Parrado, E.A. and Morgan, S.P. 2008. Intergenerational Fertility among Hispanic Women: New Evidence of Immigrant Assimilation, *Demography* 45(3), 651–71.

Passel, J.S., and Cohn, D. 2008. *U.S. Population Projections, 2005–2050*. Washington, DC: Pew Hispanic Center.

Plummer, K. 2003. *Intimate Citizenship: Private Decisions and Public Dialogues*. Seattle: University of Washington Press.

Portes, A. and Rumbaut, R.G. 2006. *Immigrant America: A Portrait*. Berkeley: University of California Press.

Rindfuss, R.R., Morgan, S.P. and Offutt, K. 1996. Education and the Changing Age Pattern of American Fertility: 1963–1989. *Demography* 33(3), 277–90.

Rostow, W.W. 1960/1971. *The Stages of Economic Growth: A Non-Communist Manifesto*. Cambridge: Cambridge University Press.

Rubin, H.J. and Rubin, I.S. 2005. *Qualitative Interviewing: The Art of Hearing Data*. Thousand Oaks: Sage.

Sennett, R. 2006. *The Culture of the New Capitalism*. New Haven: Yale University Press.

Steidel, A.G.L. and Contreras, J.M. 2003. A New Familism Scale for Use with Latino Populations. *Hispanic Journal of Behavioral Sciences* 25(3), 312–30.

Stern, S.J. 1995. *The Secret History of Gender: Women, Men and Power in Late Colonial Mexico*. Chapel Hill: University of North Carolina Press.

Swidler, A. 2001. *Talk of Love: How Culture Matters*. Chicago: University of Chicago Press.

Tuñón Páblos, J. 1987. *Mujeres en México: Una historia olvidada*. Mexico City: Planeta.

US Bureau of the Census. 2008. *Fertility of American Women: 2006*. Washington, DC: Current Population Reports.

Valenzuela, A. and Dornbusch, S.D. 1994. Familism and Social Capital in the Academic Achievement of Mexican Origin and Anglo Adolescents. *Social Science Quarterly* 75(1), 18–36.

Vega, W.A. 1995. The Study of Latino Families, in *Understanding Latino Families*, edited by R.E. Zambrana. Thousand Oaks: Sage, 3–17.

Villafuerte García, L. 1998. Los estudios del Seminario de Historia de las Mentalidades sobre la sexualidad, in *Sexualidades en México: Algunas aproximaciones desde la perspectiva de las ciencias sociales*, edited by I. Szasz and S. Lerner. Mexico City: El Colegio de México.

Westoff, C.F. and Marshall, E.A. 2010. Hispanic Fertility, Religion, and Religiousness in the US. *Population Research and Policy Review* 29(4), 441–52.

Chapter 9

Dual Pathways: Mexican Gay Immigrants, their US-Born Partners, and the Dynamics of Sexual Globalization

Héctor Carrillo

> I come from a ranch where you can't live your sexuality openly. And that's one of the reasons that I'm here. A friend brought me. He told me: "Why don't you seek new horizons, other opportunities, job opportunities? ... [You can] stay in my house and as soon as you get a job we can share the expenses." I came ... because I lost my job, but also because he told me about a gay [support] group and that fascinated me. Why? Because I was dragging with me a lot of misinformation.

With these words Santiago[1] described his reasons for moving from Mexico to San Diego, California. Santiago, like many other participants in the *Trayectos* Study[2] – my programme of research on the sexualities and HIV risk of Mexican gay and bisexual male migrants – was motivated to move to the United States by a mix of personal reasons, among which his sexuality and a desire for new forms of sexual and romantic intimacy figured prominently.

In this chapter I examine how the form of international migration that Santiago is a part of (which I call 'sexual migration' to differentiate it from primarily economic or family-related migration) is shaped by, and in turn also shapes, sexual globalization. My focus is on the mutually constitutive relationships between international migration and sexual globalization, and also on the contributions of Mexican gay men to so-called global gay sexualities. I first briefly discuss how the definition of sexual globalization has been expanded from an initial emphasis on the dissemination of sexuality-related ideas and practices from the North to the so-called Global South, to one that recognizes more complex interactions between global and local sexual discourses. Then, based on my findings, I examine whether revised conceptualization of those interactions provides an adequate framework for fully explaining the dynamics of cross-cultural sexual relations and the

---

1   The names of all research participants quoted are pseudonyms.

2   The *Trayectos* Study is supported by Award Number ROIHD042919 from the US National Institute of Child Health and Human Development. The content is solely the responsibility of the author and does not necessarily represent the official views of the National Institute of Child Health and Human Development or the National Institutes of Health.

formation of current local and global sexual cultures and intimacies. I argue that one more step is necessary: giving greater consideration to the contributions of the Global South to sexual globalization – a feature of the phenomenon that for the most part has only been hinted at in the literature and has rarely been documented empirically. Such reframing may help us rethink sexual globalization as an increasingly bidirectional exchange that is prompted, at least in part, by the flows of people across international borders, including the relocation of international sexual migrants from poor to rich countries. As I demonstrate, the relocation of gay and bisexual Mexican men to the United States prompts sexuality-related changes that affect not only the immigrant communities or their communities back in Mexico, but also the gay men with whom they interact in the United States.

Sexual Globalization and Locality

Academics have been interested in the globalization of sexual expressions, discourses, identities, and intimacies for almost 20 years. Dennis Altman (1996: 77), in an early formulation of this concept, refers to the internationalization of gay identities in these terms:

> Images of young men in baseball caps and Reeboks on the streets of Budapest or São Paulo, of "lipstick lesbians" flirting on portable telephones in Bangkok or demonstrating in the streets of Tokyo – none of which are fictitious – are part of the construction of a new category, or more accurately the expansion of an existing Western category, that is part of the rapid globalization of lifestyle and identity politics, the simultaneous disappearance of old concepts and invention of new ones.

This view, which has received some support but also has been strongly criticized as overly simplistic, reflects a sense of an accelerated dissemination of sexuality-related discourses, practices, and identities from the United States and other rich countries of the North to other nations across the globe – a dissemination that is seen as greatly facilitated by the characteristics of advanced capitalism and advances in technology, by the availability of news and cultural interpretations through the mass media, and by the ever growing numbers of people who engage in international travel. Scholars also have associated the notion of accelerated dissemination with a kind of global exchange that is perceived as qualitatively different from those of previous historical times because, as suggested by Boellstorff and Leap (2004: 5), it has 'fundamentally transform[ed] the relationship between space and subjectivity', making it possible for sexual expressions from rich countries to rapidly travel far and wide and become recognizable even in quite unlikely distant places.

Altman's argument contained nuances and qualifications that were not always acknowledged by critics.[3] But one effect of the ensuing discussion was the important clarification that sexual globalization does not erase the specificities of local sexual cultures or the effects of local histories (Johnson, Jackson and Herdt 2000, Sánchez-Eppler and Patton 2000, Adam 2001, Altman 2001, Jackson 2001, Carrillo 2004, Manalansan IV 2005). This awareness coincided with a growing sense that global (or 'modern', or 'postmodern') interpretations of the organization of sexual desires and intimacies often coexist and have become hybridized with local (or 'traditional') interpretations, often generating sexual interpretations that must simultaneously be read as both 'global' and 'local'.

Growing consensus about this interplay between global and local, however, has not necessarily translated into agreement about how best to account for the interactions between the two in analysing specific sexual interpretations or expressions within a particular location. One issue that has been raised, for instance, relates to a perceived over-generalization and naïve over-simplification of the complex processes involved in the 'exportation' of global sexuality-related ideas and practices (Johnson, Jackson and Herdt 2000, Boellstorff and Leap 2004). The concern is that, in spite of awareness about interaction between global and local discourses, the dominant views of sexual globalization treat the global dissemination of sexual expressions generated in the United States – in the case of lesbian, gay, bisexual, and transgender (LBGT) identities, in the form of the reliance on 'gay English', the adoption of rainbow flags, etc. – as signposts of a worldwide homogenization of sexuality that will eventually overcome, or erase, local sexual cultures (Boellstorff and Leap 2004, Jackson 2004, Binnie 2004).

A related concern is that, in arguing the case of sexual globalization, observers are often quick to dichotomize the global and the local. Writing about Thailand, Peter Jackson (2001: 9) notices that:

> when a gender/sex category in an Asian society happens to be labelled with an indigenous term, such as *kathoey* in Thailand, then Western analysts are often prepared to grant that category a local history. However, if a Thai man self-identifies with the label "gay", then Western observers commonly overlook the possibility of a local history for this identity, and talk instead of "globalizing influences" and the "borrowing of Western models".

This observation raises questions about how best to account for constant interactions between foreign and local interpretations, and how to recognize that as foreign concepts become incorporated into a local sexual history they usually acquire local meanings that can make them distinct (Jackson 2001, Carrillo 2002,

---

3   In his early writing on this topic Altman (1996, 79) already recognized a need to find 'the right balance between tradition and modernity, while recognizing that these terms themselves are vague, problematic, and politically contested'.

Boellstorff 2005). In this sense, such arguments sound a cautionary note that all global interpretations should always be simultaneously seen through a local lens.

Another way of thinking about this issue is that notions derived from a global discourse – say, for instance the labels 'gay' or 'lesbian' – are redefined as they travel, in order for them to fit within the cultural logics of each country or region. An interesting example is provided by the Indonesian identities associated with the labels 'gay' and 'lesbi', as identified by anthropologist Tom Boellstorff (2005), which differ significantly from the definitions of 'gay' and 'lesbian' in the United States. Boellstorff labels this process of redefinition 'dubbing culture', a reference to the process of cultural translation that accompanies the translation of dialogue in dubbed films. Similarly, in describing this process with an emphasis on the blending between foreign and local interpretation that takes place, I have labelled it 'sexual hybridity' (Carrillo 2002).[4] As Povinelli and Chauncey (1999: 441) note, attempts to capture these complex interactions between the global and the local have generated other descriptors, including the term 'glocal' and other 'conceptual conjunctions and neologisms that describe, or more simply that demarcate, the dense, variegated traffic in cultural representations, people, and capital that increasingly characterizes the social life of people around the world'.

A third related concern has to do with the assumption that sexual globalization involves a unidirectional exportation of sexuality-related interpretations from the United States and other rich countries to the rest of the world (Boellstorff and Leap 2004). Jackson (2001: 14), for instance, problematizes this assumption when he states:

> Globalization is not merely a one-way process transferring ideas, aesthetics and sex-cultural patterns from the West to "the rest". Globalization also needs to be understood as the operation of common processes in diverse locales, inciting semi-independent and parallel developments in these different places. In other words, gay and other new identities may have multiple origins in a globalizing world.

For Jackson, however, this observation does not mean that we should see sexual globalization as a bi-directional exchange between North and South. His critique instead leads him to the conclusion that sexual globalization may not be occurring at all beyond a very superficial level. Jackson (2001: 22) writes: 'there is no global gay, lesbian, or queer subject, only locally constituted g/l/t subjects, who at times appropriate elements of a global idiom and style as strategies in their locally determined and locally directed resistances'.[5]

---

4   For more on this process of appropriation and reinterpretation of sexual labels and categories see also Sánchez-Eppler and Patton (2000), Boellstorff (2004), Jackson (2004), and the various other chapters in Leap and Boellstorff (2004).

5   Of concern, as Binnie (2004: 36) points out, is the possible conclusion that the local is the only 'site of authenticity' for sexuality. Johnson, Jackson and Herdt (2000: 362)

The problem with this statement is that reducing the role of sexual global discourse to that of a mere cultural tool – a 'global idiom and style' that simply provide a language that can be adapted to meet local cultural needs and conditions – curtails opportunities to fully account for the complex dynamics of the exchange, including the potential contributions on the part of the countries of the South to global sexuality discourses. It then becomes easy to miss how the local cultural productions of the South – the complex reinterpretations and forms of hybridization that are taking place there – may in turn be put into global circulation and thus also affect the very same foreign concepts and labels that possibly prompted them in the first place.[6]

Instead, reconceiving sexual globalization as an increasingly bidirectional exchange between North and South may prove to be quite productive – assuming it can be done without discounting the profound inequalities between North and South (and the pernicious effects of colonialism, postcolonialism, and cultural imperialism),[7] which may help explain why the contributions of the South to sexual globalization may still be relatively modest. Furthermore, viewing sexual globalization as a two-way street between North and South may open the possibility of studying the sexual cultures of the North not only as 'influencers' of global sexual cultures, but also as recipients of sexual interpretations, ideas, and practices arriving from abroad, including from the Global South.

In the specific case that concerns me, reconceiving of sexual globalization as a two-way street invites us to identify not only local appropriations in Mexico of globally circulating discourses or local processes of reinterpretation, *but also* Mexicans' own efforts to circulate their interpretations within a global sexual landscape and to influence and shape global sexualities and intimacies. As I show in this chapter, Mexican gay and bisexual immigrants often find themselves forced to reflect about both 'Mexican' and 'US' interpretations about what it means to lead a gay life. Their reflections often start before they leave and only intensify after they arrive in the United States, particularly as they engage in, and learn to negotiate, cross-cultural relations (sexual and otherwise). The contrasts that they perceive are sometimes subtle and sometimes dramatic, but taken together they

---

propose an intermediate level of analysis – that of 'critical regionalities', a term that is meant to '[recognize] the historicity of world areas or regions' (e.g. Asia, Latin America, Europe) as 'both theoretically and politically useful ... "fictions" or "partial truths"'. In this reading, a slight, but possibly productive, tension emerges between the idea that all sexualities are constituted locally and the notion of shared cultures among countries with common cultural background or histories.

6 See Binnie (2004: 7–8) on the 'failure to acknowledge non-western perspectives on sexualities' and the complications of defining 'what constitutes the centre and the margins' in analyses of sexual globalization.

7 On the relationships between colonialism, postcolonialism, and sexuality, see McClintock (1995), Young (1995), Hawley (2001b), and Stoller (2002), among other authors working on these topics.

provide a window for observing the dynamics of sexual globalization that I have discussed in this section. I turn to those narratives after a brief description of the *Trayectos* study.

The *Trayectos* Study

Santiago, whom I quoted earlier, is one of the 81 self-identified gay or bisexual men who were born or raised in Mexico and who participated in the *Trayectos* study. This research is based on ethnographic observations in venues where Mexican gay immigrant men socialize and in-depth interviews with 150 men. In addition to the 81 Mexican participants, my research team and I interviewed 35 US Latinos for comparison purposes, and 34 non-Latinos who were born or raised in the United States and who had been involved in recent sexual or romantic relations with Mexican or Latino men. One-hundred and fifteen of the interviewees returned for a follow-up interview a year after their initial interview. During these follow-up interviews, we further explored issues that participants had previously discussed and obtained updates on their sexual and romantic lives during the previous year.

This chapter is primarily based on systematic analysis of the Mexican men's narratives on their motivations for migration and their cross-cultural encounters with gay men in the United States. As needed, I also draw from the interviews with American men, which provide helpful additional perspectives on the Mexicans' sexualities and intimacies. I begin by elaborating on Santiago's story and, in the process, introduce some of the key empirical themes.

Santiago's Sexual Migration to San Diego

Santiago grew up in a small town in north-western Mexico. When he was a teenager, his father, a medical doctor, scolded him for not acting in a sufficiently masculine way. By then, Santiago had begun to realize his attraction to men and also felt that this made him a sinner. Prompted by suspicion that Santiago had 'homosexual tendencies', his father took him to see a psychologist and an endocrinologist in the hope that they would intervene to prevent his son from becoming a homosexual. Eventually Santiago came to understand that he was sexually attracted to both women and men, but he strongly disagreed with bisexuality as an identity. He says, however, that later he adopted an identity as *homosexual* and *gay* 'without difficulty'.

His search for greater sexual freedom began at the age of 18, when he moved to the capital of his Mexican state where he attended college and became a journalist. Santiago was unable at that point to pursue his sexual interest in men. In his late twenties he decided to marry a woman – whom he says he loved – and stayed married to her for three years, a period that he describes as 'living in hell' because he had to be extremely vigilant about repressing his sexual desires for men. Santiago says that, prior to their marriage, he had told his wife that he felt 'different', that he was attracted to men, and that he wanted to change. At the time, his therapist had authoritatively instructed him that there was no such thing as homosexuality. He had instead diagnosed him as fixated on a dangerous adolescent obsession for young men. Santiago adds that, making matters worse, his wife's younger brother began making sexual advances toward him, which prompted him to avoid his wife's family home. Santiago, however, eventually gave in and initiated sexual contact with his brother-in-law. This was his first same-sex sexual experience since his early teenage years, when he had participated in exploratory sexual games with some of his male friends.

Two years into his marriage, while Santiago and his wife were at a newsstand, his wife noticed his interest in a gay magazine. She asked him if the magazine had caught his attention, and he told her that he was interested in learning more about the topic. She encouraged him to buy it, and this simple act opened a first window for him into the world of global gay identities. He not only read the magazine from front to back that same night, but he also decided to respond to some of the personal ads in the magazine. Santiago says that the magazine prompted him to think '*de aquí soy*' ('this is where I belong'). Santiago subsequently placed a personal ad of his own in a different American gay magazine that he picked up at a gay bar in Phoenix, Arizona, where he lived temporarily with his wife and son. In response to this ad, he received many letters from American gay men, as well as from gay men in other countries. Through this medium he also made contact with the man who eventually helped him move to San Diego.

After divorcing his wife, Santiago was now living by himself in a different Mexican city. He also had initiated a sexual life with men, which mainly consisted of sporadic sexual encounters with non-gay-identified young men from his neighbourhood. The first among these sexual partners had passed on to others word of Santiago's sexual availability, and this started a chain reaction (it helped that Santiago had a place of his own where the sex could happen, so young men who were aware of his reputation came looking for him). Santiago's descriptions of these connections make them seem at once alluring and frustrating. Santiago complains that these men never kissed him. Other *Trayectos* participants had a similar complaint. They sense that non-gay-identified Mexican men avoid kissing other men to signal their unwillingness to pursue greater intimacy. Santiago says: 'I am attracted to their bodies, but they don't stop feeling like men. When they're with you, they stress "I like women". And then you have to ask yourself, "what am I doing here?" … But one had to be very aware of that to avoid being emotionally hurt.'

Santiago had also made some gay friends in his new city and had found gay bars in the state capital – which men attended surreptitiously – but was aware of the existence of visible gay cultures in larger cities such as Mexico City. Yet he was wary of what he had heard about Mexico City: that the city was too dangerous and that there was much promiscuity there. As he explored his gay sexuality further, Santiago was particularly impressed by a letter that he received from a young gay man in San Diego. They exchanged more than 15 letters and they also talked on the phone. His conversations with this man prompted him to recognize how tired he was of, in his own words, '*vivir en el clóset*' ('living in the closet'). He incrementally told family members about his homosexuality and, when he was fired from his job for unrelated reasons (although he has a nagging suspicion that being gay was part of why he was fired), he listened carefully to his friend's advice that he should move to San Diego. He was particularly curious about what his friend described as a 'Latino organization where they provide advice to gay men'. At the time of his interview, a month after arriving in San Diego, Santiago had already attended three talks there. Santiago found these meetings:

> … very fascinating, from a cultural point of view. I have learned very much about something that I hadn't learned in many years. The more I learn, the more I feel ignorant and realize how much more I have to learn. With him [his San Diego friend] I have learned a lot, in particular about having a positive attitude about homosexuality. I feel so comfortable with him, and he feels less lonely, and I do too.

Although this friendship was not sexual or romantic, it provided Santiago with the kind of intimacy with a man that he craved, and which he had not encountered with others in Mexico. This was also Santiago's first exposure to the notion of having a roommate – something which, in his view, would be automatically suspect in his Mexican city. 'It wouldn't look good for two men [there] to live with each other', he says. He fantasized about finding the same kind of intimacy within a romantic relationship with a gay man. During his short time in San Diego he was also already participating in mainstream gay culture and attending gay dance clubs, which he really liked. He had also heard about San Diego's gay bathhouses and about a local nude beach, but he had not yet been to either.

Santiago was one of the few participants who did not return for a follow-up interview. At the time of his initial interview he was concerned that he might not find a job at his level of training, and he seemed wary about doing menial jobs, which many of his counterparts did. We lost contact with Santiago over the course of the year and we later found out that he had returned to Mexico, which suggests that San Diego provided only a temporary respite in his search for a gay identity and for new forms of intimacy. We can only wonder what he brought back with him culturally and how it may have influenced others in his local community.

Constructing Imaginaries of the Global

Other immigrant men indeed had migrated to the United States motivated in part by what other immigrants who returned to Mexico had told them. For instance, Octavio, who grew up in a small town in the southern part of Mexico, recalls hearing from migrants that people in the United States are more liberal and have different lifestyles from those that they knew in Mexico. In particular, two migrants whom he described as *homosexuales* 'who had been living in this country [the United States] for a long time' told him the following:

> They said that in this country homosexuals are not discriminated against – not like in Mexico where they are discriminated against in many places. They treat them badly; they beat them up, just for being homosexual. And they said that doesn't happen here. That here one can dress as a woman, or that you can walk on the street as who you are: gay. And no one says anything. And that was a recurrent thought – that here they're not treated badly. Plus there is the economic factor as well.

Similarly, Gonzalo, who grew up in a rural area of north-western Mexico and then moved to a large coastal resort, describes the information that he received from others as he was beginning to imagine the possibility of starting a new life in the United States. Gonzalo said,

> Acquaintances told me: "Go there. There are many gays there. You can be freer, you can work wherever you want, and ... no one makes fun of you. No one robs you. If someone insults you for being gay, you call the police and the police will defend you."

Mexican gay migrants rely on these idealizations of American sexual liberalism in deciding whether to try their own luck by moving to the United States. Their impressions contain a somewhat unrealistic sense of the widespread legal protections for gay people in the United States – 'you call the police and the police will defend you' – that not only surprise them, but also contrast greatly with their own experiences in Mexico. Indeed, some of these men bitterly complain about negative experiences that they had with the local police in their Mexican locations, where the police not only offered no protection against homophobia, but instead harassed them or extorted money from them. Their view of the United States also references a sense of the laissez-faire attitudes of American individualism – 'you can walk on the street as who you are: gay ... and no one says anything'. Their informants, and later themselves, also tend to exaggerate the freedoms that gay people actually enjoy in the United States, and they portray the whole country as homogenously progressive on LGBT issues (and, by extension, Mexico as homogenously backward).

Nonetheless, these messages, often delivered directly by those who have witnessed gay life in the United States (not only migrants, but also Mexican tourists who visited US cities and American tourists visiting Mexico), complement other representations of American gay life that Mexican gay and bisexual men access through the mass media and the Internet. These include television shows such as *Will and Grace* or the American version of *Queer as Folk*, foreign movies with gay themes, gay Internet sites, gay Internet-based social media, and the local and international Spanish news media (Carrillo 2002). These images of greater sexual freedoms in the United States, however, partially obscure the signs of local change within Mexico in relation to gay issues which, as in the United States, are more readily evident in large urban centres (Carrillo 2002, 2007).

It is not surprising, for instance, that in talking about same-sex marriage – a topic that was being heavily debated in California at the time of my interviews – most immigrant men could not imagine that same-sex marriage would ever be approved anywhere in Mexico, or opined that its approval in Mexico would only be possible long after same-sex marriage was a reality in all of the United States, if ever. Yet, not long after my team and I finished conducting these interviews, as a result of rather expedient local political processes, Mexico City and the northern Mexican state of Coahuila approved separate civil-unions laws, followed soon after by the approval of a same-sex marriage law in Mexico City. Such developments could not be anticipated by most of the *Trayectos* participants. And, indeed, we ought to consider that the successes of the Mexican LGBT movement are not just a product of globalization, but instead reflect a local history of gay and lesbian activism that dates back to the 1970s (de la Dehesa 2010).

Transporting Mexican Gay Sexual Intimacies

Importantly, these men's lack of confidence about gay rights in Mexico, or the possibility of living fully open gay lives there, does not mean that they themselves were not familiar with, or had not adopted, a Mexican gay discourse. A majority of them self-identified as gay by the time that they left Mexico and more than half were practicing sexualities and engaging in same-sex intimacies that resemble the features of so-called global gay identities and sexualities. Those features include expectations of sexual reciprocity and role versatility between partners, as well as the perception that gay men can be masculine or feminine, and also that they are gay regardless of the specific roles that they play during sex. These sexualities contrast with the *pasivo/activo* model of same-sex male sexualities that was first identified by American anthropologists in Mexico in the late 1960s, which is still pervasive and prominent in depictions of Mexican and Latino male homosexualities, particularly in the United States (Almaguer 1991, Carrier 1972, 1976, 1995, Taylor 1978, 1986). Such depictions persist in spite of the significant changes that the research on sexualities in Mexico has detected over the past four decades.[8]

---

8   For reflections on the contemporary cultural role of the *pasivo/activo* model, see Vidal Ortiz et al. (2010). See also Cantú's (2009) critique of this model, which he views as a cultural-deficit model that exoticizes Mexicans and constructs them as an 'Other'. This argument seems related to a tension noted by Altman (1996: 87) 'between political economy, which argues for universalizing trends, and anthropology, which argues for cultural specificities'.

In my own research in Guadalajara in the 1990s (Carrillo 1999, 2002, 2003), I observed that although the *pasivo/activo* model had not disappeared, it co-existed and had become hybridized with more contemporary Mexican interpretations of gay identities, as part of the emergence of significant local urban gay cultures. Mexican gay cultures indeed were already forming at the time that Joseph Carrier (1972, 1976, 1995) and Clark Taylor (1978, 1986) were conducting their ground-breaking work in Guadalajara and Mexico City (although these authors perhaps emphasized the patterns that appeared to them most distinctly Mexican at the time), and thus they now have a long local history whose origins likely date back to the decades preceding the 1960s.[9] Other recent empirical research in Mexico has also provided nuanced descriptions of gay male identities, cultures, and lives in contemporary urban Mexico (Gallego Montes 2010, Laguarda 2011, List 2005, Nuñez Noriega 1999 [1994], 2007).

Are these Mexicans' gay lives the same as those of their counterparts in the United States? They do resemble them in general form. However, once in the United States immigrant gay Mexican men discover that their discourses of gay sexuality and intimacy differ from those of American gay men in a number of interesting and significant ways.

The differences become particularly evident within their narratives of cross-cultural sexual encounters involving non-Latino US gay men. For many of the Mexican gay immigrants in my study, an important (and perhaps somewhat idealized) ingredient of sexual encounters, even casual ones, is the pursuit of passionate intimacy. These men generally believe that passionate intimacy can be fostered through kissing, embracing, full-body interaction, spontaneity, mutual surrender, and an explicit build-up of intensity leading to mutual sexual ecstasy, among other features. For instance, Leopoldo says the following:

> That word, passion, is when you feel that adrenaline running through the body. You are with a person and you feel the desire to embrace him, to hold him tightly (*estrujarlo*), to kiss him – that desire to eat him. That is, you feel that connection, that passion to say "I love it. It fascinates me. I want to touch you. I want to feel you. I don't want to let you go. I want this to last hours". That is passion.

Participants highlight that further confirmation of the passionate nature of a sexual interaction comes after orgasm in the form of extended caressing and embracing, kissing, and conversation meant to signal mutual acknowledgment. They depict sexually passionate encounters as never ending abruptly, and they appreciate the implementation of small romantic gestures as particularly essential for their successful culmination. For Alvaro, 'after finishing you stay embraced, you stay together longer, or you get up and take a shower together'. Overall, these men

---

9   Unfortunately, however, no historians to my knowledge have yet taken up the project of systematically documenting the formation of urban male homosexualities in Mexico throughout the twentieth century.

do not see this discourse of sexual passion as incompatible with one-time sexual encounters in which partners are fully aware that nothing else may happen between them afterward.

By contrast, in their sexual interactions with American gay men, particularly with white men, they perceive that expectations about intimacy are different. They often find those cross-cultural interactions to be much more instrumental, calculated, mechanical, and focused on the production of sexual pleasure instead of sexual intimacy. For those reasons they interpret those interactions as less or not sexually passionate. Horacio, for instance, says that 'Americans' (meaning whites) 'don't give you that affection. ... they don't even embrace you'. Others feel that with American white men 'it is always the same, pum, pum ... they are rather cold, like a robot' (Bonifacio), that 'they [white American men] are only interested in sex; there are fewer [romantic] details during the sexual relationship' (Armando), and that white men are 'very simple, very plastic' (Roy). In Gerardo's opinion, '... they are cold during sex; they just stay like that, like, they don't like to kiss here, to kiss there, to whisper things in your ear. For them many times it is just what they came for (*a lo que te truje*)'. These men also complain that white American men tend to end sexual interactions abruptly. 'It is just sex, they finish it and that's it', says Edwin, and Leopoldo complains that right after orgasm, an American partner said to him: '"It was a pleasure ... now dress and leave. I'm done." And maybe Latinos want to stay embraced, and want more affection. I tell you ... the human part.' Leopoldo then recalls that some American partners do not even ask his name, which he reads as meaning that they are thinking, 'Good bye ... I don't care' and as a clear confirmation of the impersonality of these sexual encounters.

A minority among these immigrant men, however, recognize that sexual passion for American white gay men may mean something different, and in some cases they express admiration for what they see as greater sexual liberalism in mainstream American urban gay cultures (which confirms imaginaries about a more sexually liberal north). As Aldo puts it, 'there are Americans who are very passionate. ... I really admire Americans. They are very liberal in bed'. For him, Mexicans, by contrast, tend to be very sexually inhibited during sex. In this view, sexual liberalism is defined in terms of directness, the existence of venues openly designed just for the pursuit of easy sex (such as gay bathhouses), an openness toward alternative partnering arrangements (including threesomes, open relationships, and group sex), and greater acceptance of the practices associated with BDSM (an acronym that encompasses practices of bondage, discipline, submission, and sadomasochism).

This does not mean that these features are not also found in Mexico; for instance, there is evidence of their presence in the form of sex clubs in large Mexican cities and of gay sex subcultures that emulate American ones. However, many of the immigrant men in my study had had no access to, or no interest in, those practices and subcultures.[10]

In the end, while some of these immigrant men adopt the practices that they perceive are more readily available within US urban gay cultures, others resist them and instead articulate alternative forms of sexual intimacy that are informed by their personal histories and socialization in Mexico. For the purposes of this chapter, I am particularly interested in the latter group (which in fact is more prevalent in my study) because their narratives provide a clearer opportunity to examine ways in which forms of sexual intimacy arriving from the South may influence those in the North.

Changing the Gay North

In the United States, many of the immigrant men who value the discourse of passionate intimacy that I described above do seek to participate in US gay life, but simultaneously seek to maintain the patterns of sexual interactions that they favour. In other words, although they are exposed to new forms of sexual intimacy – and in fact some of them do learn to like them and become adept at implementing them – these immigrant men are not just subjected to the expectations of American sexual styles. Instead, they articulate alternative interpretations of gay male sexuality that are informed by their own background and experience.

Some achieve this by choosing to seek sex or romantic relationships with other Mexicans or, alternatively, with US Latinos, with whom they feel that they share a common cultural understanding in spite of some differences caused by national origin. Yet some who are particularly sexually attracted to non-Latino men (primarily white men for the participants in my study, but in certain cases African Americans), search for partners who appear to be amenable to, or already interested in, Mexican forms of social and sexual interaction. In so doing, they sometimes look for subtle indicators of the potential for a non-Latino man to be passionate in a way that is similar to their own. In Ronaldo's experience, 'I notice it. You can tell. I don't know: how they shake hands, or how they do in a single kiss'. Some of their US-born Latino counterparts take this further by referring to their assessments of a man's ability to dance to Latin beats. 'If we see somebody that can't dance, we basically have assumed already that they are horrible in bed', says Otón. This idea is reiterated by Eugenio, also a US-born Latino, when he says, '... the way they dance, that's one of my screening [criteria]. Like, if they can't dance and they just kind of do that white boy wiggle, then it's like you don't know how to move. And if you can't move, you can't move. You know what I'm saying?'

---

10   Yet, the availability of these alternative forms of sexual intimacy may be increasing in Mexico particularly given the rapid expansion of access to the Internet.

These comments suggest that sexual passion (or its absence) is perceived as a fixed and unchangeable trait. However, some of the Mexican immigrant men feel instead that sexual passion can be taught and that they can play a role in doing that. Aurelio, for instance, views white US-born men as 'seeking passion, wanting to learn', and Reinaldo says emphatically, 'you can teach them, you can teach them'.

Indeed, Mexican gay men's cultural performances do find a receptive audience among some US non-Latino gay men, including those who are particularly sexually attracted to Mexican/Latino gay men or who feel that exposure to Mexican/Latino male partners opens new cultural horizons. For instance, Peter (US-born white) describes sex with a Mexican boyfriend in these terms:

> Like when we are having sex, he likes to look into our eyes, and to talk. And, you know, the sex with white guys that I've had, it just seems to be more like sex, and that's it, over and done with. You know, he likes to cuddle and to kiss more and to hold and to look into the eyes. ... You know, he's the first partner that I've had that likes to communicate while we're having sex on that aspect, you know. "How are you feeling?"

He then concludes: 'I guess in a way it seems like he's training me how to be more passionate.'

This group also includes American men who feel that they themselves are sexually passionate, and who feel at odds with the scripts and expectations of mainstream sexual interaction in urban US gay cultures. These men find in Mexican/Latino men particularly like-minded partners. For example, Ray (Italian American) says, 'Well I'm passionate too ... I am with them [Latinos], and ... I'm the same way'. Brian (US-born white) similarly states:

> I think I am very passion (sic) ... I like to be both aggressive and really intimate, really romantic, really touchy. I'm all about making sex an art, like a dance. ... To me like those, the intermingling of bodies in that space is so beautiful. ... I'd say I'm probably ... more passionate than the average white guy ... but I think I'm also a lot more passionate than the average Latino guy.

As these comments suggest, when American non-Latino gay men crave passionate intimacy within casual sexual encounters, they often turn to Latinos in search for it. Austin, for instance, says:

> I find that it's easier with Latino men. Because ... maybe they grew up with inter-joined intimacy. Go to [the mall]. You'll see men who are straight or heterosexual ... with their arm around each other. And I just thought that's so cool because they're not embarrassed about that. Where, heaven forbid you'd see two Caucasians from, you know, Nebraska, with their arm around each other. ... It's not a sexual thing; it's a feeling of ... the ability to show your expressions of love or caring ...

The impact of gay Mexican immigrant men on US sexual culture is underscored by the comments from several non-Latinos in the *Trayectos* study who did not discover their sexual affinity towards Mexicans or Latinos until they arrived in a city that had a large Latino population. Sometimes their first contact with Latinos took place in San Diego; and in some cases, upon arriving in San Diego they transferred to Mexicans/Latinos a previous attraction to ethnic men of Mediterranean origin – such as Greeks or Italians – who themselves have a reputation as romantic and sexually passionate.

Conclusion

In their cross-cultural relations within American gay communities, Mexican gay immigrants make their own contribution to the globalization of sexualities, in this case by assertively enacting forms of gay intimacy that they see as consistent with their own culture and upbringing in Mexico. It is perhaps not surprising that, in discussing the origins of the notion of Mexican sexual passion and intimacy, *Trayectos* participants most commonly refer to culture and family life. Some then use their own assessments of cultural difference to launch a strong critique of what they see as the excessive individuality, shallowness, and instrumentality of American society.

The question about the extent to which these Mexican immigrants' sexual intimacies affect sexual globalization is an open one. Comparatively speaking – given the enormous inequalities in terms of power and economics between the United States and Mexico – the influence of these Mexican gay immigrants in the North may admittedly be modest. But seen from a different angle, their questioning of American gay sexuality and American society, and their desire to maintain forms of sexual intimacy that they see as consistent with their own version of global gay identities, are suggestive of the ability of the 'gay subaltern to speak' – to invoke John Hawley's (2001a: 5) expansion of Gayatri Spivak's well-known provocation. As time passes, it would seem likely that more voices originating in the so-called global South will continue to be raised, not only locally but also in immigrant destination countries, such as the United States, which are typically seen as the sources of all global discourses on sexual intimacies. In fact, in addition to these Mexican men, other groups of gay immigrant similarly articulate alternative perspectives on gay sexualities and identities, including those who participated in Martin Manalansan's (2003) study of Filipino gay migrants in New York City. For instance, Manalansan reports that his participants transform Filipino religious pageantry into gay pageantry and in the process also launch a critique of American mainstream gay culture.

The data that I have presented highlight the exportation of forms of gay sexual intimacy that are deemed as more readily Mexican – albeit not necessarily 'traditionally' Mexican in the same way as the *pasivo/activo* model. Those affective exports, however, must be seen as part of a larger constellation of Mexican or

Latino cultural expressions that may increasingly play a role within the mainstream gay cultures in American cities with large Latino immigrant populations. Non-Latino participants in *Trayectos*, for instance, talk about being exposed through boyfriends to extended Mexican/Latino family life, which they sometimes see as contrasting with the less-involved and more distant relations in their own families, and they remark on the ease with which children in their boyfriends' families start referring to them as 'uncles'. In San Diego, almost every mainstream gay dance club and bar had a weekly Latino night at the time of my study, featuring Latin dance music that would normally be absent, and on those nights the participation of men of other racial or ethnic backgrounds was not negligible. Similarly, many gay men from San Diego, Latino and non-Latino, participate in the mainstream gay cultures of Tijuana, just on the other side of the US-Mexico border, in part because the drinking age in Tijuana is three years lower than in California (18 compared to 21), but also because the gay cultural expressions in Mexico have their own appeal.

Although I have suggested we attend to the exportation of Mexican gay intimacy to the US, it is important to avoid the view that all that the global South has to contribute to sexual globalization is emotions – what Dennis Altman (2001: 40), reacting to Marta Savigliano's discussion of the 'world economy of passion', notes as the perception 'that the globalization of emotions runs in one direction', from South to North. In Savigliano's (1994: 237) words:

> [p]arallelling the extraction of material goods and labor from the Third World, the passion-poor core countries of the capitalist world system have been appropriating emotional and affective practices from their colonies for several centuries ... The Third World's emotional and expressive actions and arts have been categorized, homogenized, and transformed into commodities suitable for the First World's consumption.

The discourse of passionate intimacy that Mexican gay migrants articulate indeed also represents more than an appropriation of Southern emotions on the part of the North. It also signifies the will of Mexican gay immigrants to assert themselves and their worldview within a society in which they are often marginalized, as well as their efforts to launch a broader critique of American social relations and to formulate an alternative way of being gay that challenges the notion that there is only one form of global gayness. Moreover, their project is a 'modern' one. Their formulations are not meant to produce a sense of 'feeling backward' – to reference the catchy phrase with which Heather Love (2007) describes the abjections and impossible same-sex love of a queer past – but one of 'feeling forward'. These men are not proposing a nostalgic return to abandoned traditions or old histories. They seek instead to induce a strong sense of affection into US sexual liberalism, as well as to show that there need be no contradiction between passionate intimacy and free, casual gay sex.

And yet, paradoxically, these gay migrants also use their seemingly more liberalized experiences in the United States – which, as we saw, include a relaxing sense of greater anonymity and freedom to be openly gay as well as explicit legal protections that validate their sexualities – both in justifying their decision to stay and explaining to their counterparts in Mexico what they may get from going north. They generate, together with other US gay men, an alternative 'culture of migration' that intersects with, but also differs from, the more heteronormative version – involving a mix of economics and reciprocity created through kinship – identified in the literature on Mexican migration (Kandel and Massey 2002; Massey, Goldring, and Durand 1994; Wilson 2010). In this sense, they produce dual pathways through which they themselves – and their supporters – contribute to the globalization of gay sexualities both in Mexico and in the United States.

Bibliography

Adam, B.D. 2001. Globalization and the Mobilization of Gay and Lesbian Communities, in *Globalization and Social Movements*, edited by P. Hamel, H. Lustinger-Thaler, J. Nederveen Pieterse and S. Roseneil. Houndmills: Palgrave Macmillan, 166–79.

Almaguer, T. 1991. Chicano Men: A Cartography of Homosexual Identity and Behavior. *Journal of Feminist Cultural Studies* 3(2), 75–99.

Altman, D. 1996. Rupture or Continuity? The Internalization of Gay Identities. *Social Text* 14(3), 78–94.

Altman, D. 2001. *Global Sex*. Chicago: University of Chicago Press.

Binnie, J. 2004. *The Globalization of Sexuality*. Thousand Oaks: Sage Publications.

Boellstorff, T. 2004. 'Authentic, of Course!': Gay Language in Indonesia and Cultures of Belonging, in *Speaking in Queer Tongues: Globalization and Gay Language*, edited by W.L. Leap and T. Boellstorff. Urbana: University of Illinois Press, 181–201.

Boellstorff, T. 2005. *The Gay Archipelago: Sexuality and Nation in Indonesia*. Princeton: Princeton University Press.

Boellstorff, T. and Leap, W.L. 2004. Introduction: Globalization and 'New' Articulations of Same-Sex Desire, in *Speaking in Queer Tongues: Globalization and Gay Language*, edited by W.L. Leap and T. Boellstorff. Urbana: University of Illinois Press, 1–21.

Cantú Jr., L. 2009. *The Sexuality of Migration: Border Crossings and Mexican Immigrant Men,* edited by Nancy A. Naples and Salvador Vidal-Ortiz. New York: New York University Press.

Carrier, J.M. 1972. *Urban Mexican Male Encounters: An Analysis of Participants and Coping Strategies*. Unpublished doctoral dissertation. Irvine: University of California.

Carrier, J.M. 1976. Cultural Factors Affecting Urban Mexican Male Homosexual Behavior. *Archives of Sexual Behavior* 5, 103–24.

Carrier, J.M. 1995. *De Los Otros: Intimacy and Homosexuality among Mexican Men.* New York: Columbia University Press.

Carrillo, H. 1999. Cultural Change, Hybridity and Contemporary Male Homosexuality in Mexico. *Culture, Health and Sexuality* 1(3), 223–38.

Carrillo, H. 2002. *The Night is Young: Sexuality in Mexico in the Time of AIDS.* Chicago: University of Chicago Press.

Carrillo, H. 2003. Neither Machos nor Maricones: Masculinity and Emerging Male Homosexual Identities in Mexico, in *Changing Men and Masculinities in Latin America*, edited by M.C. Gutmann. Durham: Duke University Press, 351–69.

Carrillo, H. 2004. Sexual Migration, Cross-Cultural Encounters, and Sexual Health. *Sexuality Research & Social Policy* 1(3), 58–70.

Carrillo, H. 2007. Imagining Modernity: Sexuality, Policy, and Social Change in Mexico. *Sexuality Research and Social Policy* 4(3), 74–91.

de la Dehesa, R. 2010. *Queering the Public Sphere in Mexico and Brazil: Sexual Rights Movements in Emerging Democracies.* Durham: Duke University Press.

Gallego Montes, G. 2010. *Demografía de lo otro: Biografías sexuales y trayectorias de emparejamiento entre varones de la Ciudad de México.* Mexico City: El Colegio de México.

Hawley, J. 2001a. Introduction, in *Postcolonial Queer: Theoretical Intersections*, edited by J. Hawley. Albany: State University of New York Press, 1–18.

Hawley, J. 2001b. *Postcolonial Queer: Theoretical Intersections.* Albany: State University of New York Press.

Jackson, P.A. 2001. Pre-Gay, Post-Queer: Thai Perspectives on Proliferating Gender/Sex Diversity in Asia. *Journal of Homosexuality* 40(3/4), 1–25.

Jackson, P.A. 2004. *Gay* Adaptation, *Tom-Dee* Resistance, and *Kathoey* Indifference: Thailand's Gender/Sex Minorities and the Episodic Allure of Queer English, in *Speaking in Queer Tongues: Globalization and Gay Language*, edited by W.L. Leap and T. Boellstorff. Urbana: University of Illinois Press, 181–201.

Johnson, M., Jackson, P. and Herdt, G. 2000. Critical Regionalities and the Study of Gender and Sexual Diversity in South East and East Asia. *Culture, Health & Sexuality* 2(4), 361–75.

Kandel, W. and Massey, D.S. 2002. The Culture of Mexican Migration: A Theoretical and Empirical Analysis. *Social Forces* 80(3), 981–1004.

Laguarda, R. 2011. *La calle de Amberes: Gay street de la Ciudad de México.* Mexico City: Universidad Nacional Autónoma de México.

Leap, W.L. and Boellstorff, T. 2004. *Speaking in Queer Tongues: Globalization and Gay Language.* Urbana: University of Illinois Press.

List, M. 2005. *Jóvenes corazones gay en la Ciudad de México.* Puebla: Benemérita Universidad Autónoma de Puebla, Facultad de Filosofía y Letras.

Love, H. 2007. *Feeling Backward: Loss and the Politics of Queer History.* Cambridge, Massachusetts: Harvard University Press.

Manalansan IV, M.F. 2003. *Global Divas: Filipino Gay Men in the Diaspora.* Durham: Duke University Press.

Manalansan IV, M.F. 2005. Migrancy, Modernity, Mobility: Quotidian Struggles and Queer Disaporic Intimacy, in *Queer Migrations: Sexuality, US Citizenship, and Border Crossings*, edited by E. Luibhéid and L. Cantú Jr. Minneapolis: University of Minnesota Press, 146–60.

Massey, D.S., Goldring, L. and Durand, J. 1994. Continuities in Transnational Migration: An Analysis of Nineteen Mexican Communities. *American Journal of Sociology* 99(6),1492–533.

McClintock, A. 1995. *Imperial Leather: Race, Gender, and Sexuality in the Colonial Contest*. New York: Routledge.

Nuñez Noriega, G. 1999 [1994]. *Sexo entre varones: Poder y resistencia en el campo sexual*. Mexico City: Universidad Nacional Autónoma de México.

Nuñez Noriega, G. 2007. *Masculinidad e intimidad: Identidad, sexualidad y SIDA*. Mexico City: Porrúa.

Povinelli, E.A. and Chauncey, G. 1999. Thinking Sexuality Transnationally: An Introduction. *GLQ: A Journal of Lesbian and Gay Studies* 5(4), 439–49.

Sánchez-Eppler, B. and Patton, C. 2000. Introduction: With a Passport to Eden, in *Queer Diasporas*, edited by B. Sánchez-Eppler and C. Patton. Durham: Duke University Press, 1–14.

Savigliano, M. 1994. Tango in Japan and the World Economy of Pleasure, in *Re-Made in Japan: Everyday Life and Consumer Taste in a Changing Society*, edited by J.J. Tobin. New Haven: Yale University Press, 235–52.

Stoller, A.L. 2002. *Carnal Knowledge and Imperial Power*. Berkeley: University of California Press.

Taylor, C.L. 1978. *El Ambiente: Male Homosexual Social Life in Mexico City*. Unpublished doctoral dissertation. Berkeley: University of California.

Taylor, C.L. 1986. Mexican Male Interaction in Public Context, in *The Many Faces of Homosexuality*, edited by E. Blackwood. New York: Harrington Park Press, 117–36.

Vidal-Ortiz, S., Decena, C., Carrillo, H. and Almaguer, T. 2010. Revisiting Activos and Pasivos: Toward New Cartographies of Latino/Latin American Male Same-Sex Desire, in *Latina/o Sexualities: Probing Powers, Passions, Practices, and Policies*, edited by M. Asencio. New Brunswick: Rutgers University Press, 253–73.

Wilson, T.D. 2010. The Culture of Mexican Migration. *Critique of Anthropology* 30(4), 399–420.

Young, R.J.C. 1995. *Colonial Desire: Hibridity in Theory, Culture and Race*. London: Routledge.

Index